Sociology of Everyday Life in New Zealand

Sociology of Everyday Life in New Zealand

edited by
Claudia Bell

d p
Dunmore Press

©2001 Claudia Bell
©2001 Dunmore Press Limited

First Published in 2001
by
Dunmore Press Limited
P.O. Box 5115
Palmerston North
New Zealand
http://www.dunmore.co.nz

Australian Supplier:
Federation Press
P.O. Box 45
Annandale 2038 NSW
Australia
Ph: (02) 9552-2200
Fax: (02) 9552-1681

ISBN 0 86469 387 7

Text: Times New Roman 10.5/12.5
Printer: The Dunmore Printing Company Ltd
               Palmerston North
Cover design: Murray Lock

Contents

Introduction

Claudia Bell

Everyday life is the starting point for the authors contributing to this collection. The immediate obvious question is 'whose everyday?' As New Zealand becomes more culturally diverse, the ways people live their daily lives less and less fit a standard pattern or stereotype, if they ever really did. The emphasis in this book is on individual and collective engagement in mainstream culture, to provide readers with a substantial background for understanding the ways in which the 'everyday' is acted out in New Zealand society at this time.

In these chapters the writers acknowledge that the everyday takes place in the space of ordinary people, but is heavily impinged on, informed by and directed by powerful social forces. The everyday is not innocent lived experience, but is, as **Hope and Johnson** explain at the beginning of their chapter, shaped by tradition, social institutions and social structure. While we may feel that everyday decisions are made of our own volition, there are nevertheless social patterns to the actions we take and the choices we make.

Social theorists investigating the everyday have made various observations. Raymond Williams wrote of the ordinariness of everyday life; culture is constituted by the meanings and practices of ordinary men and women.[1] While in this book we have not taken as a prescription Williams' strategy for the exploration of culture[2], we have adapted some components of it. The authors of this text deal with some omnipresent institutions of New Zealand society (for instance, the home, sport, work, food) and look at the means of cultural production and their resultant forms. They have diligently stayed with analysis of the 'ordinary'.

What is more ordinary than talking about the weather? Easy human interaction is a critical part of everyday life. **Steve Matthewman** explains that comments on the weather have an important social role. The weather is a safe topic of casual conversation, which expresses moods, opens conversations with friends or strangers, distracts from serious issues, and can be relied on for its suitability to fill in conversational gaps. Our sense of individual and collective identity is tied to facts and fictions about the local and national climate.

In their book *Popular Culture and Everyday Life* Miller and McHoul refer to theorists who offer analysis of the everyday as investigation of alienated and reified life under capitalism. [3] Accommodating capitalism is also an overarching presence in this book; but most explicitly, perhaps, in **Martin Tolich's** chapter. Tolich starts with that famous line from Marx 'Hunt in the morning, fish in the afternoon, rear cattle in the evening, criticize after dinner.' He compares this ideal with the way the day is actually spent by an Auckland cleaner, who works nights and manages her family and other commitments during the day. Her after-dinner social critique equivalent is talk-back radio.

The loss of the eight-hour work day is lamented by Tolich. He discusses the impact of the Employment Contracts Act, its impacts on women workers, the problems of the casualisation of labour, and the euphemism of 'self-employment'. Tolich makes it very clear that the future of jobs is the future of New Zealand society. He points out that those who wish to offer the next generation a better society may be unable to deliver.

Another theme of analysis of the everyday identified by McHoul and Miller is as a site of pleasure and resistance by social actors. [4] Several articles in this new collection illustrate this process. An example is the chapter on gambling by **Bruce Curtis** and **Cate Wilson**. Recent surveys in New Zealand show that up to 90 per cent of those surveyed participate in various forms of gambling. While surveys may suffer from conceptual or methodological flaws, nevertheless the snapshots they present show that gambling certainly has the status of an everyday activity. Curtis and Wilson explain to us the odds of becoming Lotto millionaires; how to play roulette; and tell us why our chances of winning are slim indeed. In New Zealand expenditure on gambling has reached around six billion dollars per year.

Giddens, in *The Constitution of Society*, explains that understanding how human activity is distributed in space is fundamental to analysis of social life. Human interaction takes place in spaces which have particular meanings. [5] This is echoed in this new text by **David Thorns** and **Harvey Perkins** when they write 'If we are to understand New Zealanders' everyday lives then we must spend some time considering our relationship with our houses and homes.' The home is where we have most control of our environment. But the meaning of the home is not created only by those who live in it, but also by far larger forces. The news media, product advertising, urban planning systems and real estate marketing contribute to the way we think about and use our domestic spaces. The home has both sentimental associations, and exchange value. It is also, increasingly, a site for home-based work, a centre for learning, a virtual shopping mall, and a technology-based entertainment centre.

The home is a place heavily invested with the labour of negotiation, explains **Ruth Habgood**. Her response to that nagging old question about how come women end up doing most of the housework is to investigate couples trying to adopt unconventional domestic arrangements. Her subjects are consciously contrary to gendered conventions about the division of paid and unpaid work. While popular claims insist that since the impacts of the second wave of feminism male partners are taking greater responsibility in the domestic sphere, there is, she points out, little concrete evidence to support those claims.

Habgood concludes that the broader social and economic context in which the household is situated, and the processes and circumstances that are an everyday feature of the broader social environment, are themselves gendered.

'We need to examine cultural phenomena in terms of their own rules, logics, development and effectivity,' writes Chris Barber in *Cultural Studies, Theory and Practice*. This is the challenge facing **Farida Tilbury** and **Mike Lloyd** as they examine friendship and relationships as an everyday part of social life. They tell us that sociology has never had a lot to say on the subject of friendship; but nevertheless they have uncovered some studies that present empirical material that shows how relationships develop, or fail to develop, in everyday situations.

While friendships suggests an area of social life in which we have freedom of choice, these authors show that in fact people mostly choose friends of similar class and ethnic background to themselves. The political climate also affects the chances for friendships to develop. They conclude that the wider context of social discourse influences friendships and maintains rules.

Ian Carter and **Angela Maynard** assert that a sociological investigation of food is a way into understanding everyday life in New Zealand. They discuss the evolution of local foods, from the use of indigenous foods by Maori, to the current vast range of international varieties of products available in most supermarkets. Food writers have long rejoiced in the abundant varieties of food available here; and manufacturers have found ways to preserve and transport it. But have we developed a New Zealand cuisine? Or has there been a decline in knowledge of food preparation (despite the all-time best-seller status of *Edmonds Cookery Book*) as supermarkets and fast food outlets supply instant meals? Why is there such frequent revision of health advice about what we should eat? Carter and Maynard explain how an enriched understanding of our everyday culture can be realised through sociological inquiry into food and food preparation.

The promotion of global food brands is central in the advertising industry. As **Wayne Hope** and **Rosser Johnson** explain, the goal is to extend the traditional association between branded merchandise and positive experiences. These authors discuss the association of lifestyle and consumer goods, explaining how sellers project atmosphere and lifestyle rather than product. Imagery may include 'New Zealandness', as presented in the Toyota or Lotto campaigns.

These authors explain how the media presents a commodified understanding of the world, and of social relationships, infiltrating our daily lives; to the point that most of us experience no discernable boundaries between media content, advertising and everyday life. We share our lives in a particular place; but beyond that what we know of one another is as likely to be from news media reports as from first-hand knowledge. Second-hand experience of everyday life has become part of everyday life.

Shopping as a mundane activity is discussed by authors **Robin Kearns, Wardlow Friesen** and **Laurence Murphy**. They explain that the processes of consumption and our own personal identities are connected through the places in which we shop. These authors note that annual retail sales totalled over $41 billion in 1999. To maintain or increase this figure, shoppers are encouraged to see this activity as recreation and self-realisation, rather than as a chore. But malls as 'palaces of consumption' have caused the decline of local shops, affecting the life world of those dependent on neighbourhood facilities.

Contemporary shopping may be viewed as an inherently democratic activity, as the market does not discriminate on the basis of identity, nationality or culture. Yet it is also a source of social exclusion, as the range of shopping experiences available throws into relief the polarities of incomes in New Zealand. It is perhaps telling that the most profitable retail chain in the 1990s was the bargain-basement-style Warehouse.

Over 93 per cent of New Zealanders participate in arts activities on a regular basis. In their chapter on aesthetic leisure, **Claudia Bell** and **John Lyall** consider this finding of the *Arts Every Day Mahi Toi Ia Ra* survey in 1999, carried out by the Hillary Commission and Creative New Zealand. That study shows that more New Zealanders spend time in arts activities than watching or participating in sport: an announcement that surprised many, and that has been used by the current Labour Government to support their new arts policies and unprecedented budget allocation to arts funding.

The authors of this chapter revisit Creative New Zealand's definition of 'arts participation' as 'all forms of creative and interpretive expression,' and show how New Zealand has always been a nation of people who create things. Indeed, that favourite traditional claim of 'kiwi ingenuity' refers to skills in creativity. New digital technologies enable ever greater private domain authoring of creative products, further increasing 'arts participation.' Yet the public status of artists, and of hobbyists, has remained modest. Given the high level of arts participation, why has this not been adopted as a major feature of the national identity of New Zealanders?

Watching sport is the theme of **Camilla Obel's** chapter. She notes that worldwide there is debate about how best to accommodate the public who wish to attend live sports events. When stadiums are upgraded, who should pay? And should cities compete for the right to stage popular sports events? She explains that a sociological understanding of sports spectating needs to consider both the experiences spectators get from major sports events, and the production of facilities to stage such events.

Obel writes that major sports events are promoted as an opportunity to participate in the celebration of national and international ideals. The more people who participate, the greater the festive atmosphere of the event; fans want to feel excitement as they support their teams. But the financial costs of being a spectator are increasing, as the capacity of stadiums has decreased; and for live coverage viewers may need to pay for SKY. The traditional activity of watching live sport is changing from a mass experience to one accessible only to more privileged members of the population.

Encounters with death have become an everyday experience, writes **Tracey McIntosh**. Ironically, while we live in times when we can expect greater personal longevity than at any time in human history, we can witness death on a daily basis. The media constantly flashes at us images of what Giddens calls 'fateful moments', from breaking news stories of dramatic crashes or accidents, fatal-disease-of-the-week dramas, reality TV, and dramas in which murder is the central motif. Our most common daily encounters with death have much in common with spectator sports: for the viewer, this is sheer entertainment.

McIntosh explains that this is an age when elaborate technological intervention can save lives. But 'death, like life, is not equal', she writes, explaining that social location, class, gender and ethnicity will play an important role in determining the probable type and cause of death for different groups. This is an everyday concern that as a society we have not successfully addressed.

The twelve chapters in this book cannot claim total coverage of everything that happens in New Zealand on a daily basis. However, the collection does show how many of the activities that we engage in as individuals, and in which we apparently make our own individual choices, are in fact social activities, determined in large measure by the culture that New Zealand is today, which in turn is shaped by global forces.

This text also reveals a wide range of research on everyday issues being undertaken in New Zealand. Some writers have drawn from their own PhD research, some from major funded research projects, and most of us from our teaching or general research interests. We hope these articles answer some queries, while raising new questions about New Zealand culture. A primary goal for the authors in assembling this text was to engender debate on taken-for-granted features of our society.

Endnotes

[1]   Williams, Raymond (1965) *The Long Revolution*, London: Penguin, p. 42.

[2]   Barber, Chris (2000) *Cultural Studies – Theory and Practice*, London: Sage, p. 40.

[3]   McHoul, Alec and Miller, Toby (1998) *Popular Culture and Everyday Life*, London: Sage, p. 10.

[4]   Ibid., p. 10.

[5]   Giddens, A. (1984) *The Constitution of Society*, Cambridge: Polity Press.

[6]   Barber, op. cit., p. 50.

The National Climate: Our Weather Culture

Steve Matthewman

Evening love
How's your day?
I'm bringing you the weather from the satellite jigsaw

Today was fine
Tears at times
A weak ridge from pressure from the hinter to the heartland.

Dave Dobbyn (1992) 'Outlook for Thursday'.

Weather and the Everyday

We commence with two conversations: one between Jack and Gwendolen in the first act of Oscar Wilde's *The Importance of Being Earnest*, the other between Roland Barthes and a woman as recorded in his autobiography. The former is fictional and the latter factual, yet both are the stuff of common exchange, at once significant and revealing. As much is recognised by Greg Dening, who notes that '[t]he medium of most of our living is conversation, of texted narrative. The clothing of our structures is the trivialities of everyday existence'.[1] Our first discussion begins when Jack passes comment on the weather, 'Charming day it has been, Miss Fairfax'. To which Gwendolen replies, 'Pray don't talk to me about the weather, Mr Worthing. Whenever people talk to me about the weather, I always feel quite certain that they mean something else. And that makes me so nervous'.[2] They may well mean something else, for Gwendolen's concerns find empirical confirmation in the work of de la Soudiere.[3]

De la Soudiere demonstrates *why* much of our weather talk constitutes 'covert' usage: we natter about the weather to express moods, open conversations, circumvent serious issues and fill conversational pauses. *How* we talk about the weather illuminates other things besides. One morning while in the bakery Barthes heard a woman say the following: *'It's still lovely but the heat's lasting too long'* [italics in original]. Used to such customary statements in this region, Barthes returned one that was not: *'And the light is so beautiful!'* His remark ended the exchange. '[O]nce again I notice that short-circuit in language of which the most trivial conversations are the sure occasion', observed Barthes, 'I realize that *seeing the light* relates to a class sensibility'.[4] That different ethnic groups may see the weather in different ways is also beyond dispute. Mary Douglas (1962) studied the ways in which neighbouring Congolese tribes make sense of their meteorological year. Despite fairly constant year-round temperatures, the Lele and the Bushong celebrate hot and cold seasons at opposite ends of the calendar.[5]

Yet a consideration of the weather can demonstrate more than personal discomfort, class position or ethnic affiliation. Weather is a part of our daily life, affecting the ways we think and feel,[6] the ways in which we use space,[7] and ultimately how we anchor ourselves to place. Consider the way that regional identity is conveyed in Basil Dowling's poem *Canterbury*, where:

> On this great plain the eye
> Sees less of land than sky,
> And men seem to inhabit here
> As much the cloud-crossed hemisphere
> As the flat earth.[8]

As we progress we will see how the weather helps forge a sense of national identity. For the moment, the point to stress is that discourses about the weather cross the nature–culture divide. When discussing weather, it is difficult to see where nature stops and culture starts. Problems have arisen from seeking their separation. In his influential work *Landscape & Memory*, Simon Schama reunites these domains, writing:

> ... although we are accustomed to separate nature and human perception into two realms, they are, in fact, indivisible. Before it can ever be a repose for the senses, landscape is the work of the mind. Its scenery is built up as much from strata of memory as from layers of rock.[9]

Landscape & Memory usefully transgresses the nature–culture binary, but one can't help enjoining Schama to look up. His is a world without weather, yet the overall impression landscape makes upon one's senses includes invisible phenomena like wind and temperature, and visible phenomena such as light and rain. Like the land, weather is a powerful component of the social memory, and these two elements are never more potent than when combined. Think of novelist Keri Hulme's favourite homeplace on the West Coast in spring, where:

> ... the mountains with a full cloak of snow burn white against the sky, and sunsets are acid-dream vivid, burnt orange and lime green, every shade of pink and maroon and scarlet with piles and bands of navy blue or silver clouds, and the sea gone weirdly pale jade. The lagoon will turn jet black, or abruptly fluoresce an unholy bright gold.[10]

Writing of Canada's climatic extremes, particularly the severity of its winters, Berland is moved to argue that '[i]n some weird way, we *are* our weather. If we have nothing else in common, our reciprocal recognition as citizens "North of the 49th" is naturalized annually by our shared encounter with the weather'.[11] Here in the Land of the Long White Cloud summer serves as our defining season. Braunias offers the following:

> Yes, this is New Zealand – open, and dazed, and you have sand in your hair and sand in your pockets, and every day is like Sunday. The sunsets are shocking pink, outrageous, would you look at that. The air in front of you is wrinkled with heat. Mt Ruapehu is as bald as a coot, Lake Tekapo needs a drink. You are walking on hard, pale clay. You are on the porch. There are monarch butterflies, and cicadas, and moths, and flies, mosquitoes, wasps, ants, and visiting aunts. We are a nation of summer islands – the beach, the dust, the light. It suits us. It *makes* us. It's the way we imagine ourselves, and brag about it to the world.[12]

He continues his themes of identity and representation thus:

> ... [s]ome of our best literature has suntan lotion on its pages – Sargeson's *That Summer*, Duggan's *Along Rideout Road,* Frame's *The Reservoir*, and if you close your eyes while reading Stead's *All Visitors Ashore* you see orchards and wharves, bare legs and open windows. *It's our time.*[13]

The strongly social significance of the seasons should come as no surprise. Trevor Turner has even written of the very real possibility 'that the weather, in ways much more profound than the minor personal problems that pass for experience in the modern world, affects our very soul'.[14]

Of course image and reality may not correspond. Counter-narratives have challenged this sun-kissed vision, and nowhere more so than in Keri Hulme's backyard. Such is the scale of precipitation on the West Coast that visitors have corrupted its title to the Wet Coast, tourists have claimed to rust rather than tan, and travel guides hint at an official cover-up. Intending tourists consulting the *Traveller's Survival Kit* are warned that:

> New Zealand's climate may come as a shock. ...Rainfall is terrifically high on the west coast of the South Island, which is where some of the country's foremost attractions are located. The New Zealand Tourist & Publicity Department plays down the fact that visitors have to be lucky to see Mount Cook or Mount Taranaki out of cloud, or to see Milford Sound in the sunshine. Their evasive description of the weather ... hardly does justice to the inconvenience to walkers and sightseers caused by frequent torrential downpours.[15]

If there is a high-level conspiracy it has yet to reach the Tourist Information Centre at Fox Glacier, which openly sells copies of the anonymous poem 'Rain':

> It rained and rained and rained
> The average fall was well maintained
> And when the tracks were simple bogs
> It started raining cats and dogs.
> After a drought of half an hour
> We had a most refreshing shower,
> And then, most curious of all
> A gentle rain began to fall.
> Next day but one was fairly dry
> Save for one deluge from the sky
> Which wetted the party to the skin,
> And then, at last - the rain set in.

Indeed, showers such as this seldom astonish residents. Rather matter-of-factly, Keri Hulme says, '[t]here's quite a lot of heavy rain on the West Coast. I have seen it bucket down at over an inch an hour for more than a day. We measure yearly rainfall in yards, or metres, here.'[16] On the Coast your calibration needs to go up an order of magnitude.

Whatever the weather on the Coast, it manages to weave its way into our wider sense of identity. For instance, the sleeve notes to Douglas Lilburn's 'Symphony No 2' (1951) inform us that:

... this symphony with its subtle allusions to ... *the oppressive pride of the West Coast weather and landscape* (third movement), the opening-up of the mountain skyline (fourth movement) or, more generally, the sweep of the horizons around us in the first movement, *has the power to arouse in New Zealanders an indefinable feeling of identity with their country*.[17]

The Coast is cartography and consciousness, a place on the map and a whole way of knowing. It is the stamping ground of Pioneer Man, a place where the past can be seen in the present (at a price). Not so much heartland as *soul* land. The 21 February 2000 screening of *Our People, Our Century* helped explain its spiritual significance: only 15 per cent of New Zealanders live outside cities, making our country one of the most urbanised in the world. As Gary McCormick writes:

The West Coast of the South Island ... does play a central role in the mythology of Kiwi life. More so to men possibly than to women. Men will often ask me if I've been down 'the Coast' (even if they saw the programme 'The Whitebaiter's Ball'). It's not that they really want to know. It is more that they are seeking an opportunity to let their eyes glaze over and relive some past real or imagined experience down there.[18]

I encountered precisely the same reaction on my only journey to the Coast. Having flown into Christchurch I took a taxi to the railway station. Unlike most places in the world, the trip from the airport to the city takes you through the finest local residential real estate. Though my taxi driver admitted that it was unusual, he remained unmoved. Dave was not a city person and had no time for novelty, social or physical. In our short ride he dismissed contemporary class composition and architectural construction. The *nouveaux riches* of Fendalton 'talked funny', like a breed apart: which they were, for this was 'Daddy had a sheep station' country. His mood did not improve upon reaching Addington Railway Station. This building had won an Artex award, despite Dave's disdain for modernist design. He thought it 'bloody terrible'. Only the mention of my ultimate destination could raise his spirits. As his eyes shifted westward he said in approving tones, 'Ah, the good country.' Clearly, he *idyllised* the Coast. Deferring to McCormick once more, we find the following note in *Heartland*: 'The West Coast is a very satisfying figment in many a Kiwi imagination, and if it didn't exist it would be necessary to invent it.'[19]

Having drifted back to that site of national authenticity, now seems as good a time as any to explore our early settler history. By doing so we will see that the weather has always been used to help consolidate the imagined national community.

The Colonial Climate

As Harvey Day has observed, '[r]ice pudding and inclement weather have contributed much to the average Englishman's stoicism and to Britain's success as a great power. There is little doubt that many of her Empire builders fled these shores for balmier lands.'[20] Of course Day's *Curries of India* may not be the most palatable source for authoritative information on matters of migration, but it expresses popular sentiment. In Oscar Wilde's tale *The Canterville Ghost* (1887), Irish writer and American character conspire around the same theme. Hiram B. Otis has our attention: '"What a monstrous climate!" said the American minister calmly as he lit a long cheroot. "I guess the old country is so overpopulated that they have not enough decent weather for everybody. I have always been of the opinion that emigration is the only thing for England." '[21]

In the middle of the nineteenth century, emigration did seem the only thing for the English. Between 1830 and 1850 Britain was in the throes of an economic crisis that threatened the very social order. At the top of the social scale there was conflict between two distinct classes: the entrenched rural aristocracy and the emergent industrial bourgeoisie. Because of 'aristocratic' impediments to capitalist agriculture's development, manufacturing stagnated. Dependent upon raw materials and foodstuffs, industry suffered from high costs and low profits. With an excess of labour and capital, reduced profits and high import prices, threats from lower down the social order also emerged. Echoing Edward Gibbon Wakefield, the Otago Scheme's promoter George Rennie saw emigration as a way 'to save the institutions of England from being swept away in an uncomfortable rebellion of the stomach',[22] which was a touch ironic since the Free Church of Scotland promoted the Otago Scheme. Ruling patrician authorities and calculating industrial capitalists joined in agreeing that systematic colonisation solved a range of problems. They had places to which to export people and capital. These would form new sources for raw materials, and new colonial markets for exported finished products.

Visions of paradise always promise good weather. New Zealand's early climatological literature eschewed mere facts in favour of attracting migrants from Britain. Competition was stiff. The United States, Canada and Australia were also in the market for British stock, and they were bigger, nearer and more established colonies.[23] A number of scholars can be blamed; here Arthur Thomson serves as the representative villain. Thomson fostered what James Belich terms 'a cult of climatic determinism'.[24] In comparison to the tropics, New Zealand's bracing weather would lead to racial improvement.

From the late 1830s to the early 1880s, propaganda designed to attract streams of British migrants and money portrayed New Zealand as a latent paradise, peculiarly destined to be brought to fruition by select British stock. As in other colonies, it was asserted that New Zealand was uniquely well-placed to deliver 'progress without the price, paradise without the serpent, and Britain without the Irish', and prophecies of a great future abounded.[25]

An early example of trans-Tasman rivalry was expressed in the observation that: 'Two generations in Australia change the children of the broad-shouldered emigrants into a lithe race more nervous and muscular. "Sydney corn-stalks", as the youth of the city are denominated, are no match in intellect against men brought up in colder countries'.[26] The preferred alternative was New Zealand. In the first volume of his national(*ist*) history, Thomson wrote: 'It is the opinion of persons who have sojourned in different parts of the world, that the Anglo-Saxon race can work and expose themselves to the climate of New Zealand without injury, during more days in the year, and for more hours in the day, than in any other country.'[27] (Nowadays the competition with Australia is over who will win the title of skin cancer capital of the world, and melanoma comes to look like karma for colonialism.) This nostrum intensified in the years to come.

Requiring capital and colonists, and in competition with other colonies for them, Canaan was relocated. *The Labourer's Union Chronicle* published pamphlets in collusion with immigration agents in the 1870s that made New Zealand the promised 'land of oil, olives and honey'.[28] Emigration leaflets produced by Shaw, Savill and Co. in the same decade informed intending British migrants that New Zealand had little if any snow.[29] More impressively still, 'Messrs. Chambers, in one of their popular publications state[d] that "*The banana and other fruits of an oriental character form immense orchards in New Zealand.*" '[30]

Between 1885 and 1901 the combination of economic depression and Australian federation seriously undermined New Zealand's settler society, decimating population levels and transforming Pakeha collective identity in the process. New Zealand's links with Britain strengthened to such an extent that Belich refers to a process of 'recolonization'. It was in this period that 'the notion that the first settlers were the cream of the British population' and that the climate cultivated further racial improvement found their strongest expression.[31] But Utopia, as its etymological origins imply, is nowhere. A decade later a disgruntled settler noted, '[n]othing is more offensive to Colonial views than to have the dark side of things in the country fairly set forth,' however, 'should anyone write very favourably of climate, productions, commerce, institutions and the wonderful future of New Zealand, well then his future is made, he is a god out here'.[32] The myth required maintenance, the viability of a rickety settler society rested on it. Here Belich adds an entirely new dimension to the notion of a weather forecast, for as he notes these myths 'began as bait for migrants', but 'became the prospectus New Zealand was considered obligated to fulfil, a history written in advance'.[33]

Constructing a Kiwi Weather Culture

Ever since Kupe's wife, Hine te aparangi, cried 'He ao! He ao!' upon sighting these shores, the weather has involved, obsessed, moulded and enmeshed us. Having discussed the ways in which weather was used to lure migrants here, we now turn to what they made of it once they arrived. Arrival 'for the ocean-weary immigrants', Jones writes, 'must have provided mixed emotion: relief, certainly, but also foreboding'.[34] It certainly did. There is a wealth of documentary evidence recording such reactions to landfall. In this regard, Dr Alexander Tinline Thomson's arrival aboard the *Agnes Muir* is particularly instructive. Setting sail from Greenock, Scotland on 14 April 1869, the P. Henderson & Co. vessel made Port Chalmers three months later 'with 150 emigrants and six saloon passengers. The hills, on our arrival', Thomson recalled, 'were covered with snow, which frightened the emigrants, who thought that they could never live in a country having snow in June or July'.[35] Clearly, stowed away among their many material possessions was a certain amount of cultural baggage. For despite being in the antipodes, the settlers were still seeing Scotland. Caledonia's seasons were being mapped onto the new colony, giving literal truth to the Neil and Tim Finn (1996) song that 'Everywhere you go, you always take the weather with you.'

Not only did these settlers conceive of Aotearoa in Eurpoean terms, they actively sought to remake it in a European image. William Pember Reeves notes this process in *The Long White Cloud. Ao Tea Roa*:

> Pastoral settlement speedily overran such a land, followed more slowly and partially by agriculture. The settler came, not with axe and fire to

ravage and deform, but as builder, planter, and gardener. Being in nineteen cases out of twenty a Briton, or a child of one, he set to work to fill this void land with everything British which he could transport or transplant.[36]

British flowers, vegetables, fruit trees, cattle, grasses, birds, bees, fish and flies all settled here too. 'The Briton of the South has indeed taken with him all that he could of the old country', Pember Reeves wrote.[37]

However, this is only *one* version of nature. The land was anything but 'void' prior to European inscription, and the people that brought the flora and fauna here caused environmental displacements of their own. What nature is and how it should be are still sorely contested. David Eggleton (Eggleton and Potton 1999:7) emphasises this very point:

> New Zealand is a site of competing versions, a site of struggle: aesthetic consideration clashes with commercial consideration; conservation clashes with exploitation; methods of ownership are disputed – individual pitted against communal, communal pitted against corporate, corporate pitted against state; Maori negotiates with Pakeha; national versus multinational; heritage versus progress ....[38]

His account is given added force by the inclusion of those crucial aspects of non-human agency, for Eggleton adds: 'meanwhile climate, geology, topography exert their own pressures in the Shaky Isles'.[39] This point is important. The ongoing battle between humanity and nature constitutes one of the strongest themes in our nation's history, running from pioneering days right up to the present. In Kevin Dew's simple phrase, '[n]ature has never been successfully contained'.[40]

The notion that we are feuding over nature and that nature is fighting back upsets many people. A contested and unconquered terrain problematises those core issues of image, identity and representation. To recycle Braunias' phrase, it troubles 'the way we imagine ourselves, and brag about it to the world'.[41] Andrew Ross has noted how '[d]ominant ideas, whether in science or technology, are legitimised and enforced at any time by presenting them as part of the natural order of things'.[42] Social groups have cemented privileged positions through the same rhetorical strategies: think of the domination of men over women, of heterosexuals over homosexuals, of colonisers over colonised, and of ruling classes over subject classes. If we can't agree on nature we can't agree on what's natural.

Often these thorny issues go unengaged, and are merely glossed over. One of the latest efforts comes from Lindsey Dawson (2000:17). She argues that 'New Zealand needs a new icon for a new century. A "Soul Brand" ... that defines who and what we are. Here it is. Consider the colour green.'[43] One can see the attraction. Choose green rather than brown, white or yellow. Focus exclusively on the land rather than on those intimately related issues of alienation, appropriation and exploitation that involve all those other colours. Dawson's rallying cry in a popular magazine is merely the latest in a long line. Many of those involved in the arts have also tried to ground our identity. By siting national identity in the topography, artists, poets and composers 'have [also] ideologically sidestepped many crucial social issues such as our ugly history of race relations, the oppression of women and the exploitation of workers'.[44] Simply put, wherever we look, cultural constructs have always sought the sanction of nature, and the weather has been made to play its part. Andrew Ross shows how this works in an American context:

> ... [i]f extreme weather conditions can cause suffering, then people's suffering can always be explained (away) in turn by weather conditions; the foreclosure of a family farm can then be seen as an inevitable component of a natural cycle. Inequalities are evenly distributed throughout the country according to the current weather configuration of highs and lows, some like it hot, some like it cold, some times are good, some times are bad, wherever there are winners, there will be losers elsewhere. Rewards and punishments are disbursed in a cost–benefit analysis that balances across the breadth of the nation. This weather system of credits and debits refers as much to a political model – the US constitutional system of checks and balances – as to an ideology – the holistic maxim that 'Mother Nature will balance everything out'. Such appeals make it seem as natural as the weather that some people must experience hardship so that others may enjoy abundance.[45]

Having signposted varying cultural perceptions of nature, and mentioned the invocation of nature to affirm particular social stations, we now consider nature's use in legitimating the entire nation. David Carter's writings on the 'ecological turn' in recent imaginings of Australian landscape are useful for the purposes of our discussion. In these narratives we see history without a human presence. Gone is the triumphal domination-of-nature narrative. Those old British myths of nature that colonised the collective consciousness no longer apply. Here history flows in the opposite direction, far into the past. Carter is intrigued by these new images of unpopulated landscapes in Australia, with their theme of the 'oldest earth on earth'. In his opinion '[t]his is nation-making at its strongest, giving one of the newest nations on earth an unexpected depth and centredness. In the primeval landscape, before society and politics, before culture and history, time and place become one'.[46] His observations have an obvious resonance with New Zealand's latest tourist campaign. Visit the New Zealand Government Online site and click on Tourist Information. Intending tourists are greeted with the promise of '100 per cent Pure NZ', the first entry of which is on wilderness – 'Idyllic, isolated, untouched'. The web page announces 'nature as it was intended: pure, untouched, energising', encouraging visitors to '[f]ly to the edges of steaming volcanoes, feel the primal legacy of giant kauri trees, walk on top of crystalline glaciers and venture into mystical and uninhabited fiords'.[47]

In the preceding discussion nature substitutes for a past and presents new possibilities for national distinctiveness. But in our history privileging the natural over the social in an attempt to cement the two is not new. Indeed, doing so helps overcome what Anderson identifies as one of the great paradoxes of nationalism: '[t]he objective modernity of nations to the historian's eye vs their subjective antiquity in the eyes of nationalists'.[48] In politician William Pember Reeves' *The Long White Cloud. Ao Tea Roa* we see an ancient entity being forged from a novel fabrication. In the preface to the first edition of September 1898 Pember Reeves states that '[i]f The Long White cloud should fail to please a discerning public, it will not prove that a good, well-written history of a colony like New Zealand is not wanted' – it will simply show that he has not tried hard enough. 'But of the quality of the material awaiting a capable writer', he continues, 'there can be no question'. The historical material 'ready to his hand' begins before civilisation and the affairs of state, prior to Maori, pioneers and colonial founders, with 'the beauty of those islands of mid-ocean, the grandeur of their alps and fiords, the strangeness of their volcanic districts, the lavishness, yet grace, of the forests'.[49]

A Nation of Weather Watchers

We remain enchanted and awed by nature, be it alpine grandeur or volcanic strangeness, yet there is still a tendency to see it as a thing apart. Television viewers switching on *One Network News* on the evening of 13 February 2000 heard the following statement from weather presenter Karen Pickersgill: 'we're pretty much a nation of weather watchers'. She did have a point: most New Zealanders are conscious of the weather; they know what it's doing. But are they aware of the weather's role in their consciousness? Do they know what the weather is doing to *them*? More to the point, 'weather watching' implies passivity, detachment, spectatorship, when our position towards the weather is one of an involved and ongoing *relationship*. As Jody Berland asserts, the weather 'mediates between our physical and social bodies. Its rhythms and irregularities, and the rituals we construct around them, shape what it means to be part of the social, both within a particular time and space, and across to other times and places, as we imagine or remember them'.[50] M. K. Joseph's 'Mercury Bay Eclogue' cuts to the heart of this connection, noting that New Zealand's commerce and leisure are tied in with the weather:

> The wind strums Aeolian lyres
> Inshore among the telephone wires
> Linking each to each
> The city and the beach.
>
> For sunburnt sleepers would not come
> If inland factories did not hum
> And this Arcadian state
> Is built on butterfat.[51]

The ability of New Zealand to operate as a South Pacific farm to feed the Mother Country relied heavily on climate – for successful agriculture it is the single most important input. This helps explain why the New Zealand Meteorological Service (founded on 21 August 1861) is our oldest continuous scientific institution. Even today, many of our foremost export industries – from forestry and fruit to flowers and wine – are heavily weather-dependent. Similarly, summer would not be our time, and beach-going would not take on 'quasi-religious' dimensions for Kiwis if we didn't have the weather for it.[52] Fun and fortune are fuelled by the same source. Good weather is a foundation for wealth and for national identity.

Let us finish with a local example that illuminates the relationships that we have with the weather. Arguably these relationships are thrown into their sharpest relief when we attempt to change it. Recall Auckland's water crisis of 1994 and the ensuing struggle to alleviate this socially unacceptable weather. Accusations flew in all directions over who was to blame for the lack of rainfall. *One Network News* looked to local government minister John Banks for some sort of resolution, but he passed the buck and blamed God. Laingholm Baptist Church followed his advice, and prayed for rain at Huia dam. This, and not the impious rituals of the Wizard of Christchurch who had been conscripted to make rain, was later said by a Henderson help-group to be the real cause of the drought's relief. The Wizard had struggled to find a venue for his rainmaking rituals because fundamentalist Christians objected to his practices. In the midst of this clash between Christianity and paganism a preacher from Remuera, showing an astounding ignorance of meteorological threats and punishments scattered through the Old and New Testaments and the Apocrypha, said that the God he worshipped had nothing to do with the weather. While the drought continued, a familiar string of scapegoats was trotted out to account for it: homosexuals, bureaucrats and leftists. If the blasphemous Hero paraders were not to blame for the drought by way of Sodom and Gomorrah-style censure, then perhaps it was the ineptitude of Watercare Services, or the Alliance-dominated Auckland Regional Services Trust that owned it. It took a sober Vincent Heeringa (1994:54) to write in *Metro,* 'It's the weather, Stupid'.[53]

Endnotes

1 Dening, G. (1996) *Performances,* Carlton, Vic.: Melbourne University Press, p. 47.

2 Wilde, O. (1955) *The Importance of Being Earnest,* London: Methuen, p. 15.

3 De la Soudiere, M. (1994) ' "It's Rather Chilly". On Some Covert Usages of Discourses About the Weather', *Recherches Sociologiques,* vol. 25, no. 2, pp. 43–60.

4 Barthes, R. (1995) *Roland Barthes,* Translated by Richard Howard, London: Papermac, pp. 175 & 6.

5 Douglas, Mary (1962) 'Lele Economy Compared with the Bushong. A Study of Economic Backwardness', in Bohannan, P. and Dalton, G. (eds), *Markets in Africa,* Evanston, Illinois: Northwestern University Press.

6 Sanders, J.L. and Brizzolara, M.S. (1982) 'Relationships between Mood and Weather', *Journal of General Psychology,* vol. 107, pp. 157–8.

7 Nash, Jeffrey E. (1981) 'Relations in Frozen Places: Observations on Winter Public Order', *Qualitative Sociology,* vol. 4, no. 3, pp. 229–43.

8 Dowling, B., 'Canterbury', quoted in Eggleton, D. and Potton, C. (1999) *Here On Earth: The Landscape in New Zealand Literature,* Nelson: Craig Potton Publishing, p. 44.

9 Schama, S. (1995) *Landscape & Memory,* London: HarperCollins, p. 6–7.

10 Hulme, K., quoted in Ihimaera, W. and Leue, H. (1989) *Aotearoa New Zealand. The Legendary Land,* Auckland: Reed, p. 150.

11 Berland, J. (1993) 'Weathering the North. Climate, Colonialism, and the Mediated Body', in Blundell, V., Shepherd, J. and Taylor, I. (eds), *Relocating Cultural Studies. Developments in Theory and Research,* London and New York: Routledge, p. 208.

12 Braunias, S. (2000) 'Summer', *Listener,* January 1, p. 94.

13 Ibid., emphasis added.

14 Turner, T. (1999) 'Seasons of the Mind, Storms of the Soul', *New Internationalist,* no. 319, December, p. 16.

15   Griffith, S. and Calder, S. (1988) *Traveller's Survival Kit*, Oxford: Vacation Work, p. 359.

16   Hulme, K. (1989) *Homeplaces: Three Coasts of the South Island of New Zealand*, Auckland: Hodder and Stoughton, p. 16.

17   Lilburn, D., quoted in Beatson, P. (1991) 'From Landscape to Environment: Representations of Nature in New Zealand Classical Music', *Sites*, vol. 22, p. 38, emphasis added.

18   McCormick, G. (1994) *Heartland*, Auckland: Moa Beckett, p. 18.

19   Ibid., p. 19.

20   Day, H. (1956) *Curries of India*, London: Nicholas Kaye, p. 39.

21   Wilde, O. (1993) 'The Canterville Ghost', *The Complete Plays, Poems, Novels and Stories of Oscar Wilde*, London: Magpie, 1887, p. 195.

22   Rennie, G., quoted in Sinclair, K. (1980) *The Pelican History of New Zealand*, Harmondsworth: Penguin, p. 92.

23   Belich, J. (1996) *Making Peoples. A History of the New Zealanders From Polynesian Settlement to the End of the Nineteenth Century*, Auckland: Penguin, p. 278.

24   Belich, J. (1997) 'Myth, Race and Identity in New Zealand', *The New Zealand Journal of History*, vol. 31, no. 1, pp. 13–4.

25   Ibid., p.13.

26   Thomson, A. S. (1859) 'Sydney Corn-Stalks', *The Story of New Zealand: Past and Present – Savage and Civilized*, London: John Murray, vol. 2, p. 230.

27   Thomson, A. S. (1859) 'Climate', *The Story of New Zealand: Past and Present – Savage and Civilized*, London: John Murray, vol. 1, p. 37.

28   Fairburn, M. (1989) *The Ideal Society and Its Enemies*, Auckland: University of Auckland Press, p. 22.

29   Ibid., p.21.

30   Quoted in Hursthouse, C. (1861) *New Zealand, the 'Britain of the South': With a Chapter on the Native War, and Our Future Native Policy*, London: Edward Stanford, p. 211, italics in original.

31   Belich (1997) op. cit., pp. 13–4.

32   Quoted in Fairburn, op. cit., p. 23.

33   Belich (1996) op. cit., p. 279.

34   Jones, L. (1999) 'Boundaries and Renewals', in Carlin, J., *Beach New Zealand*, Albany: David Bateman, p. 16.

35   Quoted in Fulton, R. V. (1922) *Medical Practice in Otago and Southland in the Early Days*, Dunedin: Otago Daily Times / Witness Newspapers, p. 250.

36   Pember Reeves, W. (1998) *The Long White Cloud. Ao Tea Roa*, Twickenham: Senate, 1924, p. 36.

37   Ibid.

38   Eggleton, D., op. cit., p. 7.

39   Ibid.

[40] Dew, K. (1999) 'A Hazardous Country: A Socio-Cultural Theory of Risk for New Zealand', in Collis, M., Munro, L. and Russell, S. (eds), *Sociology for a New Millennium. Challenges and Prospects*, Melbourne: TASA Conference Proceedings, p. 393.

[41] Braunias, op. cit., p. 94.

[42] Ross, A. (1992) 'The Drought This Time', *Strange Weather. Culture, Science and Technology in the Age of Limits*, London: Verso, p. 232.

[43] Dawson, L. (2000) 'Shades of Green ... the Colour of Our Country', *Grace*, no. 17, p. 17.

[44] Beatson, op. cit., p. 47.

[45] Ross, op. cit., p. 237.

[46] Carter, D. (1995) 'Future Pasts', in Headon, D., Hooton, J. and Horne, D. (eds), *The Abundant Culture. Meaning and Significance in Everyday Australia*, St. Leonards, NSW: Allen & Unwin, p. 9.

[47] http://www.purenz.com/wilderness.cfm

[48] Anderson, B. (1991) *Imagined Communities*, London: Verso, p. 5.

[49] Pember Reeves, op. cit., p. 14.

[50] Berland, J. (1994) 'On Reading "The Weather" ', *Cultural Studies*, vol. 8, no. 1, p. 99.

[51] Joseph, M. K. 'Mercury Bay Eclogue', quoted in Bornholt, J., O'Brien, G. and Williams, M. (eds) (1997) *An Anthology of New Zealand Poetry in English*, Auckland: Oxford University Press, p. 300.

[52] Amery, M. (2000) 'Golden Oldie Reborn', *Sunday Star-Times*, 28 May, p. F1.

[53] Heeringa, V. (1994) 'It's the Weather, Stupid', *Metro*, August, pp. 54–62, 64–6, 68.

Bibliography

Amery, Mark (2000) 'Golden Oldie Reborn', *Sunday Star-Times*, 28 May, F1.

Anderson, Benedict (1991) *Imagined Communities*, London: Verso.

Anon (2000) 'Wilderness', *100% Pure New Zealand*, Available at: http://www.purenz.com/wilderness.cfm [Accessed 2 August 2000].

Anon (1993) 'A Forecast on Pain', *Psychology Today*, no. 26, p. 3.

Barthes, Roland (1995) *Roland Barthes*, Translated by Richard Howard, London: Papermac, 1975.

Beatson, Peter (1991) 'From Landscape to Environment: Representations of Nature in New Zealand Classical Music', *Sites*, no. 22: pp. 34–53.

Belich, James (1997) 'Myth, Race and Identity in New Zealand', *The New Zealand Journal of History*, vol. 31, no. 1, pp. 9–22.

Belich, James (1996) *Making Peoples. A History of the New Zealanders from Polynesian Settlement to the End of the Nineteenth Century*, Auckland: Penguin.

Berland, Jody (1993) 'Weathering the North. Climate, Colonialism, and the Mediated Body', in Blundell, V., Shepherd, J. and Taylor, I. (eds), *Relocating Cultural Studies. Developments in Theory and Research*, London and New York: Routledge, pp. 207–25.

Berland, Jody (1994) 'On Reading "The Weather" ', *Cultural Studies*, vol. 8, no. 1, pp. 99–114.

Bornholdt, Jenny, O'Brien, Gregory and Williams, Mark (eds) (1997) *Anthology of New Zealand Poetry in English*, Auckland: Oxford University Press.

Braunias, Steve (2000) 'Summer', *Listener*, 1 January, p. 94.

Carter, David (1995) 'Future Pasts', in Headon, D., Hooton, J., and Horne, D. (eds), *The Abundant Culture. Meaning and Significance in Everyday Australia*, St Leonards, NSW: Allen & Unwin, pp. 3–15.

Dawson, Lindsey (2000) 'Shades of Green ... the Colour of Our Country', *Grace*, no. 17, pp. 16–8.

Day, Harvey (1956) *Curries of India*, London: Nicholas Kaye.

Dening, Greg (1996) *Performances*, Carlton, Vic: Melbourne University Press.

Dew, Kevin (1999) 'A Hazardous Country: A Socio-Cultural Theory of Risk for New Zealand', in Collis, M., Munro L. and Russell, S. (eds), *Sociology for a New Millennium. Challenges and Prospects*, Melbourne: TASA Conference Proceedings, pp. 389–97.

Dobbyn, Dave (1992) 'Outlook for Thursday', *The Dave Dobbyn Collection*, Festival Records.

Douglas, Mary (1962) 'Lele Economy Compared with the Bushong. A Study of Economic Backwardness', in Bohannan, P. and Dalton, G. (eds), *Markets in Africa*, Evanston, Ill.: Northwestern University Press, pp. 211–33.

Eggleton, David and Potton, Craig (1999) *Here on Earth: The Landscape in New Zealand Literature*, Nelson: Craig Potton Publishing.

Fairburn, Miles (1989) *The Ideal Society and Its Enemies*, Auckland: University of Auckland Press.

Finn, Neil and Finn, Tim (1996) 'Weather With You', *Recurring Dream. The Very Best of Crowded House*, Capitol Records.

Fulton, Robert Valpy (1922) *Medical Practice in Otago and Southland in the Early Days*, Dunedin: Otago Daily Times Witness Newspapers.

Griffith, Susan and Calder, Simon (1988) *Traveller's Survival Kit,* Oxford: Vacation Work.

Heeringa, V. (1994) 'It's the Weather, Stupid', *Metro*, August, pp. 54–62, 64–66, 68.

Hulme, Keri (1989) *Homeplaces: Three Coasts of the South Island of New Zealand*, Auckland: Hodder & Stoughton.

Hursthouse, Charles (1861) *New Zealand, the 'Britain of the South': With a Chapter on the Native War, and Our Future Native Policy*, London: Edward Stanford.

Ihimaera, Witi and Leue, Holger (1994) *Aotearoa New Zealand. The Legendary Land*, Auckland: Reed.

Jones, Lloyd (1999) 'Boundaries and Renewals', in Carlin, J., *Beach New Zealand*, Albany: David Bateman, pp. 10–23.

McCormick, Gary (1994) *Heartland*, Auckland: Moa Beckett.

Nash, Jeffrey E. (1981) 'Relations in Frozen Places: Observations on Winter Public Order', *Qualitative Sociology*, vol. 4, no. 3, pp. 229–43.

Pember Reeves, William (1998) *The Long White Cloud. Ao Tea Roa*, Twickenham: Senate, 1924.

Ross, Andrew (1992) 'The Drought This Time', *Strange Weather. Culture, Science and Technology in the Age of Limits*, London: Verso, pp. 193–267.

Ross, Andrew (1987) 'The Work of Nature in the Age of Electronic Emission', *Social Text*, vol. 18, pp. 116–28.

Sanders, J. L. and Brizzolara, M.S. (1982) 'Relationships between Mood and Weather', *Journal of General Psychology*, vol. 107, pp. 157–8.

Schama, Simon (1995) *Landscape & Memory*, London: HarperCollins.

Sinclair, Keith (1980) *The Pelican History of New Zealand*, Harmondsworth: Penguin.

de la Soudiere, Martin (1994) ' "It's Rather Chilly". On Some Covert Usages of Discourses About the Weather', *Recherches Sociologiques*, vol. 25, no. 2, pp. 43–60.

Thomson, Arthur S. (1859) 'Climate', *The Story of New Zealand: Past and Present – Savage and Civilized*, vol. 1, London: John Murray, pp. 36–50.

Thomson, Arthur S. (1859) 'Sydney Corn-Stalks', *The Story of New Zealand: Past and Present – Savage and Civilized*, vol. 2, London: John Murray, p. 230.

Turner, Trevor (1999) 'Seasons of the Mind, Storms of the Soul', *New Internationalist*, no. 319, December, pp. 16–7.

Wilde, Oscar (1993) 'The Canterville Ghost', *The Complete Plays, Poems, Novels and Stories of Oscar Wilde*, London: Magpie, 1887, pp. 193–214.

Wilde, Oscar (1955) *The Importance of Being Earnest*, London: William Heinemann, 1899.

2

Houses, Homes and New Zealanders' Everyday Lives

Harvey Perkins and David Thorns

Introduction

If we are to understand New Zealanders' everyday lives then we must spend some time considering our relationships with our houses and homes: the locale which contributes to our sense of place and helps us to develop our sense of who we are. This is the case because the everyday experiences of places help create and maintain individual and collective identity. Everyday life is therefore social *and* spatial and, paraphrasing Eyles,[1] is the reality which makes us self-aware and self-conscious individuals. It is the world of experience which we see as being both under our own control and shaped and even determined by forces and events outside of that control. Everyday life is not a static phenomenon, but is rather a dynamic process which is continually unfolding and emergent. Seen in these terms, the form, use and meaning of New Zealanders' houses and homes are also unfolding and emergent.

Before going on to discuss house and home in Aotearoa/New Zealand we need to define a few of the terms we have used above. Houses, at their most basic, are spatially organised building materials on particular sites. Homes are houses made meaningful as people live in and around them. The spatial nature of housing and the ways in which the meanings of home are constructed vary in myriad ways. Even the most casual observer of the landscapes of several countries will have noted that houses vary significantly from country to country and from region to region within countries. This, in part, is a product of the geographical, historical and contemporary material conditions of life in those places – climate, topography, mortality and morbidity rates, life expectancy, degree of urbanisation, economic activity, transportation and the availability of building materials. The spatial and symbolic nature of housing is also a product of the variation in what might generally be termed cultural factors – family form, gender relations, social class, consumption patterns, leisure participation, work, employment and interpretations of locally appropriate uses of land. To the degree that all of these factors can change, perhaps as a result of the application of new building technology, amended legislation, changes in consumption tastes or new family forms, our houses and homes can also change.

Houses and homes are types of places. Our use of the term 'place' is a little more complex than the way it is used in day-to-day speech. From our perspective, places and people are inextricably intertwined. Places have a spatial component relating to their location and physical form. In that sense they are 'containers' in which everyday life is worked out. More than that, however, places are sites which are in some way meaningful to the people who live in or are associated with them. Places, and therefore homes, are made in processes of place-making and home-making.[2] It is important to note that the meanings of places, and therefore homes, are not just created locally, by the people who inhabit them. Global forces are also at work in the creation of place-meaning.[3] In the case of houses and homes such things as news media, product advertising, administrative systems (e.g. urban planning and management) and real-estate marketing contribute to the way we think about and use them. As local and global social and economic arrangements change, so too do the meanings of places. Massey discussed this change in terms of the identity of places, arguing that it is always in a sense temporary, uncertain, and in process.[4]

This brings us to our final definitional point: the interrelationships between individual, collective and place identity. Identity may be described as the qualities, beliefs and ideas individuals or groups of people use to define who they are; often expressed in oppositional terms relating to other individuals or groups. Social scientists have spent much time recently discussing social identity. Their debates have focused on ideas such as Sennett's,[5] who wrote recently that today 'an ever shifting, external market reality disturbs fixed pictures of self'. The implication here is that people, at least in the West, no longer have well-defined and stable identities but rather experience multiple and constantly changing and fleeting identities, consistent with changes in the world around them. Suggestions such as this are also linked to the idea that 'the new capitalism has also disturbed identities based on place – that sense of "home", of belonging somewhere in the world'.[6] While not denying the importance of change in the creation of new social and place identities, our research suggests that in Aotearoa/New

Zealand, at least, most people's identities change temporally but not in the quite spectacular ways discussed by Sennett. One of the factors that create relatively stable identities is people's close relationship with places, family and friends, particularly centred on their homes. As Ley argued:

> Place is a negotiated reality, a social construction by a purposeful set of actors. But the relationship is mutual, for places in turn develop and reinforce the social identity of the social groups that claim them. [7]

The everyday lives of most New Zealanders are closely related to their houses and homes, which are in turn central to the creation and maintenance of their identities, their sense of who they are. In saying this it is also necessary to acknowledge that not all people's experiences of home are positive ones, resulting from consensual negotiation. For some New Zealanders home is a place in which others dominate them.

Welcome to our Place

Our research into the meaning of house and home for New Zealanders was recently described in the cover story of *Outlook*, a magazine published by Lincoln University. The editor of the magazine asked a Wellington illustrator, Fifi Colston, to create a cover depicting aspects of house and home (Figure 2.1). We want to use that illustration to introduce a number of important matters in the discussion of house and home in Aotearoa/New Zealand.

Figure 2.1 offers an idealised picture of New Zealanders' relationships with their houses and homes. The heart shape embedded in a blue sky with soft white clouds and resting on twenty dollar notes is a very rosy picture. No sign of homelessness or poverty here. To be fair to the illustrator, the story was about people and their homes so, in this part of the chapter, we won't dwell too long on the question of whether or not people do have homes. The heart shape is important because it highlights the strong sentimental attachments many New Zealanders have with their houses and homes. This sentiment is often strongest among those who have lived in one place for a long time or who have had a strong hand in the making of a particular residential environment.

Within the heart are people engaged in a number of activities. Some of these activities could be classified as work, as being productive in some way (e.g. laying bricks or pavers, decorating a room, wallpapering and painting). Other activities could be classed as leisure (e.g. gardening, drinking

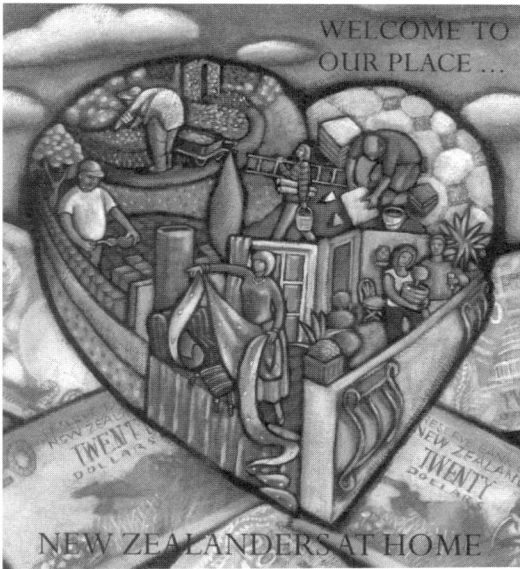

Figure 2.1: Welcome to our place: New Zealanders at home[8]

wine, choosing a potted plant from the garden shop). There is, however, a measure of ambiguity, particularly in a New Zealand context, because many of these work activities are also leisure activities for those who enjoy do-it-yourself home building, decoration and maintenance. A closer look at the figures engaging in these activities also highlights the gendered nature of house and home. The bricks and pavers are being laid by men, the flower gardening and room decoration are being done by women.

Leaving activities aside for a moment and looking at the images, the illustrator captures contemporary concerns about fashionable house interiors and exteriors, as exhibited in the consumption of often expensive stylish products and associated consumer lifestyles. This leads us on to an analysis of what is missing from the picture. There is no attempt, for example, to depict mundane domestic work (such as cleaning, ironing or bed making). Nor do children, cultural and ethnic diversity, pets, the aged and infirm, and those in dire financial straits have a place in this characterisation of house and home. Colston's illustration presents house and home as a secure and peaceful place where individuals can express their individuality and autonomy. Such views, however, ignore the fact that home can also be a place of negative values, of marginalisation, or of fear and violence, as shown by the debate about 'home invasion'. The illustration is a very partial, monocultural and sanitised representation of house and home in Aotearoa/ New Zealand.

The literature on house and home, and our research to date, sheds light on some of the issues raised above and it is to that part of our story that we now turn.[9] We will focus particularly on those parts of the literature which contribute to an understanding of home-making.

Home-centredness, Sentiment and Attachment

In different cultures home has greater or lesser impact, depending on the extent of privatism and home-centredness. Some writers see the growth of technologies which permit the development of home-based work and individualised leisure practices as factors likely to strengthen the home as the centre of future activity.[10] This home-centredness, for philosophers, is the existential space of being.[11]

Sentimental attachment to home is often discussed either explicitly or implicitly by those social scientists who are interested in the taken-for-granted nature of people's relationships with the world around them. These researchers have noted that while people are very strongly connected in their everyday lives with their houses, and with the people and activities associated with them, household members have difficulty articulating in any detailed way how those connections are created and maintained. They simply take the connections for granted. This research finding has much in common with the characterisation of home made by psychoanalytical psychologists. For them, home is a centre, a place in which possessions and display represent identity: home and self become merged. Home in these terms means different things to different individuals at different stages of development.[12] Marcus Cooper developed these ideas further in her recent book, which drew on a series of interviews where people were encouraged to talk about their houses.[13] She suggested that the home is a place of memories, a refuge from the outside world, which changes through our lives as we move from childhood to old age. Increasing attention is focused here upon the experience of children and young people, rather than on simply adult experiences.[14] The focus in this work is on individuals and their shifts and changes through life. It pays less attention to the wider social, economic and political context in which individuals and their homes are set.

Turning a Profit

Housing has both a use and exchange value. It both provides shelter and is a potential source of income and wealth. In societies in which owner-occupation of houses has become well established (e.g. Australia, Aotearoa/New Zealand, Canada and the USA), houses are the most significant source of wealth for the majority of the population.[15] Rates of financial return from home-ownership and the buying and selling of houses are time and place specific, and generally flow most strongly to those who already have assets.[16] Wealth stored in the house also forms a potentially transferable asset which can be passed on through inheritance to succeeding generations.[17] Home-owners are therefore usually vigorously protective of their housing investments and will work hard to resist the activities of neighbours, commercial interests or local authorities which may threaten house values.

Gender and Home

Homes are also gendered spaces. Feminist analysis is therefore important for an understanding of house and home. Home, for women, has a variety of meanings. It may be a site of security and empowerment but it can also be a place where power is exercised in a way that inhibits and controls their lives, creating a place of fear rather than one of peace, security and safety.[18] The development of the city under industrial capitalism led to the spatial segregation of many women and men, creating the duality of 'private suburb' and 'public city' where work, business and political life exist. Women are increasingly engaged in paid employment *and* domestic work at home, so new spatial urban forms and activities are emerging. These include new forms of dwelling and changed practices within existing dwellings. Further research has challenged dominant conceptions of home as heterosexual, showing how for lesbians, sharing the heterosexual 'family' home has been an experience of oppression and has limited their capacity to create their own sense of identity.[19]

Shelter and Homelessness

If having a permanent, secure home provides a range of significant economic, social and emotional benefits, being 'homeless' clearly provides a very marginal status. In the *Nelson Evening Mail* (September 1998), for example, a story described how a homeless man was refused help from a government agency because he did not have an address. His homelessness effectively made him a 'non person'. There are many pathways into homelessness – composed of a mix of personal circumstances and structural changes such as redundancy and unemployment, level of benefits, and cost of accommodation. Data from New Zealand research have shown that the last two decades have seen a rise in the numbers of homeless people. In the 1987 study by the National Housing Commission, 17,500 households were found to be homeless. Of these 51 per cent were Maori, 32 per cent Pacific Island People and 17 per cent Pakeha. This displays a clear over-representation of Maori and Pacific Island people amongst the homeless.[20] The rising cost of accommodation relative to incomes has created an affordability problem. The restructuring of the job market, along with reforms to such areas of social provision as state housing and the mental health system (which has 'de-institutionalised' former patients of large institutions) has contributed to this increase.[21] By the mid-1990s it was estimated that around 48,000 families were 'homeless' and that housing costs were one of the most significant contributing factors.[22]

House and Home in Aotearoa/New Zealand

Home-making is an interactive and ongoing process. Places are made and re-made through life as relationships change, as people age and pass through different life stages, and as the external and local environment shifts through both the conscious action of individuals and households and through the decisions and activities of external agents such as local and national government, business firms and environmental groups. An understanding of New Zealanders' creation of and attachment to their homes must, therefore, be set within a framework that takes account of the specific features of the New Zealand context. The next section will discuss the urban and suburban world in which home-making is taking place, the nature of the households, families and individuals involved in it, and the range of activities that are based in and around the home and which are thus integral to home-making in 2000.

Urban and Suburban Worlds

Low residential building densities have dominated New Zealand's urban areas. A rapid growth of this suburban form occurred in the 1950s and 1960s as a result of migration (both internal and from overseas) and the baby boom

(Figure 2.2). Suburbia was composed of single-family, one-storey houses, typically the three-bedroom 'bungalow', each on its own 'quarter acre section'. Over time the size of the section has decreased, so that subdivisions are now more likely to be one fifth of an acre (around 600 square metres). The presence of sections around most houses has resulted in gardening – both for production and leisure – being a significant part of many people's experience. The nuclear family comprising mum, dad and two kids was seen as the ideal, and suburbs were held to be great places to bring up children because they offered clean living in fresh surroundings. During the same period the nuclear family became the unit of consumption, where the products of the growing manufacturing industries of the 1950s and 1960s (whiteware, televisions, cars, mowers, telephones, and so on) were required to maintain and enhance the 'suburban lifestyle'.

(Source: *Housing in New Zealand*. Report of the Commission of Inquiry into Housing, 1971)

Figure 2.2: Suburban housing

The speed of suburban construction meant that houses were often built in advance of such facilities and services as shops, community centres, public transport and telephone connections. Suburbs tended to be 'dormitories' from which mainly men went out to work in paid employment. This led to the semi-isolation of many women and children and the rise of 'suburban neurosis'. By 1970 Aotearoa/New Zealand's suburbs were often seen as bland, monotonous and boring places of conformist activity, where leisure was typified by work on the house and section.[23] Some residential place-making took on largely negative connotations, especially in areas where the state was strongly involved in the creation of the new suburbs.[24] Good examples include suburban Wellington and the growth of Porirua East, Naenae and Wainuiomata; suburban South Auckland and Otara, or suburban West Auckland and Henderson and Massey.[25] Negative images, once created, have been hard for the suburbs to throw off, despite changes since their development.[26]

Suburban Change

During the 1980s and 1990s the pattern of suburban living changed. Household production and consumption patterns were influenced by far-reaching restructuring of many other aspects of New Zealand society as a result of economic reforms leading to market liberalisation. These shifts have been so significant that the typification of leisure and the kiwi weekend centred on suburban domestic activity has undergone many changes. These changes have had a considerable influence on the ways people construct their sense of self and place.[27]

The 1980s and 1990s also saw dramatic changes in the use of time. The changes to both work hours and leisure activities led to seven days a week shopping, and significantly influenced leisure patterns. City centres are no longer deserted at the weekend and New Zealanders have experienced the rise of a 'café culture' in the main cities, stimulated by the emergence of yuppies in the late 1980s. More spending power, amongst at least a proportion of city dwellers, has been aided by the growth of dual-income households.[28] Wealth and income distributions have been affected by employment and tax changes and by the booms and slumps within the housing market. The result has been a much greater degree of income inequality and the emergence of a high-consuming section of the population. This has stimulated the development of 'new landscapes of consumption' often associated with inner-city revival (Figures 3a and 3b) and the growth of a café society.[29] Further encouragement for these consumption-oriented lifestyles is found in the growth of lifestyle magazines and city promotional activity.[30]

Changes in, and liberalisation of, government policy associated with environmental management, including urban planning (the Resource Management Act 1991), house construction (the Building Act 1991) and local government administration (the Local Government Act 1989 No.2 and 1996) have been influential in this process.[31] They have led to changes in the pattern of suburban and inner-city development. Suburban infill has occurred and the conversion of unused central city office accommodation to apartments has been particularly popular in Auckland and Wellington.

(Source: *Housing in New Zealand*. Report of the Commission of Inquiry into Housing, 1971)

Figure 2. 3a: Inner-city housing – the late nineteenth and early twentieth centuries' legacy

Figure 2.3b: Inner-city housing – revival, infill and gentrification

Home Ownership

Housing tenure issues lie at the centre of home-making in Aotearoa/New Zealand. Home ownership is a central objective for most New Zealanders. At the 1991 Census, over 73 per cent of households were classified as being owners and in 1996, 70 per cent were similarly classified (Table 2.1). Despite this small decrease between 1991 and 1996, home ownership rates in Aotearoa/New Zealand are extremely high by international standards. This is the case even though New Zealanders have faced rapid economic and social change, increased interest rates, and housing price instability in the 1980s and 1990s. The slight reduction in home-ownership between 1991 and 1996 is a reflection of the changing economic circumstances affecting particularly younger households as they struggle with a more difficult job market, higher interest rates, and greater debts from tertiary study, for example. The continuing high rates of ownership also reflect the absence of rental properties and thus of viable renting alternatives. Of significance is the variation in home ownership across the population. As Table 2.1 shows, Maori and Pacific Island people have much lower ownership rates. This affects their ability to accumulate wealth via home ownership and so contributes to continuing inequality across the ethnic communities in Aotearoa/New Zealand.[32] Research among Maori undertaken by Te Puni Kokiri in 1998 found a strong desire to own a home as it provides shelter, stability and security for children and other whanau.[33]

Table 2.1: Occupancy of Dwellings 1991, 1996

	All Population		Maori		Pacific Island People	
	1991	1996	1991	1996	1991	1996
Owned with mortgage	39.4	36.7	40.4	37.6	38.9	33.6
Owned without mortgage	34.2	32.3	14.9	12.8	8.1	8.4
Not specified		1.5		1.0		1.3
Total owned	73.6	70.5	55.3	51.4	47.0	43.3
Rented	23.1	25.6	44.7	46.8	50.9	54.3
Not specified	3.3	3.9		1.8	2.1	2.4
Total	100.00	100.00	100.00	100.00	100.00	100.00

(Source: Census of Population 1991, 1996).

The promotion of home ownership has a long history in New Zealand public policy. It has consistently been associated with positive virtues and has been seen as a way of creating model citizens, integrated into the mainstream of New Zealand social and economic life. This mainstream of policy, however, has been patriarchal and women and men have not had equal access to home ownership.[34] From the 1950s to the 1970s support for home ownership in the form of government-subsidised loans and capitalisation of family benefits meant that most newly formed households could buy a house. The majority were low-cost houses supplied by group builders in new subdivisions. This was also a reflection of the fact that government policy was directed at increasing the supply of housing, so was restricted to the purchase of new – rather than existing – housing.

Home for most New Zealanders has thus been constituted through ownership; owning one's house has been seen as a secure base for the development of a household and family. Other forms of housing tenure, particularly renting, have been seen as morally acceptable for members of society who are not yet fully fledged (such as young adults), but owning one's own house (or at least having secured a mortgage) has been an important source of social respectability in Aotearoa/New Zealand for many years.

Household Formation

Patterns of household formation are also of significance, with a trend towards a greater number of single-person, sole-parent and childless-couple households. This leads to a greater variety of life stages and increased diversity in the material conditions of life in Aotearoa/New Zealand. This may indicate that over the next decade the factors which constitute a home are also likely to become increasingly diverse – if so, this will have implications for the ways in which New Zealanders construct their sense of identity, their sense of place and their housing requirements. Changes in the way that home is interpreted also occur with movements through the life course. These includes forming a new household or living alone, ageing, having or not having children, being a two-income post-children family, and retiring from the paid workforce. All these shifts potentially affect how home is seen and how it is reconstructed in both its physical and social forms. In older age such events as the death of a spouse, ill-health and diminished capacity are likely to be key factors. This is especially true in

Aotearoa/New Zealand, where household occupants have often been actively involved in maintenance of house and garden.

What Gets Done?

The activities which are pursued at home or by using the home as a new form of activity-centre have also changed in importance with changes in family relationships. The home was seen traditionally as the 'heart of family life', a place where the most intimate and special times and activities were located and experienced. Homes were where families met and shared social and other leisure activities. Houses and homes now serve a greater variety of functions and their use for leisure and work is changing. In a recent study the author suggested that 'future homes would be multifunctional spaces', providing 'an office for home-based work, a substitute for short-term hospital and long-term care, centre for learning, virtual shopping mall, virtual community center, technology based entertainment center and for some a prison (as the popularity of home detention increases).[35] These suggestions show how extensively many assume the work/leisure/home relationship will be reshaped over the next decade.

Opportunities to work at home have increased as a result of both telecommunication changes and widespread use of personal computers. This new technology, coupled with the economic restructuring which has occurred in Aotearoa/New Zealand over the 1980s and into the 1990s, has resulted in many mid-life employment redundancies and an increase in self-employed people who have established small home-based business activities. It is important to appreciate that tele-working comes in many different forms, from routine data-entry activities to independent self-employed professionals working at home. The degree of autonomy and control that tele-working provides depends on the segment of the knowledge/information economy in which the worker is engaged. This has created an interesting redesigning of space within the home – with some establishing 'offices' and keeping office hours while others, especially women, juggle their work and other family and household activities often without the benefit of a designated space for their work.[36] The changing use of space here impacts upon family life and relationships, although as yet this has not been extensively researched.

These changes are influenced by the latest phase in the development of global capitalism, based around information as the driving force. In these terms Kumar argued that the home has become an increasingly important site around which leisure and entertainment revolve with 'going out' being replaced by 'staying in'.[37] This new version of home is, in Kumar's analysis, a place where individuals live largely independent of each other, each occupying their own space and pursuing their own highly individualistic leisure activities. This suggests that 'the home is becoming less of a haven in a heartless world for the family and more like a hotel for paying (and non-paying) guests'.[38] The further privatisation of leisure and tele-shopping will continue to redefine the range of activities that can be done from our houses and may well reshape our understanding of the meaning of home in Aotearoa/ New Zealand.

Gender also impinges on questions of home-based activity but this is an area which has not been extensively researched in Aotearoa/New Zealand. Fiction and writing in the popular media have, however, drawn attention to the ways in which the home is constituted differently for women and men.[39] Janet Frame[40] and Robin Hyde,[41] for example, wrote ironically of suburbia, exposing the different gender experiences of New Zealanders from the 1930s to the 1950s. Existing social scientific work supports these experiences. In studies of older New Zealanders, for example, clear differences have emerged between the ways women and men talk about what home means to them.[42] Men's retirement was also found to be a significant stage. At this time many women's sole occupancy of the house during working hours changes, and they have to share space with their partner. This requires a renegotiation of how the household's space is to be used and understood.

Further gender-related data on the ways in which activities are carried out in the home can be derived from the Census, which in 1996 explored the area of unpaid work in the home by sex and age group. These data show that more women than men in each of the age groups covered are engaged in household work. The greatest differences are found in the areas of caring for children and for the aged, ill or disabled. With respect to childcare, the proportion of men ranges from 30 per cent (20–24 years) to 42 per cent (35–39 years) whereas for women the figures are 69 per cent (20–24 years) to 58 per cent (35–39 years). Caring for the aged is also more likely to be done by women in each age group than men. The distribution of unpaid work shows a nine to ten per cent difference between women and men: around 45 to 46 per cent of men participate in unpaid work in the home, whereas for women the proportion is 54 to 55 per cent.

The significance of particular forms of home-based domestic work, do-it-yourself maintenance and building, has meant that many New Zealanders have developed a special type of relationship with their houses, which has seen them continually renovating and changing the physical shape of house and garden – painting the roof or the house, putting up and staining fences, extending the living areas or building on rumpus rooms. The weekends were often punctuated with the sounds of the home-handyman's tools, the growl of the motor-mower and chainsaw and the whine of the power drill, as New Zealand men demonstrated their ingenuity and commitment to a culture of 'do-it-yourself', based around fixing and producing rather than artistic creativity. Inside the house their female partners pursued similar activities. The garden was also a site of activity where adult members of the house grew and maintained vegetables or flowers for family consumption. Gardening was often gendered, with men working in the vegetable garden and women taking charge of the flowerbeds. Children were also 'press-ganged' into these gardening efforts, which were a combination of work and leisure for adults, but for children an often unwanted diversion from play. The burgeoning number of garden and outdoor living centres with their designer courtyards, terraces, decks, patios, arches, terracotta pots and landscape architectural advice have now turned many house sections from a site of vegetable production into a landscape of consumption, thus indicating how gardening has changed.

Conclusion

This chapter has explored the making of home in contemporary Aotearoa/ New Zealand. We have argued that this is an ongoing and contingent activity. Both macro and micro social processes shape it. Over the past two decades significant macro processes have included the restructuring of economic and social life as a result of shifts in economic and social policy; the impact of new information technologies; shifts in the urban planning environment; and the changing dynamics of population composition and household formation. The continuing significance of home ownership and the way that housing functions as a source of shelter, wealth accumulation and location for the development of individual and family identity are also important. At the micro level we explored 'what gets done in the home'. Here we drew attention to the significance of life-course changes and the idea that what constitutes home is a product of social interaction and negotiation between and amongst household members. Gender is another significant marker of home-making. Women and men often participate in different activities in the home and have different understandings of what constitutes a home. Here change is also occurring, with the rise of dual-earner families and the increased use of the home as a site for work as well as leisure activity. Home remains for most New Zealanders a special kind of place where in their everyday lives they can exercise some autonomy and carve out a sense of place and identity. Home-making is becoming a more varied and differentiated activity, and it is increasingly difficult to speak easily about the typical New Zealand home. This is a trend which is likely to continue in a world where difference and fragmentation are increasingly common.

Acknowledgements

Research for this chapter was conducted as part of a combined University of Canterbury and Lincoln University study of the meaning of house and home in Aotearoa/New Zealand. The authors gratefully acknowledge financial support from the New Zealand Foundation for Research Science and Technology.

Endnotes

[1]   Eyles, J. (1989) 'The geography of everyday life', in Gregory D. and Walford R. (eds), *Horizons of Human Geography,* Totowa, N.J: Barnes and Noble.

[2]   Jackson, P. (1986) 'Social geography: the rediscovery of place', *Progress in Human Geography* vol. 10, pp. 118–124.

[3]   Massey, D. (1995) 'Places and their pasts', *History Workshop Journal* vol. 39, pp. 182–192.

[4]   Ibid.

[5]   Sennett, R. (2000) 'Street and office: Two sources of identity', in Hutton, W. and Giddens, A. (eds), *On the Edge: Living with Global Capitalism,* London: Johnathon Cape, p. 176.

[6]   Ibid.

[7]   Ley, D. (1981) 'Behavioural geography and the philosophies of meaning', in Cox, K. R. and Gollege, R. G. (eds), *Behavioural Problems in Geography Revisited,* London: Methuen, p. 219.

[8]   Colston, F. (1998) 'Welcome to our place: New Zealanders at home', Cover Illustration of *Outlook,* Lincoln University, April.

[9]   Perkins, H. C., Thorns, D. C. and Winstanley, A. (1999*) The Study of 'Home' from a Social Scientific Perspective: An Annotated Bibliography,* University of Canterbury and Lincoln University, House and Home Project, Christchurch and Lincoln; Perkins, H. C. and Thorns, D. C. (1999) 'House and home and their interactions with changes in New Zealand's urban systems, households and family structures', *Housing, Theory and Society* vol. 16, no. 3, pp. 124–135.

[10]   Townsend, M. (2000) 'Building the future from the fragments: Women's views on 21st century housing and neighbourhoods'. Paper presented at the European

Network Housing Research Conference, Gavle, Sweden.

11   Young, I. M. (1997) *Intersecting Voices: Dilemmas of Gender, Political Philosophy and Policy*, New Jersey: Princeton University Press.

12   O'Doyle, K. (1992) 'The symbolic meaning of house and home', *American Behavioral Scientist* vol. 35, no. 6, pp. 790–802.

13   Marcus Cooper, C. (1995) *House as a Mirror of Self*, Berkeley: Conari Press.

14   Nilsen, R. (2000) 'Children in houses: preliminary results from a study with girls and boys'. Paper presented at the European Network Housing Research Conference, Gavle, Sweden; Ruud, M.E. (2000) 'Youth and housing. Preferences, options and limitations'. Paper presented at the European Network Housing Research Conference, Gavle, Sweden.

15   Dupuis, C. A. (1997) 'Housing Wealth and Inheritance: A Theoretical and Empirical Exploration', unpublished PhD thesis, Department of Sociology, Christchurch: University of Canterbury.

16   Badcock, B. (1994) 'Snakes and ladders? The housing market and wealth distribution in Australia', *International Journal of Urban and Regional Research* vol. 18, no. 4, pp. 609–627; Dupuis, A. and Thorns, D.C. (1997), 'Housing and wealth accumulation: the New Zealand case', *Urban Policy and Research* vol. 15, no.3, pp. 189–202; Hamnett, C. (1998) *Winners and Losers*, London: London University Press.

17   Thorns, D.C. (1995) 'Housing inheritance and class reproduction', in Forrest, R. and Murie, A. (eds), *Housing and Family Wealth in Comparative Perspective*, London: Routledge.

18   Young, I.M. (1997) *Intersecting Voices: Dilemmas of Gender, Political Philosophy and Policy*.

19   Johnston, L. and Valentine G. (1995) 'Wherever I lay my girlfriend, that's my home', in Bell, D. and Valentine, G. (eds), *Mapping Desire: Geographies of Sexualities*, London: Routledge.

20   Thorns, D.C. (1989) 'The production of homelessness: From individual failure to system inadequacies', *Housing Studies* vol 4, no.4, pp. 267–280.

21   Kearns, R. (1995) 'Worried sick about housing: Extending the debate on housing and health', *Community Mental Health in New Zealand* vol. 9, no. 1, pp. 5–11.

22   Thorns, D.C. (2000) 'Housing policy in the 1990s – New Zealand a decade of change', *Housing Studies* vol 15, no. 1, pp. 129–138; Waldergrave, C. and Sawrey, R. (1994) *The Extent of Serious Housing Need in New Zealand 1992 and 1993,* Social Policy Unit, The Family Centre, Lower Hutt.

23   Commission of Inquiry 1971, *Housing in New Zealand,* Report of the Commission of Inquiry into Housing, Wellington.

24   Schrader, B., Kirkpatrick, R., Williams, J. and Fraser, T. (1997) Plate 74: 'Housing and the family: Public and private housing in Wellington, 1930 to 1950s', in McKinnon, M. (ed.) with Bradley, B. and Kirkpatrick, R., *New Zealand Historical Atlas – Ko Paptuanuku e Takoto Nei,* Auckland: David Bateman in association with Historical Branch, Department of Internal Affairs.

25   Schrader, B. (1996) 'A brave new world? Ideal versus reality in postwar Naenae', *New Zealand Journal of History* vol 30, no.1, pp. 61–79.

26   De Bruin, A. and Dupuis, A. (1995) 'The implications of housing policy for women in non- nuclear families', Paper presented at the Eighteenth Conference of the New Zealand Geographical Society, Christchurch: University of Canterbury; Le Heron, R. and Pawson, E. (eds) (1996) *Changing Places: New Zealand in the Nineties*, Auckland: Longman Paul; Thorns, D.C. (1992) *Fragmenting Societies?*, London: Routledge.

27   Le Heron, R. and Pawson, E. (eds) (1996) *Changing Places: New Zealand in the Nineties*, Auckland: Longman Paul; Thorns, D.C. (1992) *Fragmenting Societies?*, London: Routledge.

28   Goodger, K., O'Brien, P., McPherson, M., Meha, R., Spellerberg, A. and Brown, D. (1993) *All about Women in New Zealand*, Wellington: Statistics New Zealand; Perkins, H. C. and Gidlow, B. (1996) 'New social arrangements – case study: The dual-career family', in Le Heron, R. and Pawson, E. (eds), *Changing Places: New Zealand in the Nineties*, Auckland: Longman Paul.

29   Dupuis, A. (2000) 'City life', in McLennon, G., Ryan A. and Spoonley, P. (eds), *Exploring Society*, Auckland: Pearson Education.

30   Perkins, H. C. and Thorns, D. C. (2000) 'The impact of place promotion strategies on urban planning and development', in Memon, P. A. and Perkins, H. C. (eds), *Environmental Planning and Management in New Zealand*, Palmerston North: Dunmore Press.

31   Memon, P.A. and Perkins, H.C. (eds) (1993) *Environmental Planning in New Zealand*, Palmerston North: Dunmore Press; Memon, P.A. and Perkins, H.C. (eds) (2000) *Environmental Planning and Management in New Zealand*, Palmerston North: Dunmore Press.

32   Thorns, D.C. (1995) 'Housing inheritance and class reproduction', in Forrest, R. and Murie, A. (eds), *Housing and Family Wealth in Comparative Perspective*, London: Routledge.

33   Te Puni Kokiri (1998) *Regional Housing Issues: Feedback from Maori*, Ministry of Maori Development, Wellington.

34   Ferguson, G. (1994) *Building the New Zealand Dream*, Palmerston North: Dunmore Press; De Bruin, A. and Dupuis, A. (1995) 'The implications of housing policy for women in non-nuclear families'.

35   Townsend, M. (2000) 'Building the future from the fragments: Women's views on 21st century housing and neighbourhoods'.

36   Armstrong, N. (1997) 'Flexible Work and Disciplined Selves: Telework, Gender and Discourses of Subjectivity', unpublished PhD thesis, Department of Sociology, Massey University, Palmerston North.

37   Kumar, K. (1995) *From Post-Industrial to Post-Modern Society*, Oxford: Blackwell.

38   Ibid., p. 159.

39   Winstanley, A. (forthcoming) 'Housing, Home and Women's Identities',

unpublished PhD thesis, Department of Sociology, University of Canterbury.
[40]   Frame, J. (1957) *Owls Do Cry,* Christchurch: Pegasus Press.
[41]   Hyde, R. (1938) *The Godwits Fly*, Auckland: Hurst and Blackett (republished 1970, Auckland University Press).
[42]   Dupuis, A. and Thorns, D.C. (1998) 'Home, home ownership and the search for ontological security', *Sociological Review* vol. 46, no.1, pp. 24–47; Mansvelt, J. (1997a) 'Working at leisure – critical geographies of aging', *Area* vol. 29, no. 4, pp. 289–298; Mansvelt, J. (1997b) 'Playing at home? Emplacement, embodiment and the active retiree in New Zealand/Aotearoa', *New Zealand Geographer* vol. 53, no. 2, pp. 57–61; Mansvelt, J. and Perkins, H.C. (1998) 'Putting recreation and leisure in their place: The geography of leisure', in Perkins, H. C. and Cushman, G. (eds), *Time Out? Leisure, Recreation and Tourism in New Zealand and Australia*, Auckland: Addison Wesley Longman.

Bibliography

Armstrong, N. (1997) 'Flexible Work and Disciplined Selves: Telework, Gender and Discourses of Subjectivity', unpublished PhD thesis, Department of Sociology, Massey University, Palmerston North.

Badcock, B. (1994) 'Snakes and ladders? The housing market and wealth distribution in Australia', *International Journal of Urban and Regional Research* vol. 18, no. 4, pp. 609–627.

Colston, F. (1998) 'Welcome to our place: New Zealanders at home', Cover Illustration of *Outlook,* Lincoln University, April.

Commission of Inquiry (1971) *Housing in New Zealand*, Report of the Commission of Inquiry into Housing, Wellington.

De Bruin, A. and Dupuis, A. (1995) 'The implications of housing policy for women in non-nuclear families', Paper presented at the Eighteenth Conference of the New Zealand Geographical Society, Christchurch: University of Canterbury.

Dupuis, C. A. (1997) 'Housing Wealth and Inheritance: A Theoretical and Empirical Exploration', unpublished PhD thesis, Department of Sociology, Christchurch: University of Canterbury.

Dupuis, A. (2000) 'City life', in McLennon, G., Ryan, A. and Spoonley, P. (eds) *Exploring Society*, Auckland: Pearson Education.

Dupuis, A. and Thorns, D.C. (1996) 'Meaning of home for home owners', *Housing Studies* vol. 11, no. 4, pp. 485–501.

Dupuis, A. and Thorns, D.C. (1997) 'Housing and wealth accumulation: The New Zealand case', *Urban Policy and Research* vol. 15, no.3, pp. 189–202.

Dupuis, A. and Thorns, D.C. (1998) 'Home, home ownership and the search for ontological security', *Sociological Review* vol. 46, no.1, pp. 24–47.

Eyles, J. (1989) 'The geography of everyday life', in Gregory, D. and Walford, R. (eds) *Horizons of Human Geography,* Totowa, N.J: Barnes and Noble.

Ferguson, G. (1994) *Building the New Zealand Dream,* Palmerston North: Dunmore Press.

Frame, J. (1957) *Owls Do Cry,* Christchurch: Pegasus Press.

Goodger, K., O' Brien, P., McPherson, M., Meha, R., Spellerberg, A. and Brown, D. (1993) *All About Women in New Zealand,* Wellington: Statistics New Zealand.

Hamnett, C. (1998) *Winners and Losers,* London: London University Press.

Hyde, R. (1938) *The Godwits Fly,* Auckland: Hurst and Blackett (Republished 1970, Auckland University Press).

Jackson, P. (1986) 'Social geography: the rediscovery of place', *Progress in Human Geography* vol. 10, pp. 118–124.

Johnston, L. and Valentine G. (1995) 'Wherever I lay my girlfriend that's my home', in Bell, D. and Valentine, G. (eds) *Mapping Desire: Geographies of Sexualities,* London: Routledge.

Kearns, R. (1995) 'Worried sick about housing: Extending the debate on housing and health', *Community Mental Health in New Zealand* vol. 9, no. 1, pp. 5–11.

Kumar, K. (1995) *From Post-Industrial to Post Modern Society,* Oxford: Blackwell.

Le Heron, R. and Pawson, E. (eds) (1996) *Changing Places: New Zealand in the Nineties,* Auckland: Longman Paul.

Ley, D. (1981) 'Behavioural geography and the philosophies of meaning', in Cox, K. R. and Gollege, R. G. (eds) *Behavioural Problems in Geography Revisited,* London: Methuen.

Mansvelt, J. (1997a) 'Working at leisure – critical geographies of aging', *Area* vol. 29, no. 4, pp. 289–298.

Mansvelt, J. (1997b) 'Playing at home? Emplacement, embodiment and the active retiree in New Zealand/Aotearoa', *New Zealand Geographer* vol. 53, no. 2, pp. 57–61.

Mansvelt, J. and Perkins, H.C. (1998) 'Putting recreation and leisure in their place: The geography of leisure', in Perkins, H. C. and Cushman, G. (eds) *Time Out? Leisure, Recreation and Tourism in New Zealand and Australia,* Auckland: Addison Wesley Longman.

Marcus Cooper, C. (1995) *House as a Mirror of Self,* Berkeley: Conari Press.

Massey, D. (1995) 'Places and their pasts', *History Workshop Journal* vol. 39, pp. 182–192.

Memon, P.A. and Perkins, H.C. (eds) (1993) *Environmental Planning in New Zealand*, Palmerston North: Dunmore Press.

Memon, P.A. and Perkins, H.C. (eds) (2000) *Environmental Planning and Management in New Zealand*, Palmerston North: Dunmore Press.

Nilsen, R. (2000) 'Children in houses: preliminary results from a study with girls and boys'. Paper presented at the European Network Housing Research Conference, Gavle, Sweden.

O'Doyle, K. (1992) 'The symbolic meaning of house and home', *American Behavioral Scientist* vol. 35, no. 6, pp. 790–802.

Perkins, H. C. and Cushman, G. (eds) (1998) *Time Out? Leisure, Recreation and Tourism in New Zealand and Australia*, Auckland: Addison Wesley Longman.

Perkins, H.C. and Gidlow, B. (1996) 'New social arrangements – case study: the dual-career family', in Le Heron, R. and Pawson, E. (eds) *Changing Places: New Zealand in the Nineties*, Auckland: Longman Paul.

Perkins, H.C. and Gidlow, B. (1991) 'Leisure research in New Zealand: patterns, problems and prospects', *Leisure Studies* vol. 10, pp. 93–104.

Perkins, H.C. and Thorns D.C. (1999) 'House and home and their interactions with changes in New Zealand's urban systems, households and family structures', *Housing, Theory and Society* vol. 16, no. 3, pp. 124–135.

Perkins, H. C. and Thorns, D. C. (2000) 'The impact of place promotion strategies on urban planning and development', in Memon, P. A. and Perkins, H. C. (eds) *Environmental Planning and Management in New Zealand,* Palmerston North: Dunmore Press.

Perkins, H. C., Thorns, D. C. and Winstanley, A. (1999) *The Study of 'Home' from a Social Scientific Perspective: An Annotated Bibliography,* University of Canterbury and Lincoln University, House and Home Project, Christchurch and Lincoln.

Ruud, M.E. (2000) 'Youth and housing. Preferences, options and limitations'. Paper presented at the European Network Housing Research Conference, Gavle, Sweden.

Schrader, B. (1996) 'A brave new world? Ideal versus reality in postwar Naenae', *New Zealand Journal of History* vol. 30, no.1, pp. 61–79.

Schrader, B., Kirkpatrick, R., Williams, J. and Fraser, T. (1997) Plate 74: 'Housing and the family: public and private housing in Wellington, 1930 to 1950s', in McKinnon, M. (ed.) with Bradley, B. and Kirkpatrick, R. *New Zealand Historical Atlas – Ko Paptuanuku e Takoto Nei*, Auckland: David Bateman in association with Historical Branch, Department of Internal Affairs.

Sennett, R. (2000) 'Street and office: Two sources of identity', in Hutton,

W. and Giddens, A. (eds) *On the Edge: Living with Global Capitalism,* London: Johnathon Cape.

Te Puni Kokiri (1998) *Regional Housing Issues: Feedback from Maori,* Wellington: Ministry of Maori Development.

Thorns, D.C. (1989) 'The production of homelessness: From individual failure to system inadequacies', *Housing Studies* vol. 4, no.4, pp. 267–280.

Thorns, D.C. (1992) *Fragmenting Societies?,* London: Routledge.

Thorns, D.C. (1995) 'Housing inheritance and class reproduction', in Forrest, R. and Murie, A. (eds) *Housing and Family Wealth in Comparative Perspective,* London: Routledge.

Thorns, D.C. (2000) 'Housing policy in the 1990s – New Zealand: A decade of change', *Housing Studies* vol. 15, no. 1, pp.129–138.

Townsend, M. (2000) 'Building the future from the fragments: Women's views on 21st century housing and neighbourhoods'. Paper presented at the European Network Housing Research Conference, Gavle, Sweden.

Waldergrave, C. and Sawrey, R. (1994) *The Extent of Serious Housing Need in New Zealand 1992 and 1993,* Social Policy Unit, The Family Centre, Lower Hutt.

Winstanley, A. (forthcoming) 'Housing, Home and Women's Identities', unpublished PhD thesis, Department of Sociology, University of Canterbury.

3

Negotiating Housework

Ruth Habgood

Everyday life in most New Zealand households continues to be characterised by gender inequalities in tasks and responsibilities. Despite popular and sociological claims that male partners have begun to take more responsibility in the domestic sphere there is little evidence to support these assertions. Studies of domestic work from around the world have consistently shown that few heterosexual couples, especially those who are parents, depart in any significant ways from the dominant 'conventional' patterns of female responsibility for domestic work and childcare. Variations cross-nationally, historically and within specific societies have been small, and patterns of women's responsibility for domestic work and childcare remain pervasive, predominant and remarkably stable.[1] It is, McMahon[2] suggests, 'one of the few sociological phenomena of which this can be said'.

There is no evidence to suggest that everyday life in New Zealand households is any different, and the evidence suggests that things are much the same here as in other Western economies.[3] May's study of inter-generational change and the more general studies such as those of Barrington and Gray and Bell and Adair, as well as the historical work of Olssen and Levesque and Toynbee all provide support for the assumption that the findings of the studies from similar countries are broadly applicable in the New Zealand context.[4] These patterns are both ordinary and remarkable. They have resisted major social changes and shown little response to the changes that have reworked women's lives.

The More Things Change, the More They Stay the Same

Since the beginning of the twentieth century, many aspects of women's lives have changed significantly. Women's access to educational and employment opportunities have increased markedly. The greatest changes have been in married women's participation in paid employment from the 1960s onwards. In New Zealand, married women's participation in full-time paid employment rose from around four per cent of all married women in the 1930s to over 60 per cent by 1996. As a result women now have greater access to money than in previous generations. By 1984 women's weekly earnings had risen to 76.3 per cent of men's and currently stand at around 79 per cent. However, while their weekly wages have risen, increases in overall incomes have been less dramatic due to many women withdrawing from paid employment to raise children. The median income of women relative to men stood at 51 per cent by 1986, and by 1996 it had risen to only just over 57 per cent, with much of this rise due to a reduction in male incomes in the 1990s.[5]

Compared to their mothers or grandmothers, women now have more choice over when they have children, giving birth to fewer and raising them for a much smaller proportion of their lives. The average number of children in families fell from 4.3 in 1961 to 1.95 in 1996. Alongside this fall was a steady rise in women's age at marriage from its lowest point of the century, 21.7 years in 1971, to 30.7 years in 1996.[6] This means that most women in the 1980s and 90s spent a longer time in paid employment before they married, raised fewer children and were likely to be employed as they did so, and were likely to have their last child leave home when they were still in their early forties.

By the mid 1980s the dual-earner nuclear family had become the dominant arrangement for raising children. The proportion of breadwinner nuclear families continued to fall from 30.3 per cent of two-parent families in 1986 to only 18.8 per cent in 1996. By 1996, dual-earner families were not only the most common family type for raising children, but 31.2 per cent of all two-parent families had both parents in full-time employment. More than one third of women are now employed from the time their children are born, and almost 80 per cent will be employed by the time their children are teenagers.[7]

Changes to divorce laws and the introduction of the domestic purposes benefit for single parents have assisted women wanting to leave unsatisfactory or violent relationships. Divorce after two years' separation became possible in 1980. The divorce rate peaked sharply before settling at just under 12.5 per thousand until 1994 and then began to slowly rise again. High divorce rates have contributed to the increasing numbers of single-parent households throughout the 1980s and 1990s. In 1996 17.7 per cent of all families were solo-parent families, an increase of 11 per cent since 1991. The majority of these households consist of women and children.[8] This means that everyday life for many women and children will be that of living in a single-parent household for at least some of their lives.

Not only have the demands on mothers undergone a major transformation, but domestic tasks themselves have also changed. Shopping and cooking have been simplified. There have been changes in household furnishings and levels of cleanliness, improved transport and the introduction of domestic appliances such as refrigerators, electric stoves, and vacuum cleaners, all of which have made domestic work less arduous (though not less time-consuming).[9]

Despite these changes the gender division of labour persists. While men's contributions to domestic responsibilities have shown small changes in the actual tasks they undertake, the overall extent of these domestic contributions has not increased.[10] Do these differences matter? For most women, the answer is yes.

What Difference Does Difference Make?

Despite declining rates of marriage and fertility and growing divorce rates, the majority of heterosexual women still live with a male partner for a significant proportion of their adult lives. Most will also raise children. Thus, for most women, continued responsibility for domestic work and childcare has significant consequences. It means that taking care of families and the mechanics of domesticity remain central and defining features of their lives, regardless of their participation in other activities. Because women have retained responsibility for domestic life, those who are raising children either withdraw from paid employment or continue to participate on different and disadvantageous terms relative to men. This means that heterosexual women in long-term relationships are far more likely than men to be economically dependent on their partners. Not only will they shoulder the greater share of housework and childcare responsibilities, but as those defined as 'natural' specialists in nurturance and care, they are also likely to provide more personal services, care and emotional support to male partners than they will receive in return. These patterns mean that women's work has intensified and their leisure time has decreased as they have taken on wage-earning responsibilities outside the home without relinquishing responsibilities within it.

Women's responsibilities for domestic work and childrearing also affect their lives more broadly. Women's roles as mothers and wives in nuclear-family households are seen as both 'natural' and desirable. The lives of all women, whether or not they are wives and mothers, have been shaped by this presumption. These kinds of ideologies and responsibilities have served to inhibit women's opportunities to participate in arenas outside the household – such as paid employment – and have had the effect of constraining their participation in 'public' life.

Why So Little Change?

This was the central puzzle of some research I recently completed, which sought to identify some of the sources of stability and change in gendered domestic arrangements and relationships. This was approached through an investigation of the processes and conditions which allowed twenty New Zealand couples, with dependent children, to adopt unconventional domestic arrangements and responsibilities. It focused in particular on the sources of support they encountered in doing so, and on the processes and circumstances which acted to limit or unravel their attempts to innovate or 'do things differently'.

Although the study focused on 'unusual' couples, its purpose was to illuminate the processes that shape and sustain the patterns of everyday life in more conventional families. By moving contrary to gendered conventions about the division of paid and unpaid work, it was argued that couples with unusual arrangements would be more likely to feel the pressures which act to shape more dominant patterns. It was expected that their 'non-conventional' arrangements would need to be actively discussed and negotiated to be achieved, and so were likely to make them especially aware of the structures and practices they needed to work around and against, in order to sustain these arrangements. The stresses they experienced as a consequence, and the fact that they had to think about alternatives, were likely to make them more able to articulate and reflect about their experiences, their actions and their feelings. These couples were therefore seen to be well placed to provide insights into the processes which shape and sustain more conventional patterns, and to highlight constraints and possibilities for change in the way everyday domestic life is experienced in New Zealand.

The study included both heterosexual and gay/lesbian couples with dependent children. Families with two parents and dependent children were chosen because, despite a gradual decline in recent years, the dominant family experience for most people in contemporary New Zealand society remains that of being raised in a nuclear family (i.e. a two-parent family that may or may not include both biological parents) and living as a heterosexual couple before and after child-rearing in a nuclear family environment. Census data shows that in 1996, 76 per cent of dependent children and 32 per cent of adults were living in nuclear family households and a further 25 per cent in heterosexual-couple-only households.[11]

Dual-earner families were chosen because they have outnumbered breadwinner families since 1991 and they continue to increase both in number and as a proportion of all two-parent families.[12] When both partners earn, the possibilities for equity and innovation are also increased.

Becoming Different – What Does It Take, What Does It Tell Us?

Whether or not they are perceived to have been freely made, choices about the division of labour in a household are structured and shaped not only by individual circumstances and personalities but also by culture, history, economic circumstances and by specific social arrangements. The social and economic changes noted above provide a backdrop – a social framework of conditions and opportunities – that the couples in my study have utilised to develop non-conventional and more equitable ways of organising their domestic lives. The experiences of these couples as they devised and negotiated strategies to balance and weave together their needs, priorities and resources to construct their daily lives highlighted some of these connections and the ways that they have shaped their decisions and actions.

The couples interviewed had access to different sets of resources and differed in many respects from each other. Their accounts, different as they are, throw into relief some of the common threads in their experiences. This is not to say that these shared experiences or commonalities 'cause' or even promote certain kinds of 'differences' in themselves, but rather that when present *in combination with each other* they have helped to create the options that these couples were motivated to take up and to support and maintain unconventional arrangements. Where a number of these elements were weak or absent, the degree of 'difference' that could be established and the stability of the arrangement itself was threatened.

While, for example, a couple's economic circumstances, relative incomes, employment situations and a variety of other kinds of resources were important in facilitating their ability to innovate, they were not in themselves sufficient as motivating factors. On the other hand, couples who were motivated to innovate primarily as a means of realising particular sets of ideals about domestic life and relationships were to find such goals ineffective as sources of change in the absence of other kinds of supports. Couples who would be economically disadvantaged by adopting alternative arrangements, for example, faced strong disincentives to innovation, even if other motivating/supporting features existed. Successful innovation required that these various dimensions reinforced each other.

There were a variety of values, circumstances or events that motivated or pushed these couples to adopt their arrangements, and they had arrived at them via different paths. The strategies required to put the various plans into action depended not only on the kind of arrangement adopted and the material implications of the arrangement, but also on whether both partners shared motivating pressures.

I begin by looking at commonalities in the experiences of those whose arrangements were relatively stable and had worked out according to plan. The remaining parts of the chapter draw on the experiences of the couples whose relationships and arrangements were less straightforward, less 'equal' or less stable. The purpose of this discussion is to highlight sources of pressure and constraint which threaten innovation and reinforce the status quo. It includes the experiences of the gay couples, which despite the absence of gender differences were found to experience similar pressures.

Couples Sharing Domestic Commitments: Working Out as Planned

The couples who most actively pursued and successfully established and maintained innovative arrangements were those where his priorities, interests and sense of identity or self worth were not primarily or exclusively employment-based. They were also couples where both partners put a high value on her employment and career/employment aspirations, where male partners gave priority to balancing employment, domestic/family life and relationships, and where both partners took a pragmatic/utilitarian rather than a gendered approach to domestic work and childcare.

The domestic arrangements of these couples showed a high degree of consensus regarding the principles and priorities around which they were organised. What was different about these couples was not just their domestic arrangements but the processes by which they had come to adopt them. They had all jointly planned their employment and domestic arrangements around shared principles of equity and justice. They had also planned them prior to, and as a part of their decision to have children. Since their arrangements were driven by principle rather than by specific forms of organisation, they were flexible and showed little sign of the tensions, contradictions and vulnerability to change that characterised the arrangements of the couples whose arrangements had been arrived at by other processes.

These couples shared domestic work and childcare to a significant degree and central to their arrangements was a sense of fairness and joint responsibility for, and commitment to, the smooth day-to-day running of domestic affairs. This involved rather more than a simple 'acceptance in principle' of generalised notions of domestic equality – notions which have been shown to be widespread but which do not in practice translate into equitable domestic arrangements.[13]

Family responsibilities were also central to both partners' calculations about life choices and both partners were actively engaged in balancing employment and family priorities. Both partners described their domestic responsibilities as central priorities, to be balanced with other demands.

> ... basically I think it's actually more a matter of a commitment to the domestic situation on the part of both partners that kind of characterises what we're doing and fitting everything in around that, I mean, someone's got to earn some money to keep body and soul together, someone's got to look after the kids. (Patrick)

Women's employment was valued by both partners in these couples not simply, or even primarily, for the economic security it provided, but because it was something that the woman wanted to do. Nevertheless, it was also important for the economic feasibility of arrangements where women were the primary earners, or for 'alternating' arrangements in which women's incomes were not only sufficient to support their families but also similar to or greater than their partner's.

The male partner having a source of self worth, identity and purpose which had its roots outside of paid employment was important not only for increasing the appeal of alternative arrangements and decreasing personal barriers to innovation, but for the survival of these arrangements over time.

For one man, fatherhood itself became a significant source of identity and self worth.

> I found I liked looking after kids although ... I never saw myself much as a dad. I don't know why... I found it to be one of the major mysteries of my life don't know why I never saw myself in that role. ... I don't care if I never work again in a paid capacity. I'd be happy to stay home for the next 10 years and look after the kids. (George)

None of the men in these arrangements focused on employment as their primary interest or source of satisfaction. Even Louis, a man who found his job interesting and satisfying and would not willingly give it up, did not pursue it as a 'career' and had allowed a number of opportunities for advancement to slip by. His experiences at work, which resulted from his sharing domestic and childcare responsibilities, point to a significant source of pressure on sharing arrangements.

Louis works for a large manufacturing company. The management reacted very badly to his request for half a day off to alternate the minding of a sick child with his wife, even though his employment contract allows his own sick leave to be taken for this purpose.

> We had a huge hassle last year when Annie had the chicken pox. He took time off, I took time off and they got really upset about him taking time off. ... From my perspective as a manager that's certainly better because, he's taking half the time needed off. I can't see how managers can't see it ... you know I feel like shaking them. (Marion)

One of the reasons 'they can't see it' is because they were 'policing' gender as well as 'productivity'. Although many women face equally restrictive employment conditions, in this case management's rules were differentially applied according to gender. Louis works independently to deadlines and his absence would have little if any effect on anyone else. Yet when a female secretary on whom a number of people depend took a whole day off for the same purpose management was quite accepting and made no fuss. The management was also unhelpful about Louis taking leave around the births of his children and has remained rigid over the possibility of him working flexitime. Another man had also experienced this kind of gender 'policing', finding it hard to be taken seriously when he sought part-time work with a friend. These values are expressed and policed not only by management but also, in the case of males, by workmates, particularly other men:

> I'm getting constantly pressured by other men at work and razed because I do all the washing of the clothes, we share the cooking arrangements and all the other things that you know we do ... and there's a lot of people ... you'd be amazed. (Louis)

Louis had wanted to push for changes at work and reword his contract when it comes up for renewal but the strength of his boss's reaction to his requests for leave and flexibility 'stirred up the hornets' nest'. His sense of insecurity due to uncertainties in the job market meant that he has decided 'not to push it for now'. He can see, however, that situations are likely to arise where he has no choice but to make demands, and he sees this as 'a worry'.

Because they share domestic responsibilities, Louis and his wife Marion are *both* under pressure to challenge the status quo at work to secure flexibility in their employment conditions to cope with family demands. For these couples there are challenges in two workplaces and, given gender segregation in most workplaces and occupations, their male partners are likely to be making these attempts in situations where there may have been few or no women pioneers. The male partner is also the 'wrong' gender to be making such demands. Because Marion's employment conditions are more flexible and family-friendly, the reaction of Louis's employers means that she will end up making the compromises, taking on more of these kinds of responsibilities – effectively pushing their arrangements toward more conventional patterns.

The career women in this study who worked in rigid male-defined career environments managed because they had partners who were willing in some senses to be 'wives' – to work part-time or use flexible employment arrangements. These men were mainly employed in the kinds of occupations where there was shift work, where women were employed in significant numbers and where both sexes commonly participated on a part-time or intermittent basis. These occupations included teaching, tutoring, nursing and market research.

Women are concentrated in relatively few occupations compared to men. Family-friendly employment conditions are more likely to be won in contexts where women have collective bargaining power. The situation of Louis and Marion is therefore likely to be repeated and act to undermine the efforts of couples to share domestic and childcare responsibilities.

Couples Sharing Domestic Commitments: Mixed Commitments, Mixed Results

For the other couples in the study, attempts at sharing were less straightforward, less 'equal' and usually less stable. The negotiations and arrangements that had 'worked out' for the first set of couples relied on characteristics that were either absent or weak for the remaining couples, or contradicted by other features of their lives and relationships.

These couples fell into two distinct categories. The first group were those where attempts to innovate were driven by the female partner's desire for sharing, and the second were those where innovation was driven by the male partner's dissatisfaction with his current employment or desire to pursue other activities. The men in the second group already had or were searching for alternative sources of satisfaction and self worth, or were simply disillusioned with their employment situations. Although they had made organisational choices which often saw them spending greater amounts of time with their children and taking on more domestic tasks than they might otherwise have, increased involvement with domesticity and with their children had not been the primary motivation for change. This had implications for both the meaning and extent of domestic sharing in these households. Some of these men had political, artistic or self-development goals; for one man it was simply: 'my decision, that I had wanted to do that anyway some time ago, I decided I didn't want to do full-time work. Not really, I don't really like going to work much.'

The partner who was doing things 'differently' (i.e. the male partner), was doing so as an active choice primarily motivated by personal – rather than shared, domestic or child-focused – agendas. As a consequence, they had not taken on domestic responsibilities to the same extent as either their wives or as the men in the initial group. They participated on their own terms and two had remained 'helpers' more than equal participants. In this respect they were different from those in the earlier group who were as involved with their children as their partners, and who juggled their other priorities as much as their partners did. These arrangements appeared to be quite stable, but because these men chose to participate domestically for their own reasons, reading shifts in power relations from changes in domestic participation is problematic – at least in these kinds of cases.

The couples where some form of sharing was initiated by career-committed female partners had arrangements that were changing, coming unravelled or under stress. The men in this group were also the most employment-oriented of those I interviewed, deriving their sense of identity primarily from their employment. In this sense, they were much more conventional than the men in the previous two groups. In contrast to the earlier two groups these men did not have significant alternative interests, commitments or identity sources outside of employment, and this drew them even more strongly away from domestic commitments.

The women in this group found that achieving their ideals of equality in domestic affairs was far from straightforward, and they had varying degrees of success in trying to establish things as they wanted them. These women had all worked part-time and taken time out of the workforce completely after children were born. At this point, they had found themselves taking on traditional domestic arrangements and responsibilities. While housework had previously sometimes been shared, almost all of it became the woman's responsibility once she was at home full-time. It was these women's commitment to pursuing their employment that was the primary source for change. Circumstances and working conditions dictated that for all of these families the route to regaining, maintaining or advancing the woman's employment required the man to make adjustments to his own employment plans and take on significant domestic and childcare responsibilities. This was often difficult to achieve and especially to maintain.

The women's own employment commitments, their employment status and relative earning capacity were important in helping to facilitate male domestic participation, as was the notion of 'her commitment to work' and of 'wasting her training'. In a curious reversal of the influence of paid work on domestic participation the men in these couples felt pressure to participate domestically because they applied 'market values' to their partners in their domestic negotiations. The notion of 'wasting her training' was raised a number of times and clearly carried weight in this kind of situation, as did the status of her employment, as Phillip's comments reveal:

> If I didn't have any respect for Sarah's ambitions … I mean the fact that she's a professional woman she's in a career which I consider to have some importance as worth pursuing which means that I feel that she has the right to develop that. Now if she was, I don't know, working in a shop or something, I would probably feel that my career is more important than hers and that I had more right to pursue my career than hers and, as I say, the income's probably a reflection of that. (Phillip)

In another case, where a couple worked alternating shifts and both partners' employment status was very similar, it was not so much a case of valuing the woman's employment as being unable to deny its worth.

The demands of employment and family compete with and contradict each other. The satisfaction of both, as Oakley[14] has put it, are mutually exclusive because each 'calls for more time, energy, and commitment than one person can reasonably supply, and because … the full realisation of one role threatens defeat in the other'.

Compromise, however, is not straightforward, nor is it entirely in the hands of the individual. Job security, promotion, status and respect are dependent on being seen to be committed to and serious about work. Being 'serious' about work means working full-time and the same hours as others. Those with family responsibilities come under particular pressure in these environments.

Minimising family involvements, however, remains easier for men than women. Women with children usually have little choice about family responsibilities and commitments. Men have usually felt more able to make a choice. When there is a choice, pressures to conform to the demands of employment have the effect of drawing those without strong commitments to childcare and domestic responsibilities away from the family.

Phillip had agreed to alternate taking a year off for childcare with his wife, but when the time came, he couldn't bring himself to give up his job. They ended up employing a nanny. She offered to do housework as well, and many of Phillip's domestic jobs disappeared. He was now coming back from work much later than his wife and their son needed to be fed earlier. Then they got a dishwasher, 'and I sort of probably abrogated my responsibility, filling up and tidying and emptying the dishwasher as well, so that task was removed so the equity of the arrangement fell apart.'

His wife was not happy. Despite well-laid plans, detailed negotiations and agreements and a salary to match his, they were rapidly moving towards the very situation she had gone to considerable effort to avoid.

The men in this group did not include fatherhood as central to their identities and priorities as the first group had done, nor did they have the alternative priorities or employment dissatisfactions of the second. With no alternative to balance it, employment exerted a much stronger pull away from domesticity than Phillip had expected. Even though he was not career-oriented or ambitious, he found himself increasing his hours, getting drawn further into his work culture, and defining success, satisfaction and self respect on those terms.

Phillip's situation and the dilemmas he faced help to, identify a series of processes, rewards and disincentives that drew him progressively away from his domestic commitments despite having negotiated more family-friendly working conditions than most parents could hope for. Workplace culture, values and camaraderie were elements in his desire to fit in with a set of practices and demands that devalue family involvement. Equally important were the opportunities which would become open to him if he continued to participate on the terms set by those without primary family responsibilities. A further source of pressure to maintain the status quo came from Phillip's sense that taking a year at home would involve more than a temporary change of activities or time out from employment. As he saw it staying home for a year would involve rejecting the values and activities with which he currently identified and which formed the basis of his sense of self worth, and taking on a new 'alternative' identity:

... it's not like going to work in a supermarket, it's like going to live on the Coromandel, it's an alternative lifestyle ... I'm not sure that the status thing is that important ... people don't look at you and say oh he's a house-husband therefore he's less worthy. (Phillip)

In theory at least, an alternative lifestyle *was* an option which Phillip found attractive. But he also described taking time out not as temporary parental leave, with perhaps some loss of ground in 'establishing' himself in his career, but as giving up a job he enjoyed and to which he was unsure of being able to return. Given the significance his employment had for him, making such a choice had large sanctions and costs for uncertain rewards, while the costs of maintaining the status quo were limited to the displeasure of his wife. As a consequence he remained ambivalent and torn, oscillating between what he thought and felt, unable to take the 'quality of life' decision they had planned. While he was aware of the contradictions between his beliefs and his actions, this was a dilemma that Phillip was not able to resolve for himself. He tried to rationalise his choices, but as they were made on emotional rather than rational grounds they were not defensible on those terms, as he himself recognised.

Phillip is not alone in his fears, nor are they uncommon or unfounded. A Norwegian study[15] found that men who took up parental leave did so from secure roots in paid employment. They had established themselves in their employment/fields, they maintained contact with their jobs, and they had protected jobs to which they could return. In other words those who felt they lacked this kind of security had not taken up this parental leave option. Nor did Phillip, despite his flexible and supportive working environment.

I have discussed the adoption of alternative arrangements predominantly in terms of male motivations. This is because the motivations of the women interviewed were indistinguishable between the groups. They had all been keen to continue with their employment and none had wanted to stay at home with children full-time. Most wanted a balance between family and employment rather than an exclusive focus on either. They wanted this balance not just for themselves, but for their partners as well.

In most respects they were little different to other employment-oriented women in more traditionally organised two-income families. One significant distinguishing feature of their experience, however, has been their higher relative earnings and the extent to which their families are dependent for financial security or lifestyle goals on these earnings. This has opened up opportunities and choices for these families which are not available where women have lower incomes or earn much less than their partners. While higher female income or earning power opens up options and may even provide incentives, it does not, in the absence of some of the other requirements discussed, necessarily or even commonly lead to these kinds of domestic arrangements. None of the couples in this study saw it as a reason for adopting the arrangements they had. McRae's study of families in Britain showed that in most families where women's employment had higher income and status than their male partners, women were still responsible for the bulk of childcare and domestic tasks.[16]

Burgoyne has also found that higher female earnings do not necessarily translate into greater control over money or influence the balance of power in households, as higher earnings would usually do for men.[17] Men may simply contribute less when women earn an independent income, forcing her contribution to be used for and disappear into the housekeeping. A study of income distribution in New Zealand households has found that women who contribute more than one-third to the family income do share at least in the control of household money.[18]

Couples Sharing Domestic Commitments: Gay and Lesbian Couples

The pressures and issues which combined to shape the domestic choices of the couples described above had similar effects on the arrangements of the gay and lesbian couples who participated in this study. One woman commented on the similarities between the micro-politics of her own domestic arrangements and those of her heterosexual friends:

> I know there's something Mary's said to me that some of the struggles we've had in our household, the rows, or how much housework, and who does what, is very similar ... I think they are quite trivial relatively ... the problems, but it's interesting they have been similar. (Alison)

In the gay/lesbian households, the partner who was most committed to or involved in employment had the greater ability to distance themselves from routine domestic responsibilities, while the partners less committed to work or who had only part-time employment found resisting these pressures more difficult.

This is consistent with patterns in heterosexual families where men are more often employment-committed and women give priority to family, are employed part-time, or juggle these commitments. Looking at these couples in terms of the issues identified above lends further weight to these issues' significance in shaping domestic arrangements and relationships.

Conclusions

The processes of establishing and maintaining non-conventional patterns for domestic responsibilities are complex and multifaceted. Wanting, or even needing to develop equitable or innovative domestic arrangements was insufficient on its own for the realisation of these ideals. The experiences of the couples in my study suggest that to establish and maintain unusual or innovative domestic arrangements, particular sets of circumstances, resources, and attitudes need to occur together. Shifts away from conventional patterns needed to be supported from a number of directions. This multiplicity suggests the extent to which the gendered social processes supporting conventional arrangements are also multiple and embedded in many (all?) of the conditions and interactions of everyday life. Familiar gendered outcomes resulted even when major shifts had been made in some aspects of domestic life, suggesting multiple sources of reinforcement of the gendered status quo.

The pressures shaping domestic arrangements and relationships have similar effects in homosexual and heterosexual households, pointing to some of the ways in which these arrangements go beyond individual gendered identities and activities to reflect the effects of wider (gendered) processes, practices and social arrangements.

This suggests that the rate of change in gendered domestic relations and arrangements is likely to continue to be extremely slow and will require concerted effort on a number of fronts to have any discernible effects. Having said this, the study found some conditions that seemed more significant in promoting rather than simply facilitating change. In a reversal of the usual effects of the culture and practices of paid employment on domestic affairs, it was the employment-based values men accorded to their partner's work status ('she has a career worth pursuing, if she was a shop assistant/dental nurse we wouldn't be doing this'), the value put on her training ('it would be a waste of her training'), and the acceptance of her right to pursue employment and gain satisfaction from it, that provided a motivation to participate more fully in domestic affairs. Even where they did not feel obligated in this way, some simply found it difficult to justify their non-participation in domestic work when the grounds for this were the same for their partner.

The choices the couples in the study made were also facilitated by some of the broader social changes which have occurred over the last century, suggesting that more equitable domestic options may potentially be available to a larger number. Men may not take up these options because for most of them there is no incentive and possibly some costs to do so. Their lack of participation is supported by gendered cultural and structural arrangements, and the study found no pressures for men, of the kind experienced by the women, to take on domestic responsibilities. The pressures which these men experienced remain largely individualised and a matter for private negotiation. Everyday life in New Zealand households and elsewhere is likely to remain unequal for some time yet.

Endnotes

[1] Dempsey, 1997; Bittman, 1991; Baxter, 1994.
[2] McMahon, 1999.
[3] James, 1987; James, 1985; Ritchie and Ritchie, 1997; Society for Research on Women, 1984.
[4] May, 1992; Barrington and Gray, 1981; Gray, 1983; Bell and Adair, 1985; Olssen and Levesque, 1978; Toynbee, 1986; Toynbee, 1995.
[5] Statistics New Zealand, 1999b pp.85, 108, 121; Statistics New Zealand, 1999a pp.15, 20; Novitz, 1987 p. 216.
[6] Statistics New Zealand, 1999a p. 15, 20.
[7] Statistics New Zealand, 1999b; Statistics New Zealand, 1999a p. 13; Statistics New Zealand, 1998.
[8] Statistics New Zealand, 1999a p. 14; Statistics New Zealand, 1999b; Statistics New Zealand, 1997.
[9] O'Donnell, 1992.
[10] Bittman, 1991.
[11] Statistics New Zealand, 1996.
[12] Statistics New Zealand, 1999a.
[13] Dempsey, 1997.
[14] Oakley, 1974 p. 81.
[15] Brandth and Kvande, 1998.
[16] McRae, 1986.
[17] Burgoyne, 1990.
[18] Fleming, 1997.

Bibliography

Barrington, R. and Gray, A. (1981) *The Smith Women: 100 New Zealand Women Talk About Their Lives*, Wellington: AH & AW Reed.

Baxter, J. (1994) *Work at Home: The Domestic Division of Labour*, St Lucia: University of Queensland Press.

Bell, C. and Adair, V. (1985) *Women and Change*, Wellington: National Council of Women.

Bittman, M. (1991) *Juggling Time: How Australian Families Use Time*, Canberra: Office of the Status of Women, Department of the Prime Minister and Cabinet.

Brandth, B. and Kvande, E. (1998) 'Masculinity and Child Care: The Reconstruction of Fathering', *The Sociological Review* 46, pp. 293–314.

Burgoyne, C. E. (1990) Money in Marriage: How Patterns of Allocation Both Reflect and Conceal Power', *The Sociological Review* 38, pp. 634–665.

Dempsey, K. (1997) *Inequalities in Work and Marriage: Australia and Beyond*, Melbourne: Oxford University Press.

Fleming, R. (1997) *The Common Purse: Income Sharing in New Zealand Families*, Auckland and Wellington: Auckland University Press and Bridget Williams Books.

Gray, A. (1983) *The Jones Men: 100 New Zealand Men Talk About Their Lives*, Wellington: AH & AW Reed.

James, B. (1985) 'Mill Wives: A Study of Gender Relations, Family and Work in a Single Industry Town', D.Phil. Thesis, Sociology, University of Waikato.

James, B. (1987) 'Millworkers' Wives', in Cox, S. (ed.) *Public and Private Worlds: Women in Contemporary New Zealand*, Wellington: Allen & Unwin.

May, H. (1992) *Minding Children, Managing Men*, Wellington: Bridget Williams Books.

McMahon, A. (1999) *Taking Care of Men*, Cambridge: Cambridge University Press.

McRae, S. (1986) *Cross-Class Families: A Study of Wives' Occupational Superiority*, Oxford: Oxford University Press.

Novitz, R. (1987) 'Bridging the Gap: Paid and Unpaid Work', in Cox, S. (ed.) *Public and Private Worlds: Women in Contemporary New Zealand*, Wellington: Allen & Unwin.

Oakley, A. (1974) *Women's Work: The Housewife Past and Present*. New York: Random House.

O'Donnell, J.-M. (1992) ' "Electric Servants" and the Science of Housework: Changing Patterns of Domestic Work, 1935–1956', in Brookes, B., McDonald, C. and Tennant, M. (eds), *Women in History 2*, Wellington: Bridget Williams Books.

Olssen, E. and Levesque, A. (1978) 'Towards a History of the European Family in New Zealand', in Boyden, P. K. (ed.) *Families in New Zealand Society*, Wellington: Koopman-Methuen.

Ritchie, J. and Ritchie, J. (1997) *The Next Generation: Child Rearing in*

New Zealand, Auckland: Penguin.

Society for Research on Women (1984) *Jobs, Children and Chores: A Study of Mothers in Paid Employment in the Christchurch Area*, Christchurch: Society for Research on Women in New Zealand (Inc.).

Statistics New Zealand (1996) *Census '96*, Statistics New Zealand.

Statistics New Zealand (1997) *Hot off the Press: Divorce Statistics 1996*, Statistics New Zealand.

Statistics New Zealand (1998) 1996 Provisional Statistics, Vol. 1998, Statistics New Zealand.

Statistics New Zealand (1999a) *New Zealand Now: Families and Households, 1998 Edition*, Statistics New Zealand.

Statistics New Zealand (1999b) *New Zealand Now: Women*, Statistics New Zealand.

Toynbee, C. (1986) 'Her Work, His Work and Theirs: The Household Economy and the Family in New Zealand 1900–1923', in *Sociology*, Wellington: Victoria University of Wellington.

Toynbee, C. (1995) *Her Work and His: Family Kin and Community in New Zealand 1900–1930*, Wellington: Victoria University Press.

4

Friendship and Relationships in Everyday Life

Farida Tilbury and Mike Lloyd

Sociology of Friendship

The word 'sociology' can be translated from its Latin and Greek stems as 'the study of the processes of companionship'.[1] This might suggest that sociologists know a great deal about friendship, but reviews of the literature in this area find it dominated by social psychologists, with work by sociologists much less significant.[2,3] If this lack of work by the supposed experts isn't confusing enough, one can read famous social theorists making distinctly unfriendly statements, a good example being Sartre's quip, 'Hell is other people'.[4] So why does sociology, the 'study of companionship', not have much to say about friendship?

As a partial answer, let us consider a statement from one of the best introductions to sociology. In *Thinking Sociologically* Bauman[5] begins the first chapter by stating: 'Being free and unfree at the same time is perhaps the most common of our experiences.' Bauman's notion of 'two things at the same time' is useful here because it takes us away from the idea that 'friendship' has an unproblematic core: if something can be (at least) two things at the same time, then could friendship also involve elements of dislike, hate, indifference and intolerance, for example? Many contemporary sociologists would probably answer 'yes', as the discipline as a whole has embraced a move from either/or to both/and logics.[6] If this seems a little abstract, consider a concrete example – Bech's reflections on the contemporary city:

> The city is there. Instead of trying to get away from it, you can enter it; instead of closing your eyes to it, you can open them, and see what

comes of it. The brief contacts and one-off meetings are one way of tackling the reality of the city: the fact that you are among strangers; that there are lots of them and that there are constantly new ones; that you yourself are exposed surface and hidden interior, clandestine receiver and live signal; that the mixture of proximity and distance, surface and depth, crowd and loneliness is at once attractive and alarming.[7]

Like Bech's suggestion that the city is both attractive and alarming, we want to press 'two things at the same time' – connections and transformations – as a useful way to think sociologically about 'friendship' and 'relationships'. This may seem to put us immediately at risk of not clearly defining our objects of study. Many people want concepts and words to be clear and unambiguous in their meaning, hence the word 'friend' should be a category into which we could easily place some people, but not others, in a consistent rule-like manner. Allan has suggested 'voluntary informal relationship' as a definition of friendship,[8] but the obvious trouble with this is that there are relative degrees of freedom, constraint and formality, not to mention different styles of relationship. Some researchers suggest we imagine concentric circles, putting our closest friends in the smallest circles, and more distant friends in the outer ones. But where does one put one's partner, children, parents and other relatives? What about friends you feel very close to, but who are physically distant; what about neighbours, workmates, and those increasingly common 'virtual' Internet friends? These simple questions exemplify difficulties with the categorisation of friendship.

Thought experiments and definitional discussions can be useful, but here we want to do things somewhat differently. We will not be discussing theories that attempt to define once and for all the nature of friendship. Nor do we wish to attempt a review of the literature on friendship.[9] We will discuss relevant literature along the way, but the main focus of this chapter is to present and analyse some empirical material showing how people connect, and fail to connect, with others in everyday-life situations. Not all of our material is New Zealand based; for example, we look at interactions between male beggars and female passers-by in New York. In defence of using 'foreign' material in a book on everyday life in New Zealand, we would note that sociology has never been a purely local endeavour.[11] Moreover, the above example helps us to develop an analytical understanding of relationships that is carried over to the subsequent discussion, including significant material on inter-ethnic friendships in New Zealand.

Connecting and Transforming: Approaches and Rebuffs

As the above passage from Bech indicates, social and cultural theorists are increasingly interested in cities as a defining feature of contemporary social life – it is suggested that in our everyday lives we cannot escape the influence of cities. Conjoint with this interest in cities has been explosive growth of research on globalisation. The two have developed together because it is argued that global cities like London, Paris, New York, Sydney, Tokyo (and maybe Auckland) are both the evidence for, and carriers of globalising forces. But globalisation is uneven in nature: on the one hand groups of people live in global flows, cities and culture, and on the other, groups of people are increasingly immobilised, excluded, impoverished and deprived. We know of no better finely detailed study of the latter than Duneier and Molotch's research[12] on 'panhandlers' (beggars or 'street men') in Manhattan's Greenwich Village, a place of extremes of wealth as well as marked ethnic difference. This is worth brief discussion here as it is a good example of how difficult it can be to make friendly contact with fellow humans.

Duneier and Molotch focus on encounters between black panhandlers and middle-class (mostly white) women. A point of context here is that in 1996 New York City passed an anti-panhandling statute in order to control street people, so panhandling is often practised by 'pretending' to sell something (for instance, second-hand books) or simply by breaking the law and openly begging. What Duneier and Molotch are fascinated by is how, despite having to get some minimal contact to successfully beg, street men make trouble in the street, and engage in 'interactional vandalism'. More often than not, the street men are simply ignored, as in the following vignettes from observational research[13]:

1. Mudrick: I love you baby.
She crosses her arms and quickens her walk, ignoring the comment.
2. Mudrick: Marry me.
Next, it is two white women, also probably in their midtwenties:
3. Mudrick: Hi girls, you all look very nice today. You have some money? Buy some books.
They ignore him. Next it is a young black woman.
4. Mudrick: Hey pretty. Hey pretty.
She keeps walking without acknowledging him.
5. Mudrick: 'Scuse me. 'Scuse me. I know you hear me.

The natural question to be asked about the panhandler's approach is, 'Why is he so rude?' When asked by the participant–observer researcher (Duneier) why such an abrasive approach was taken, Mudrick elaborates: 'It make me feel good and I try to make them happy, the things I say to them, you understand? The things I say, they can't accept. They gotta deal with it.' 'I try to make them happy' appears somewhat ironic, but whatever we make of Mudrick's statement, a good summary of the connection is that, 'The two individuals are actively failing to collaborate in accomplishing a "normal" interaction'[14]. It would seem that neither side connects with the other.

Why would this account of interactional 'failure' be useful to a chapter on friendship and relationships? First, a key thing to note is that the street men are breaching the basic 'civility' which is a fundamental feature of everyday social life: the abuses, rudeness and annoying tactics that the men engage in are their methods ... of depriving the women of something profoundly crucial, not just to them but to everyone – the ability to assume in others the practices behind the social bond. That another cannot be presumed to *of course* socially collaborate, even if to substantively disagree on what that world actually is, undermines trust – the 'great civility' at the base of all human accomplishment, great or small.[15]

Second, they are breaching this civility in a particular public space, the sidewalk, which is a place characterised by what Goffman called 'civil inattention'.[16] In other words, in these situations people construct a sense of 'nice distance' or 'friendly unfriendliness'. What the panhandler example shows us is that people are aware of these unspoken rules: it seems that the panhandlers have to resort to unusual interaction partly to get beyond the constraints of civil inattention.

Finally, the story of the street men nicely illustrates our central motif. Obviously, there is much that is going on, but clearly two things that we see working at the same time are inclusion and exclusion. To survive by begging the men must make some contact with those in a position to give them money – they must connect with these people – but at the same time they are all too aware of their real exclusion from the 'normal' world of earning and spending money, having a place to live, and so on. When the women disregard their gaze, walk past them as if they were not there, return their compliments with silence, 'the women appear to men as beyond human empathy and, in their coldness and lack of respect, [are therefore] appropriate as men's interactional toys'.[17] In other words, the rudeness and abrasiveness could be seen to second-guess likely responses, and hence disrupt or pre-empt the normal civil inattention by effectively being 'in your face'. In this social world, the street men naturally wish to get 'something over' their passers-by; their means to do this is 'interactional vandalism'. Hence, inclusion and exclusion are caught up at the same time, sometimes in the dynamic space of a few seconds. The streetmen try to garner sympathy, invite social intercourse, maintain the fragments of human contact; but at the same time they are all too aware of the near-futility of their situation, so 'naturally' they threaten, abuse, play 'macho' games and attempt to get their own back. To use an evocative phrase the life of these men is like having 'a dollar in a two dollar shop'[18]. Hence, it is partially understandable that they resort to these forms of 'rough urban' discursive interaction.

Tentative Connections

There are times when interaction between strangers is perfectly normal and in fact invited. Take a pub or nightclub in any New Zealand city. On Friday and Saturday nights a ritual is played out between men and women who up until then are strangers to each other. Ending the night 'not as strangers' can be achieved by careful attention to the rules of the game. Verbal contact should not begin until after some basic eye contact and perhaps even smiling. Strangers may then approach, confident that they will not be openly rebuffed, but they must then take care with their 'opening line'. Perhaps safest is an offer to buy a drink, but of course whole books have been written on the 'art of pickups' and there are many other possibilities. Whichever line is chosen, unlike the panhandlers' situation, there is relative safety. If the other party is not interested they will of course indicate so, but this is highly unlikely to involve direct rudeness. This is simply because it is tacitly understood that pubs and nightclubs on Friday and Saturday nights are places where strangers can be approached in a much more open manner. Still, there are boundaries, and just as the panhandlers broke with accepted modes of interaction, strangers in pubs can be upset by inappropriate invitations. Perhaps most frequent are instances where acceptable distance between bodies is violated. These examples serve to highlight how finely socially organised are the roles of stranger or friend-in-the-making.

So what happens when there are no bodies involved, and no space? The Internet offers a unique environment for the connection and transformation which we are interested in. Some researchers have argued that the lack of embodied selves and physical space gives a particular character to Internet interactions. Nigel Clark, in a study of computer networking and virtual communities, describes a situation where he is propositioned by a blonde woman he has just met, who says she loves him. While flattered, he has his doubts about the relationship, particularly since his appearance is actually that of a bulge-eyed coloured fish! Of course, Clark is describing an encounter in an Internet 'space' – a place where people can meet and get to know each other, or where they can experiment with other versions of themselves. The point he makes is that he is obviously not 'really' a fish, and most likely the blonde is probably not even 'really' a woman.[19] But being unconstrained by physical proximity liberates their relationship and allows them to transform and connect, if only for a moment.

Even if you have never interacted in one of these virtual spaces, you are probably aware of the particular flavour which email conversations take on – the quick and easy intimacy, the informality, exemplified by the lapse in punctuation, and the flirty last lines. And we have all heard about relationships developed over the Net which have resulted in marriage. This has caused some to see the Internet as the basis for a new form of communion. It has been argued that virtual communities have emerged as a response to a lack of meaningful interaction in urbanised, mass-media-saturated environments such as the city, but this entails a rather romantic view of traditional communities, and is overly critical of the forms of intimacy which cities do afford. Others have argued that the Internet is simply the logical extension of the types of relationships already found in the city, where there is more openness to strangers than in traditional communities.

Suburban Contact

Keeping with the theme of the city and how relationships are at once made freer and more constrained, existing studies of neighbouring in New Zealand indicate that suburban neighbourhoods can be both places for connection and of isolation. In a well-known study of the lives of a group of New Zealand women, the experience of living in suburbia is described as wonderfully connecting by some, and sadly isolating for others:

> When we first moved into this area we had a marvellous time really. There were about six of us in a row, all with several kids; no tele, all very hard up sitting on boxes, that sort of thing. ...We all got on well. ... The men pooled their labour and got things done. ...You'd be out in the back yard on a weekday and Viv over the fence would yell, 'Like a cup of tea? Come in! Have a cup of tea on the wing' ... they are the sort of days you'll always remember. [20]

Contrast this picture of a close-knit community with the following description of the experience of an upper-middle-class woman in a new housing area:

> I'm sure I had suburban neurosis out there …We lived there five years.
> … It was just a back section and I hated that. … You couldn't even see
> life going by. You were just stuck there. You couldn't very well go and
> sit at the gate or letter box just to see people! You can't be on other
> people's doorsteps all the time. There was no community feeling there.
> It was so new.[21]

Glenda obviously felt very connected with the neighbours surrounding her, but Miriam's description is one of social isolation. Without knowing more about the particular circumstances of each woman, and the suburbs in which they lived, we can only suggest possible reasons for these marked differences. One might be class. Glenda's experience seems to spring from a need to share home-related work between neighbours. The other families in Miriam's suburb may have been out at work most of the day, causing the feeling of emptiness that many community researchers have noted. Their networks of interaction may have been based more around work than home, an increasingly common feature of modern life. Here, gender differences are clearly important. As Julie Park found, neighbourhood friendships were important sources of support for stressed Pakuranga housewives, but their upwardly-mobile husbands' desire to move to better areas often disrupted this support.[22] Traditionally, the workplace has been the focus of friendship-making for men,[23, 24] whereas for women the home has been more central.

Ethnicity, Friendship and Impression Management

Ethnicity is another frequent factor in exclusion in neighbourhoods,[25-27] and it is the effect of ethnicity on interaction in friendship relationships that we will now examine. The remainder of the chapter focuses on data taken from a study by one of the current authors[28] which investigated the effects of Maori–Pakeha friendships on ethnic identity and attitudes to 'race relations' issues.

Friendship is often seen as an area of social life in which we have total freedom of choice, but in fact we tend to choose friends who share our class and ethnic background, our values, and our gender and sexuality. How is it that friendships develop, and what are they based on? One of the strongest themes in definitions of friendship provided by participants in this study was that close friendships are characterised by trust, honesty and openness, reflecting a sense of freedom and lack of constraint. Respondents were asked what it means to be a friend and about the differences between a friend and a good friend. While they were able to list their closest friends (although significantly most 'forgot' to include their partner) many had difficulty describing what it was about the relationship that was significant. Most concluded that close friendships are based on trust and openness.

The following examples illustrate our earlier contention that at least two things can be going on at the same time in relationships. They demonstrate that despite identifying openness and trust as key features of close relationships, New Zealanders are simultaneously aware of a degree of guardedness in their closest relationships, and that this guardedness may be related to recognition of ethnic difference. Despite saying that they didn't notice the ethnicity of their friends, respondents described being careful about the topics they talked about with particular friends, about which groups of friends they brought together, and even noted that they felt less close to some friends because of these differences. For example, where respondents[29] were aware that their friends did not share their views, race relations was often avoided as a topic:

> Dan is a Maori and Marilyn is an Islander, the other couple we were talking about, so you know, you do tend to be a little more careful, it's a bit like Sue and Turoa, isn't it. Um ... the friends that we have, that are ... Maori or Islanders or that ... are very, they're not just, Maoris. They're very involved in their, um like Hanson eh, they live out on the Marae, they partake in all the cultural thing. Turoa [brother-in-law] speaks fluent Maori. Um, he's, his grandparents were the last arranged marriage in the Waikato. He was given to his grandparents because he was the eldest son, so as you can imagine, their ... their view of their culture and that is very very ... strong. So you have to be very, very careful ... you .... well I think you do, and I tend to be very, very careful, and I think we, I, and I'm very very sensitive.
>
> Elizabeth (Pakeha)

Elizabeth takes care to avoid contentious topics when interacting with Maori friends and relatives who hold different views. Goffman's insights[30] into the dramaturgical nature of social life are relevant to an understanding of how we can feel our relationships are open and honest, but also characterised by 'impression management'. By managing the way she presents *herself* in her interactions, by being 'very, very careful', Elizabeth manages the entire interaction, allowing for the smooth flow of the relationship. Her approach resonates with Hochschild's analysis of emotion work[31] and shows that 'deep acting' is not confined to the workplace, nor to gendered interactions. Our everyday interactions are characterised by conscious and unconscious monitoring and control of our emotions and presentation of self. The ultimate outcome is the ordinary civility of everyday life – the smooth flow of untroubled interaction.

Elizabeth's approach is both civil and one which does not 'give herself away'. While avoidance of taboo topics may be a useful strategy at the early stage of friendship development,[32] this state of dissonance between the friends may cause too much friction. The result may be a dissolution of the friendship, or a modification of views by one or both parties. Such a modification is an example of the idea that connection between individuals is transformative. Elizabeth seems able to continue the relationship despite the need for constant management of what she says. The result is a transformation in how she presents herself; she becomes a different person depending on with whom she is interacting.

The degree of trust and openness as opposed to constraint and impression management is likely to vary, depending on the general social climate. The wider context of social discourse influences supposedly 'private' relationships. For example, some respondents felt that their relationships had actually changed as a result of the changing 'race relations climate' in New Zealand. Several felt that discussing New Zealand's race relations with friends of other ethnic groups had become more difficult in recent years due to the rising profile of Maori activism. While this argument tended to be more common among respondents with conservative views, consider the following extract from Awhina, who had a very strong sense of her ethnicity as Maori and who held strong opinions on issues of biculturalism and Maori sovereignty:

> Awhina: I think that at the moment New Zealand's race relations are pretty bad. I find it more difficult now to talk to my Pakeha friends about controversial issues like land claims.
> Farida: More difficult now than it was what 5 years ago or 10 years ago or something?
> Awhina: Yeah.
> Farida: And do you think that they've sort of closed off, or how do you find it more difficult?
> Awhina: I think because my opinions are stronger. That I don't want us to argue, because that's what usually happens. You know I've changed quite a bit, because of the place I work in. The things I like about them are not Maori culture things. I like them because they've got a sense of humour or they're fun to be with, they're supportive, they're friendly, they're caring. So I wouldn't want that to taint our friendship and it would if that's what we talked about. It would actually come to the

point where I'd say well you and I can agree to disagree or we can part
company, you know, if we didn't agree to disagree. And sometimes I
think maybe that we might not agree to disagree so I'd rather we didn't
talk about things like that.

Awhina (Maori)

Awhina ascribes the change in her relationships with her friends to a
change in her own views, as much as to a political change in the general
race relations 'climate', although the two are connected. Her friendships
with Pakeha are based on humour, caring and support, rather than on shared
perspectives on issues of concern to Maori. Rather than 'taint' her friendship
with honesty about her views on these issues, she avoids such topics. Like
Elizabeth, she presents a particular side of herself in the relationship and
conceals another, in order to sustain that relationship.

Awhina goes on to describe how she manages the relationship between
different circles of friends, being, so to speak, a different person in each.
Awhina's views, and consequently her sense of herself, had changed
significantly in recent years. Friends whom she had made more recently
tended to have much more radical views than friends made earlier in her
life. Awhina related being careful not to mix these groups of her friends, as
well as managing her own behaviour, so as not to create embarrassing or
hurtful situations:

Awhina: There are certain situations that I would not invite them along
to because, I don't know if it's racist or not, but it could be hurtful if you
heard it. I think just with any cultures I suppose, what Maori say when
they are alone is very different from what they say when they're in a
mixed group. I'm not sure if that happens with Pakeha because I've
never been privy to an all-Pakeha conversation.
Farida: Yeah, it probably is the same.
Awhina: I behave differently with one group when I'm with them and I
behave differently with another group when I'm with them. I sort of try
to walk the tightrope, but trying also to shed a little light on both sides.
Because my colleagues at work are very, what is it, strong on their Maori
side, and I try to explain to them that no that didn't happen because of
that, it happened because of this, and the same with my Pakeha
colleagues, you know, it didn't happen because of this, it happened
because of that. ... I'd like us to be bicultural. I would like it to be. It's
a very long and very hard road.

Awhina (Maori)

What is significant about this discussion is Awhina's contention that she is not entirely constrained in her relationships, saying that she aims to gradually enlighten each group about alternative perspectives on race relations issues in New Zealand, all the while being careful not to fall out with either group. Thus, her connections with people are also attempts to transform, not only at an individual level but also at the level of social values generally. Awhina was quite unusual in her awareness of the strategies she used in order to attempt such transformations, and her conscious admission of these. We see that she does '*of course*, socially collaborate, even if to substantively disagree on what that world actually is', a position which ironically maintains trust through vigilant guardedness, producing the 'great civility' which Duneier and Molotch maintain is 'at the base of all human accomplishment, great or small'. [33] This civility allows the connection between Awhina and her friend to be potentially transformative. At the same time, Awhina is able to maintain courteous and close relationships with each group of friends, but not without careful self-monitoring and impression management.

Related to this strongly Goffmanesque approach to friendship is a very interesting theme voiced by several of the Maori respondents. They described a sense of wariness in their interactions with Pakeha. Here Eddy, displaying a slight sense of embarrassment and hesitance about describing a feeling which he thinks he perhaps shouldn't have, says that he does not feel as completely at ease with Pakeha as he does with Maori – he refers to this as 'letting go'. He finds this difficult to explain or justify, but specifically denies that it might be prejudice:

> And sure I've got some good friends that I call … that are Pakeha friends, that I am real close to and but I'm still, there's always this … be wary of. I feel that way. Perhaps that's a bit of prejudice on my side, but I don't think so …. I mean when I'm with Pakeha and they're my good friends, you still, you're not fully let go to them. You don't fully cling to them. Whereas with Maori I can feel really… let go. I don't know, I haven't really looked at this.
>
> Eddy (Maori)

Implied within this theme of guardedness is a sense of mistrust. Given that trust was one of the strongest themes in respondents' attempts to define close friendship, Eddy's comment is significant. The history of race relations in Aotearoa/New Zealand provides plenty of justification for such a sense of mistrust of Pakeha; however, in interpersonal interactions mistrust is rarely openly sustainable. If, in interpersonal interactions, one takes the step of putting doubt and mistrust 'on the table', this constitutes a substantial transformation to the grounds of such interaction: the historical and national, which are 'imagined' entities, do not easily translate into useful resources for organising the to-and-fro of *open* face-to-face interaction. If they are raised in Maori–Pakeha interactions the response of 'action at a distance' is likely to be given, that is, these events occurred long ago and 'that had nothing to do with me!'. Referring to our earlier example, this is equivalent to the panhandlers and passers-by grounding their interaction not in the immediacy of their situation, but in 'national issues' like the growth in homelessness, or the rising incidence of muggings on the street. That such broader social issues are put in the background in social interaction, and are not often directly talked about, is testament to the finely organised nature of face-to-face relationships.

Conclusion

While we have been highly selective in what has been presented above, we hope that there is much to stimulate sociological thinking in this material. Our discussion has traversed trust, civil inattention, impression management, social collaboration and exclusion. This reflects a long tradition of sociological and cultural work that shows our contemporary social worlds consist of a heterogeneous mix of norms, values and lifestyles. Within 'liquid' modernity, as Bauman[34] calls it, it is commonly suggested that individuals pay a high psychological price for survival, and there is much analysis of anomie, alienation, homeless selves, sub-cultural discontent, resistance and so on. This resonates with our above examples: in the women's minimal engagement with the panhandlers, the 'blonde' propositioning the 'fish', and Eddie's 'not fully letting go' with Pakeha, we see that trust and connection are shot through with a sense of threat, potential mistrust and dissociation. Whichever of these terms is used, following Bauman it can be argued that in circumstances of unease there are two key responses for individuals: first, the taking up of responsibility, or second, seeking a shelter where responsibility for one's own actions need not be taken. Bauman quotes Kristeva: 'it is a rare person who does not invoke a primal shelter to compensate for personal disarray'.[35] Perhaps we would all like to have more close friendships and relationships, but in a world full of people who appear to have their own self-interest at heart, it is no wonder that we often resort to a 'leave-me-alone' response.

The sociological point to be made here is that if we seek shelter from the other, whether stranger or friend, we are also running from ourselves, exiling ourselves. If this is realised, then the alternative option – taking up responsibility – becomes more likely. In his recent challenging book Scott Lash points to a way of taking such realisation beyond a simple self–other model. He comments on difference as a third term in the self–other equation:

> Difference is thus primordial, 'older' than both being and time, and the condition of possibility of both same and other. Here both same and other are constituted in this space of difference. This space of difference can also be ground, can have a materiality. Its signifying substance is not so much symbol or iconic as indexical and tactile, the most material and grounded sort of signification. ... Difference has a grain, the grain of desire, of the material and sensory, the grain of sociality, the radical empiricism of tradition and community. [36]

Difference is felt, experienced, visible at a glance. It is both the grounds for, and the product of, all human connections and transformations. This is not an empty, high-theoretical point: consider the rough urbanity of Mudrick's 'interactional vandalism' and the panhandlers' constant undercurrent of sexual innuendo; consider the tensions in Maori–Pakeha conversation and friendship.

In saying that this difference is tangible and central we also have to avoid what has been called a 'production view of self'. That is, a view where a person moves out from their core self to expand their connections and influence, then in times of disarray retreats to a core or minimal self. Individuals do extend themselves through connections, but we have to see that 'in the process of extension, one is never travelling out from a place (the core self) and then returning. Rather ... the only movement is one of circulation: around and around from figure to figure – one figure picking up on what the other excludes'.[37] This may seem counterintuitive, but what must be emphasised is that this view does not focus on individuals, but on the situations or 'events' in which individuals are able to act, to be constituted as 'selves' or 'others'.

Again, this focus on events is far from abstract, for there are materialities and spatialities involved in the movement of circulation and difference. As Munro puts it, 'Since we are always "in" extension ... any movement, and hence magnification, remains within the limits of *what can be attached and what is detached*'.[38] Eddy is attached to those who share his ethnic origins – he can 'fully cling' to other Maori in a way that he can't with Pakeha, for he shares a 'primal shelter' or sense of commonality with them. He can't completely be himself or 'let go' with Pakeha because of a perception of a realised fundamental difference. On a larger scale, Maori attach themselves to the land, and much circulation flows from this 'grounding', whereas

Pakeha New Zealanders are still working through their spatial attachments (some are attached here, some elsewhere). Whatever form the Pakeha attachment takes, it is different from Maori attachment to *te whenua*. This is not difference in any essential sense, but in a *definitional* sense, that is, to call oneself Maori is to enter into socially organised activities saturated with definitions, and as these currently exist they heavily involve *whakapapa* and its historical and spatial grounding.[39]

What all this produces, despite the apparent fixity of material and spatial groundings, is, in a word, contingency. Perhaps even the 'self' is contingent, for as Munro nicely puts it, 'we may never, so to speak, step in the same self twice. We remain in extension ...' [40] This point about the radical situatedness, or indexicality of human life needs to be extended beyond self to community and society. Nancy has put this particularly well in his work on 'community', and is worth quoting at some length:

> ... the thinking of community as essence ... constitutes a closure because it assigns to community a common being, whereas community is a matter of something quite different, namely, of existence inasmuch as it is in common, but without letting itself be absorbed into a common substance. Being in common has nothing to do with communion, with fusion into a body, into a unique and ultimate identity that would no longer be exposed. Being in common means, to the contrary, no longer having, in any form, in any empirical or ideal place, such a substantial identity, and sharing this (narcissistic) "lack of identity". ... That is, community is made or is formed by the retreat or by the subtraction of something. [41]

Nancy's work requires much more discussion than we have the space for here; let us merely suggest that a key to interpreting this passage is to read 'identity' not in the sense of a personal attribute, but in the sense of connection, oneness, or togetherness. This focus on 'lack of identity' can be nicely connected to our two examples. The women passers-by do *not* want to interact with the street men, who for their part do *not* want to accord the women the common decencies of civil interaction. They both subtract something from the other, and in doing this, is it not the case that on the sidewalk the street men and the middle-class women are inextricably *in* common? Whether they communicate or not, whether they give a dollar or not, whether they give a damn or not, they are connected and transformed by their subtractive activities, by their *differences*. Whether they care or not is actually immaterial; what is material is the fact of them being there together having to resolve the problems of their interactional situation, which are both *placed upon them* and which they *jointly construct anew*.

Equally, in Aotearoa/New Zealand the relationships and friendships between Maori and Pakeha are based upon, and constitute, differences. There is no final 'adding up', for we are not one community, let alone one nation.[42] Yet we have to be able to talk to and connect with strangers, remembering at the same time that we are and remain strangers. Could it be that the simultaneous nearness and remoteness of strangers forces the self not just outwards towards empathy for the other, but also 'inwards towards a recognition of our strangeness to ourselves?'.[43] In this view, the word 'stranger' would no longer have the negative connotations that are so commonly attached to it. Rather, it would simply involve an acceptance of difference, a recognition that what we have *in common* are 'partial connections'. [44] It is in the 'more or less' of partial connections that relationships and friendships are formed.

Endnotes

[1]   Abercrombie, N., Hill, S. and Turner, B.S. (1984) *The Penguin Dictionary of Sociology*, Harmondsworth: Penguin.

[2]   Allan, G. (1989) *Friendship: Developing a Sociological Perspective*, Hemel Hempstead: Harvester, Wheatsheaf.

[3]   Tilbury, F. (2000a) ' "Some of my best friends are Maori but...": Cross-ethnic friendships, ethnic identity and attitudes to race relations in Aotearoa/New Zealand', unpublished PhD thesis, Victoria University of Wellington.

[4]   Partington, A. (1992) *The Oxford Dictionary of Quotations*, Fourth Edition. Oxford: Oxford University Press, p. 566.

[5]   Bauman, Z. (1990) *Thinking Sociologically*, Oxford: Blackwell.

[6]   Latour, B. (1993) *We Have Never Been Modern*, Hemel Hempstead: Harvester Wheatsheaf, p. 20.

[7]   Bech, H. (1997) *When Men Meet: Homosexuality and modernity*, Cambridge: Polity Press, p. 111–112, emphasis added.

[8]   Allan, op. cit.

[9]   Duck, S. (ed.) (1997) *Handbook of Personal Relationships*, Chichester: Wiley.

[10] Willmott, P. (1987) *Friendship Networks and Social Support*, London: Policy Studies Institute.

[11] Lloyd, M. (1998) Our way looks distant, *New Zealand Sociology* 13(2): 239–264.

[12] Duneier, M. and Molotch, H. (1999) 'Talking city trouble: interactional vandalism, social inequality, and the "urban interaction problem"', *American Journal of Sociology* 104(5): 1263–1295.

[13] Ibid., pp. 1273–1274.

[14] Ibid., pp. 1274–1275.

[15] Duneier and Mulotch, ibid., pp. 1290.

[16] Goffman, E. (1963) *Behaviour in Public Places*, New York: Free Press.

[17] Duneier and Molotch, op. cit., p. 1291.

[18] Lyssiotis, P. and Petroulias, N. (1999) 'A dollar in a two dollar shop', *Meanjin* 58(4): 61–77.

[19] Clark, N. (1997) 'Life on the Line: Computer Networking and Virtual Communities', in Bell, C. (ed.) *Community Issues in New Zealand*, Palmerston North: Dunmore Press.

[20] Barrington, R. and Gray, A. (1981) *The Smith Women*, Wellington: Reed, p. 121–122.

[21] Ibid., p. 123.

[22] Park, J. (1982) *Doing Well: An ethnography of coping*, Auckland: Department of Anthropology, University of Auckland.

[23] Phillips, J. (1996) *A Man's Country?: The image of the pakeha male, a history*, Auckland: Penguin.

[24] King, M. (ed.) (1988) *One of the Boys?: Changing views of masculinity in New Zealand*, Auckland: Heinemann.

[25] Richards, L. (1990) *Nobody's Home: Dreams and realities in a new suburb*, Melbourne: Oxford University Press.

[26] Loomis, T. (1980) 'Tinkers Gully: Perspectives on social change in an Auckland renovation neighbourhood', *Urban Anthropology* 9(2): 163–197.

[27] Tilbury, F. (1997) *When Good Neighbours Become Friends: Neighbouring interactions in a New Zealand street*, Department of Sociology and Social Policy Working Paper No 11, Wellington: Department of Sociology and Social Policy, Victoria University of Wellington.

[28] Tilbury, F (2000a) ' "Some of my best friends are Maori but ...": Cross-ethnic friendships, ethnic identity and attitudes to race relations in Aotearoa/New Zealand', unpublished PhD thesis, Victoria University of Wellington.

[29] Ibid. Note that all names used in interview extracts below are pseudonyms.

[30] Goffman, E. (1990 [1959]) *The Presentation of Self in Everyday Life*, London: Penguin.

[31] Hochschild, A.R. (1983) *The Managed Heart: The commercialization of human feeling*, Berkeley: University of California Press.

[32] Miell, D. and Duck, S. (1986) Strategies in developing friendships, in Derlega, V. and Winstead, B. (eds) *Friendship and Social Interaction*, New York: Springer-Verlag.

[33] Duneier and Molotch, op. cit., p. 1290.

[34] Bauman, Z. (2000) 'On writing: On writing sociology', *Theory, Culture and Society* 17(1).

[35] Ibid., p. 88.

[36] Lash, S. (1999) *Another Modernity, a Different Rationality*, Oxford: Blackwell, p. 11.

[37] Munro, R. (1996) 'The consumption view of self: Extension, exchange and

identity', in S. Edgell, K. Hetherington and A. Warde (eds), *Consumption Matters*, Oxford: Blackwell/*The Sociological Review*, pp. 248–273.

[38] Ibid., p. 267 (emphasis added).

[39] Tilbury, F. (2001) 'Haunting traces of *différance*: Applications of Derrida to Kiwi identities', in Worth, H. and Simmons, L. (eds) *Derrida Downunder*, Palmerston North: Dunmore Press.

[40] Munro, op. cit., p 269.

[41] Nancy, J-L. (1991) *The Inoperative Community*, Minneapolis: University of Minnesota Press, p. xxxvii; original emphasis.

[42] Turner, S. (1999) 'A legacy of colonialism: The uncivil society of Aotearoa/ New Zealand', *Cultural Studies* 13(3): 408–422. In this article Turner argues that the legacy of colonialism has been to produce Aotearoa / New Zealand as an 'uncivil society'.

[43] Donald, J. (1999) *Imagining the Modern City*, London: Athlone Press.

[44] Strathern, M. (1991) *Partial Connections*, Maryland: Rowland and Little.

Bibliography

Abercrombie, N., Hill, S. and Turner, B.S. (1984) *The Penguin Dictionary of Sociology*, Harmondsworth: Penguin.

Allan, G. (1989) *Friendship: Developing a Sociological Perspective*, Hemel Hempstead: Harvester Wheatsheaf.

Barrington, R. and Gray, A. (1981) *The Smith Women*, Wellington: Reed,

Bauman, Z. (2000) 'On writing: On writing sociology', *Theory, Culture and Society* 17(1).

Bech, H. (1997) *When Men Meet: Homosexuality and Modernity*, Cambridge.

Clark, N. (1997) 'Life on the Line: Computer Networking and Virtual Communities', in Bell, C. (ed.) *Community Issues in New Zealand*, Palmerston North: Dunmore Press.

Donald, J. (1999) *Imagining the Modern City,* London: Athlone Press.

Duck, S. (ed.) (1997) *Handbook of Personal Relationships*, Chichester: Wiley.

Duneier, M. and Molotch, H. (1999) 'Talking city trouble: Interactional vandalism, social inequality, and the "urban interaction problem"', *American Journal of Sociology* 104(5): 1263–1295.

Goffman, E. (1963) *Behaviour in Public Places*, New York: Free Press.

Hochschild, A.R. (1983) *The Managed Heart: The commercialization of human feeling*, Berkeley: University of California Press.

King, M (ed.) (1988) *One of the Boys? : Changing views of masculinity in New Zealand*, Auckland: Heinemann.

Lash, S. (1999) *Another Modernity, a Different Rationality*, Oxford: Blackwell.

Latour, B. (1993) *We Have Never Been Modern*, Hemel Hempstead: Harvester Wheatsheaf.

Lloyd, M. (1998) 'Our way looks distant', *New Zealand Sociology* 13(2): 239–264.

Loomis, T. (1980) 'Tinkers Gully: Perspectives on social change in an Auckland renovation neighbourhood', *Urban Anthropology* 9(2): 163–197.

Lyssiotis, P. and Petroulias, N. (1999) 'A dollar in a two dollar shop', *Meanjin*, 58(4): 61–77.

Miell, D. and Duck, S. (1986) 'Strategies in developing friendships', in Derlega, V. and Winstead, B. (eds), *Friendship and Social Interaction*, New York: Springer-Verlag.

Munro, R. (1996) 'The consumption view of self: Extension, exchange and identity', in Edgell, S., Hetherington, K. & Warde, A. (eds), *Consumption Matters*, Oxford: Blackwell/*The Sociological Review*, pp. 248–273.

Nancy, J-L. (1991) *The Inoperative Community*, Minneapolis: University of Minnesota Press.

Park, J. (1982) *Doing Well: An ethnography of coping*, Auckland: Department of Anthropology, University of Auckland.

Partington, A. (1992) *The Oxford Dictionary of Quotations*, Fourth Edition, Oxford: Oxford University Press.

Phillips, J. (1996) *A Man's Country?: The Image of the Pakeha Male, a History*, Auckland: Penguin.

Richards, L. (1990) *Nobody's Home: Dreams and Realities in a New Suburb*, Melbourne: Oxford University Press.

Strathern, M. (1991) *Partial Connections*, Maryland: Rowland and Little.

Tilbury, F. (1997) *When Good Neighbours Become Friends: Neighbouring Interactions in a New Zealand Street*, Department of Sociology and Social Policy, Working Paper No 11, Wellington: Department of Sociology and Social Policy, Victoria University of Wellington.

Tilbury, F. (2000) ' "Some of my best friends are Maori but ...": Cross ethnic friendships, ethnic identity and attitudes to race relations in Aotearoa/New Zealand', unpublished PhD thesis, Victoria University of Wellington.

Tilbury, F. (2001) 'Haunting traces of *différance*: Applications of Derrida to Kiwi identities', in Worth, H. and Simmons, L. (eds), *Derrida Downunder*, Palmerston North: Dunmore Press.

Turner, S. (1999) 'A legacy of colonialism: The uncivil society of Aotearoa/ New Zealand', *Cultural Studies* 13(3): 408–422.

Willmott, P. (1987) *Friendship Networks and Social Support*, London: Policy Studies Institute.

5

Tell Me What You Eat …

Ian Carter and Angela Maynard

Introduction

'Tell me what you eat,' the French gourmet Anthelme Brillat-Savarin said in 1825, 'and I will tell you who you are.' This aphorism signals food's value in helping us understand everyday life in New Zealand, and everywhere else on this planet. The process of producing (through hunting, gathering, cultivating or herding) and consuming foodstuffs is the most fundamental constraint on human action. In a generous climate we could live without housing, and amble about unclothed. Refuse us adequate nourishment and we would decline. At the limit, we would starve to death.

Given its overwhelming individual and social significance, we might expect to find extensive sociological literatures on food in Aotearoa/New Zealand. We would be disappointed. Beyond some pioneering work in the sociology of agricultural production,[1] until recently local scholars have ignored this broad research field. Much the same could be said about other countries. Explanations for sociologists' remarkable tardiness in taking food seriously direct our attention to some of this discipline's birthmarks. A covert distinction between *public* and *private* worlds granted high status to research on topics located in the public realm. Political struggle, social stratification, paid work; these things mattered. Topics located in the private realm, by contrast, enjoyed little prestige – sociology of the family is an excellent example. It needed brave and stroppy feminist sociologists (exemplified, perhaps, by Anne Oakley's pioneering study[2]) to point out that these emphases deformed sociology by generalising from only half the population's routine experience. Public/private divisions are gendered; and transitions to modernity (that social formation which sociology was invented to study) strengthened rather than weakened gender boundaries. Sociological studies told us a great deal about predominantly male productive arrangements, but little about entirely female reproduction. Enjoying well-developed analyses of predominantly men's paid work, we could show none which investigated almost entirely women's unpaid work. The broad field of consumption lay fallow among welters of information about production. Trapped in a private, reproductive, consumptive and female domain, food could not become a significant sociological topic until (almost) all sociologists were jolted into taking women's experience seriously.

Today, research on the sociology of food expands rapidly in some overseas settings.[3] As Germov and Williams report from Australia, 'The study of food and eating has been one of the fastest growing areas in sociology.'[4] This is not the case in New Zealand. In this chapter we can do no more than sketch how investigations centring on food might enrich sociological understandings of this country's everyday life. This sketch will have three elements. First, we will say something about changes over time in local food patterns. Second, we will use two Kiwi food icons – Watties tomato sauce and the Edmonds cookery book – to open up spaces for different investigations in New Zealand. We conclude with some brief comments about eating out.

The Past is a Foreign Country

'The past is a foreign country,' the novelist L. P. Hartley insisted. 'They do things differently there.' Yes, of course; but what we eat today, and where, when and how we eat it is influenced (though not wholly determined) by what happened in that other country which was New Zealand's past. Before discussing current food patterns we must spend a little time looking backwards. Some other nation states[5] can show developed social historical accounts of their *provisioning systems*:[6] production and consumption arrangements combining over time to generate distinctive national – and increasingly international[7] – food patterns. There is no sophisticated social history of the nation's food patterns available to New Zealanders. What follows is therefore largely borrowed from three books. One of these is a cookery book. The second was written by a semi-amateur historian, and the third by a biochemist and a food technologist.[8] Space exists here for good social historical and sociological work on changes over time in this country's system of provision. When completed, Angela Maynard's work on New Zealand cuisine will help remedy this deficiency.

Before European contact Maori people identified and exploited a wide range of indigenous food plants, birds, fish, shellfish, insects and reptiles. These native resources were eked out with plants and animals carried in canoes from elsewhere – taro, kumara, kiore, dogs. If not eaten raw, then three cooking methods prepared these foodstuffs: steaming, grilling and boiling.[9] Contact with other peoples put pigs on the Maori menu from 1793, when two chiefs returned from Norfolk Island bearing these huge and delicious stores of protein. Potatoes arrived at much the same time, through barter with European sealers and whalers.

Anchored at Anaura Bay (on the East Cape) on 20 October 1769, the crew of James Cook's ship *Endeavour* is reported to have breakfasted on a potage compounding oatmeal from the ship's stores with local wild celery. For Burton (1983: 16) this meal marked a fateful marriage between imported British and indigenous Aotearoan foodstuffs. As is not uncommon, one partner in this marriage proved more enthusiastic than the other. We are all conservative where food is concerned, preferring the familiar to the novel. Though early settlers faced a choice between eating indigenous foods and going hungry, as the settler numbers increased so Pakeha consumption patterns reverted to those established in a more or less vaguely remembered 'Home'. Always alert for new economic opportunities, tangata whenua quickly learnt how to grow unfamiliar vegetables and farm unfamiliar animals. Expert Maori cultivators developed commercial market gardening enterprises to supply demand from settled towns and villages – until further waves of settlers extruded them from this trade.

As the weight of colonial New Zealand's economy shifted from extraction (whale and seal products, timber, gold) to pastoral production (wool, chilled and frozen meat, dairy produce), so firmer bases were laid for Pakeha to revert to familiar consumption patterns. Or rather to consumption *aspirations* entertained by those whom they had left behind. Forget the roast beef of socially comfortable Old England: most nineteenth and early twentieth-century emigrants to New Zealand came from labouring backgrounds – classes raised on debilitating grain-based diets.[10] One attraction drawing emigrants to the other side of the world was the much-hawked image of New Zealand as Canaan: a land flowing with milk and honey, a country where labouring folk could gorge on foods far beyond their reach in the Old Country.[11] Thus Pakeha settlers chose to eat a diet radically different from that of their parents, but remarkably akin to diets in other 'settler capitalist' European colonies: the United States of America, Uruguay, Argentina, South Africa, Australia.[12] This diet was carnivorous: astoundingly vast quantities of meat (and alcohol)[13], supplemented largely by bread. Few vegetables and fruit were consumed, fish was disparaged (because stigmatised as lower-class food in Britain), and shellfish utterly disdained.[14] These food preferences led to tragic and unanticipated consequences in the First World War. Forced to fight a total war with soldiers inheriting industrialisation's inadequate dietaries, British generals turned to meat-fed colonial troops – Australians, Canadians, New Zealanders, South Africans – when facing knotty military challenges. Hence the Gallipoli disaster: where, in nationalist accounts, a distinctive New Zealand identity formed through the 'mateship' born from bone-headed British staff blundering.[15] Hence the worst day in New Zealand's military history when, on 12 October 1917, the flower of Australian and New Zealand infantry was ordered to attack a fiercely defended ridge-top village – Passchendaele, still a name to send shudders down any spine – on a slope of liquid mud. The soldiers were repulsed, with terrible casualties.[16] Undaunted, next day the British high command found themselves able to celebrate Passchendaele's capture: by Canadian troops. No wonder that New Zealand disputed with Newfoundland for a vile palm, as the political unit which lost the largest proportion of its total male population in the Great War – with all that this meant for mothers, wives and sweethearts left bereft in remote districts of the British Empire. Clearly food provisioning systems' impacts on everyday life are more complicated than we might expect. Certainly they cannot be predicted with accuracy.

Walk around a New Zealand supermarket today, and count the foodstuffs which would have been familar to Maori in Cook's day: kumara, mussels, oysters. That's it. Sharing between Maori and Pakeha food cultures has proved remarkably uneven. Much the same could be said for other non-European food cultures. First imported to goldfields as indentured labourers in the 1860s, Chinese people have a long presence in New Zealand, but until the 1970s their food culture (with its distinguished cuisine history, some thousands of years older than the European) sank into social invisibility. The same held true for southern European foodstuffs – olives, olive oil and wine – carried to Northland gumfields from the late nineteenth century by Croatian immigrants ('Austrians' then 'Dalmatians' in contemporary political geographies). Attracted to fill depleted unskilled labour ranks after the Second World War, Pacific Islands migrants brought to New Zealand food patterns already transformed by contact with Western missionaries and traders. As local fish and vegetables' central place in local dietaries yielded to imported meat and fats, so Pacific Islanders' food patterns, like Maori's, borrowed more from Palangi than they lent.

TWO KIWI ICONS

1　*Wattie's Tomato Sauce*

Like Snifters and Buzzy Bees, the thought of Wattie's tomato sauce can wring floods of tears from the toughest Kiwi away on the Big OE. Marooned in Baron's Court or Manhattan, Vogel's bread and Wattie's sauce transubstantiate into a secular sacrament. Liberally splashing tomato sauce over fish and chips, meat pies and a remarkably wide range of other dishes, we consume – and reaffirm our attachment to – a shared sense of what it means to be a New Zealander. We swallow James Wattie's labour as he sweats away boiling down all those tomatoes in Hawke's Bay; we swallow more labour from hosts of vegetable growers supplying his cannery. Demographically urban but culturally rural, [17] our national image lies mirrored in the sticky red goo which has gushed from Wattie's production line since 1944.[18]

This icon's packaging has changed many times over the years, but the Christian millenium witnessed a radical makeover. 'New Zealand's favourite taste,' the new bottle screams. True enough. 'New space-saving shape for easy storage,' it yelled. Few would notice that: much more obvious was the new label. 'Wattie's, established 1934' it crooned, setting us back to those tomatoes bubbling away almost sixty years ago. But this familiar message now comes emblazoned on an angular, dentillated, and round-topped shield. Instantly recognisable in any country around the world, this shield tells us that Wattie's tomato sauce is manufactured by a subsidiary company in the American Heinz corporation. Brute multinational reality disrupts wistful Kiwi dreaming. Combined in 1986 with New Zealand flour miller Goodman Fielder (which, by then, itself controlled most of the nation's meat-processing capacity),[19] then compounded with Australian food processors before being swallowed by giant Heinz, the Wattie company's fate springs important tensions between local identification and foreign control.

Foreign ownership is nothing new for New Zealand's provisioning system. In the late nineteenth and first half of the twentieth century, local export meat works largely were owned by British or American capital. That ownership and control was repatriated later, flowing against international trends, tells us much about declining profitability (particularly in the sheepmeat sector) as overseas consumer tastes spurned the New Zealand meat industry's staple products.[20] Wattie's experience is much more typical for the food manufacturing sector. Around the world, cross-national integration binds this sector in ever tighter coils, in an industry blighted by Engel's Law: the remorseless tendency for consumers to spend a declining proportion of household income on food as total disposable income rises. One countervailing strategy has seen further stages added to some food processing, 'adding value' to goods for which a higher price – and higher profits – could then be demanded. The burgeoning diet-food industry provides one bizarre example of this strategy, with major multinational corporations lurking behind marketing fig-leaves suggesting ownership by individuals (Jenny Craig) or self-help groups (Weight Watchers) to sell a paradox – 'lite' foods selling for higher prices than 'regular' alternatives – to a predominantly female clientele.[21] This could be no more than a niche strategy, of course; though (like the rapidly growing sports food and drink sector) this niche's worldwide size is surprisingly large, and still expanding through determined advertising. A more general strategy has seen corporations seeking to maintain profit levels through economies of scale spread across national boundaries. So pervasive has corporate international integration become that the notion of a distinct New Zealand food manufacturing sector makes little sense today. In July 2000 politicians' toes stubbed against this awkward fact. The Labour/Alliance coalition government needed Green Party votes in Parliament. Fronted by the 'pure food' campaigner Sue Kedgley,[22] Green politicians exploited a rising moral panic over genetically modified food, pressing for stringent new labelling regulations. They failed – because Australian regulatory agencies already had been persuaded to entertain more friendly attitudes to corporate interests. An integrated Australasian food manufacturing sector (and increasingly integration over much wider geographical spreads than this, as Wattie's experience shows) could not be unscrambled to satisfy demands from a small New Zealand interest group punching its puny weight in a local 'food fight'.[23]

This tale shows why we need serious work on the political economy of New Zealand food manufacturing. Bruce Jesson's pioneer investigation of corporate restructuring under the third Labour government provides groundworks for such a study; Susan Sargent's account of the Australian food manufacturing sector provides a model.[24] Indeed, so tightly integrated is New Zealand capital with Australian in this sector (and, of course, in many others) that the best route to an adequate political economy of New Zealand food manufacturing today might well be a revised edition of Sargent's book. Since Engel's Law presses no less heavily on wholesalers and retailers than on manufacturers, we also need political economical work on transformations over time in New Zealand food distribution: increasing scale and impersonality as supermarkets drove out specialist grocers, butchers and the rest; retailing conglomerates' attempts to raise profit levels by adding value (or at least price) through shop-prepared 'ready meals' in initiatives like The Foodtown Kitchen.[25] For this topic we lack even the modest quantum of earlier work that exists for the food manufacturing sector: one chapter in Bailey and Earle alone hints at what this might look like.[26] The sociology of food wholesaling and retailing in New Zealand is a blank slate. Who will write on it?

2 *The Edmonds Cookery Book*

Cookbooks might seem unpromising territory for sociologists. Not so. Building on Norbert Elias' idea of the civilising process, Stephen Mennell analysed French and English cookery manuals, exploring how France developed a high cuisine, while English élite cooking came to be an international joke.[27] His answer need not detain us (it turns on differences in court society); what is important is that cookery books should matter for us.

Many cookbooks have been published here.[28] And, of course, cook books continue to pour from New Zealand's presses. At the centre of this rushing flood stands one stern rock. First published in 1907 as an offshoot from Thomas Edmonds' baking powder business in Christchurch, the *Edmonds Sure to Rise Cookery Book* now has sold over three million copies. This astounding figure makes this the biggest-selling book of any kind ever published in this country: early years saw every New Zealand couple who announced their engagement receiving a free copy. Reading recipes in the latest edition[29] still wafts us back to the social world analysed in Crawford Somerset's pioneer sociological community study; a place of plain home cooking, heavy on meat dishes and sweetened by cakes, with little time for 'foreign muck'.[30] Like Wattie's sauce, the Edmonds cookery book is a Kiwi icon. Ask the right questions of the book and it yields interesting sociological material. We shall group this material under three headings: problems of order, gender, and medical imperialism.

Problems of Order

Cookery books never tell us only how to cook. Squeeze them and information about public troubles drips out as they articulate broad concerns over social integration. Thus for Harvey Levenstein late nineteenth and early twentieth-century American cookbooks meshed with public philanthropy and state policy, attempting to channel floods of variously-origined immigrants through New England's (meaning old England's at one remove) strait and plain culinary gate in the name of nation building.[31] Ethnic integration in the American 'melting pot' enjoyed highest cultural priority here. As so often, things were different on the other side of the Atlantic. The first New Zealand recipes published in book form appeared in 'An Australian Aristologist's' *The English and Australian Cookery Book: Cooking for the Many, as Well as the 'Upper Ten Thousand'* (1864). This title hints at alarms about class, not ethnic, integration; about a pressing need to educate working-class women in preparing foods which their middle- and upper-class mistresses wished to eat, but not to cook. Precisely this challenge lay behind early editions of the most famous cookery book written in English, Isabella Beeton's 1861 *Book of Household Management* (only from the 1890 edition did the now-familiar title – *Mrs Beeton's Cookery Book and Household Guide* – emerge). As the earlier title suggests, Mrs Beeton's tome was less a cookery book than a systematic guide for young brides in burgeoning lower-middle-class sectors of mid-Victorian Britain on managing (and occasionally working alongside) the servant whom their working-class mothers could never have afforded to employ.

Today, when cookery books are the safest gamble in a risky publishing industry, these intriguing cultural objects still trade in anticipation rather than reflection. (Who *cooks* the dishes displayed so lasciviously in all those coffee-table volumes cluttering our bookshops?) Read against American and British templates the Edmonds' cookery book seems complacent. As edition succeeded edition, plain recipes for plain folk conjured New Zealand as a place marked by comfortable sufficiency and a democratic civic culture. With Maori socially and physically marginalised until postwar years, with Pakeha populations drawn overwhelmingly from working-class British stock and protected by a covert 'white' immigration policy, Edmonds did not need to proselytise ethnic or class integration through food. Bland but safe: this may be a world which Pakeha New Zealand has lost (for good or ill), but the Edmonds' cookery book's enormous commercial success suggests both that this world once existed and that inhabitants were not displeased with it.

Gender

Most New Zealand food is prepared at home, by women. Some overseas sociologists have attributed increasing sales of takeaway food and ready meals to historically unprecedented labour market shifts, as female labour force participation rates have risen sharply over recent decades.[32] We might be tempted to import this argument; but some factors urge caution. First, home consumption of convenience foods is not unique to late capitalist (or, heaven help us, postmodern) times: precisely similar arguments were advanced for the significance of sugary jam and shop-bought fish and chips in sustaining calorific intake among Britain's industrial working class.[33] Second, we know that in New Zealand (as elsewhere) women's increasing involvement in paid labour has entailed little reduction in domestic responsibilities. Just because a woman works, it doesn't mean that somebody else cooks dinner. Third, while evidence suggests that takeaway food consumption increases with rising disposable family incomes, in New Zealand (as elsewhere) the replacement of full-time male jobs by largely part-time female employment has not brought higher household incomes; and we know that takeaway food purchases rise when disposable incomes rise, falling when hard times arrive.[34] All this means that women's deeper involvement in paid work does not translate directly to changes in household food patterns.

Much more persuasive is work by feminist sociologists on food preferences. Erected on pioneering studies by Mary Douglas and her students, Nicky Charles and Marion Kerr's landmark York study showed that while women overwhelmingly prepare home-cooked meals, what is to be eaten is controlled by husbands' (and behind that, by children's) food preferences.[35] This study cries out for replication in New Zealand: after all, our first locally produced cookery book was Mrs Murdock of Napier's *Dainties: or, How to Please our Lords and Masters* (1887). Any local study must recognise that class and gender (factors recognised by Charles and Kerr) also are inflected here by ethnicity and by age. This was one of the many virtues present in the ethnographic work on New Zealand women's relationships with food undertaken by social anthropologist Julie Park and her co-workers.[36] Their study cries out for replication through more systematic sociological research of the kind pioneered by Charles and Kerr.

Generalising from their results, Charles and Kerr asserted that food presents British women with a range of difficult problems. Pleasing husbands and kids is one. A second is mirrored in the strikingly large proportion of women dieting at any one time, and the even larger proportion who have tried to diet. No less true for New Zealand, this second factor guides us to the last sociological topic which we can excavate from the Edmonds cookery book.[37]

Medical imperialism

Until very recent decades, humankind's great difficulty with food was to get enough of it. With hunger and malnutrition stalking all societies, a stout figure signified high social position. Hence (among European women) Peter

Paul Rubens' chubby nudes, and all those curvaceous actresses who offended Queen Victoria, but captivated the Prince of Wales' attention with such distressing regularity. Postwar changes in global provisioning systems have changed all that. Endemic hunger and periodic famine still stalk around far too many places in this world,[38] and socially deprived subpopulations in advanced societies still suffer disfiguring malnutrition,[39] but now, for the first time in human history, advanced societies' dominant food problem is that people eat too much food, not too little. In New Zealand today, 35 per cent of the adult population is overweight when measured against actuarial height/weight ratios, and a further 17 per cent is obese.[40] Hence those Xenical television adverts, with their blood-curdling warnings that the average New Zealander gains one gram in body weight each day. No longer a marker for high social position, our heavy bodies now signify disreputable failure to take responsibility for our personal wellbeing as we risk weight-related 'diseases of civilisation': hypertension, heart infarctions, strokes, diabetes.

The Xenical adverts commodify fear for pharmaceutical profit; but can occur only because so much discourse about food has been medicalised. As the people principally responsible for household food provision, this discourse bears most heavily on women. Average weights for men and women rise at much the same rate in New Zealand, but women worry much more about weight gain than men. Hence commercial assaults on women's self-image – through the diet industry and the sweaty gym mafia, for instance. Hence paradoxical panics about largely female *underconsumption* of food in vaguely-specified 'syndromes' anorexia nervosa and bulimia. As critics have noted, these panics nest comfortably within broader male-dominated medical strategies concerned to discipline and control female bodies – strategies focused on women's key responsibility for human reproduction. These insights have generated a spirited literature concerned to liberate women from repressively fat and repressively thin body imagery, as part of a broader effort to challenge male control over female bodies.[41]

All very interesting, no doubt; but how might we connect these struggles with the *Edmonds Sure to Rise Cookery Book*? The answer is through sociological work on dietetics, such as that which Ian Carter is undertaking. Edmonds' latest edition opens with a puff for the tome's distinguished history. Next we find eight pages defining weights and measures, ingredients, cooking terms, and advice on proper hygiene and food storage. Next are five pages outlining 'good nutrition'. At the centre of this brief chapter lies that familiar 'healthy food pyramid' which was invented in the United States Department of Agriculture, but now stares at us from so many New Zealand cookery

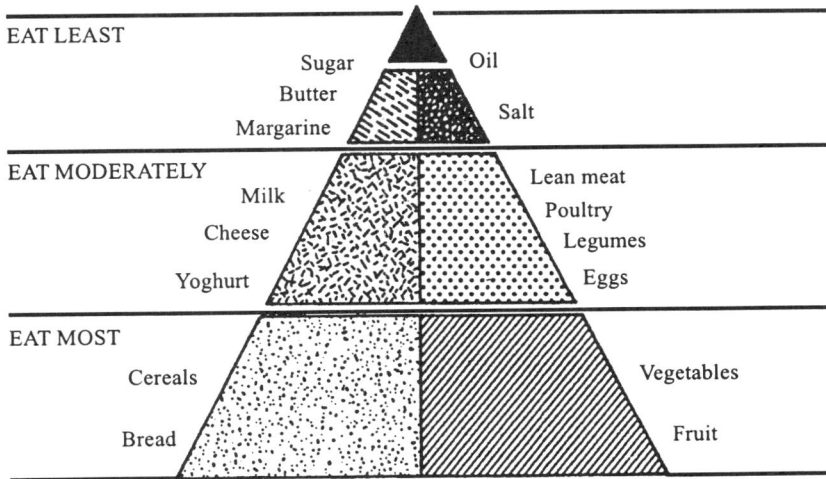

EAT LEAST
Sugar   Oil
Butter
Margarine   Salt

EAT MODERATELY
Milk   Lean meat
Cheese   Poultry
Legumes
Yoghurt   Eggs

EAT MOST
Cereals   Vegetables
Bread   Fruit

Figure 5.1   Healthy Food Pyramid

books and cereal packets.

In the Edmonds cookery book, words glossing this image define a good diet: 'New Zealanders should eat more from the fruit, vegetable, bread and cereal group (especially the wholegrain types). These foods should be balanced with moderate servings of lean meats, skinned chicken, fish, low-fat dairy products, eggs, dried beans, nuts and seeds. Sugar, added fat, salt and alcohol should only play a small role. It is not necessary to totally ban these foods.'[42]

What justifies moralising like this? One thing: *scientific mana*. 'Attempts to change nutrition opinion should only be made when the evidence for such a change is based on well-conducted and confirmed scientific enquiry and analysis,' a key government report boomed. 'A shift in nutrition opinion can easily damage a segment of the food industry, but the greatest threat to us all comes from zealots or evangelists pushing recommendations, the implications of which have not been fully investigated.'[43] This passage lives and breathes a religious discourse. Here we see – rather more clearly than its authors might intend, perhaps – that nutrition is a science in bed not only with powerful sectional interests in New Zealand's provisioning system, but also with an uninterrogated medical scientism.

In dietetics no less than law, historical amnesia protects professional practice. Writing about American experience, Harvey Levenstein noticed 'the alacrity with which experts, often backed by the flimsiest of evidence, have recommended fundamental changes in the nation's diet.'[44] His point holds well beyond America's borders. New Zealand dieticians' faith in the 'healthy food pyramid' survives only by blanking out nutritional guidelines' twisted past. Scientific advice about best practice for human diets one century ago produced patterns found today only in television adverts for cat food. Freighted with fatty meat and bereft of fruit and vegetables, to us nineteenth-century Pakeha dietaries look like recipes for a short and constipated life. But competent contemporary authorities judged Pakeha food patterns far healthier than grain-based British proletarian diets – because their recommendations rested on analytical techniques which burned fruit and vegetables to nutritionally useless ash.[45] Only once subtler techniqes allowed new substances to be identified and recommended (vitamins from the twentieth century's earliest years, then certain mineral salts) did the pattern familiar to us today crystallise: a 'food science' built around protein, carbohydrates, fats, vitamins and minerals.[46] Adjusted by minor tinkering, this orthodoxy has ruled for some nine decades.

This seems very simple – except that over time this rather stable 'normal science'[47] generated wildly lurching prescriptions for healthy eating. With vitamins' scientific status established after a generation's vehement contestation, interwar years saw a tsunami of scientifically-validated *vitamania* wash around the world. Top scientific experts recommended human diets heavy on *protective* foods like meat, milk, eggs and cheese which supplied vitamins and minerals to the body, and light on calorie-rich *energy-bearing* foods like cereals and vegetables.[48] Thus when the New Zealand Government first laid down dietary prescriptions for our citizens, the most nutritious substances turned out to be milk, eggs, meat, liver, and cheese: things calculated to give today's dieticians palpitations.[49] One widely praised overseas text insisted that one sixth of total food intake must comprise fats, half of it from dairy produce.[50] Nutritionists now recommend eating lots of carbohydrate and less protein. With fat enjoying all the popularity of a cigar smoker at an ASH convention, the Plimmers' expert scientific advice appears positively irresponsible today.

'Ah,' we may say, 'but that was sixty years ago. Science has pushed so much further forward today. Trust the experts.' This is not good advice. Food science's picayne history has reached no calm conclusion. As two American dieticians imagined their students wailing, 'What should I do, when scientists keep changing their minds?'[51]

Today, bits are falling off even the hallowed food pyramid. Rifling through her files, another American dietician found that this scientifically validated artefact had spawned lots of little brothers: healthy food pyramids for vegetarians and for people born in particular localities (Mediterranean countries, Puerto Rico, the Phillipines, Latin America, Asia); pyramids for blacks in the South and for predominantly white populations in northern states; pyramids for old people and for children.[52] Enthusiastic amateurs' effusions[53] might be dismissed with a smile (or perhaps a snarl) by food scientists, but work by scientifically literate sceptics may not be put aside so easily.[54] Scientist, lawyer, journalist and foodie Jeffrey Steingarten identified that damnably awkward French paradox: Gallic citizens' disinclination to die from circulatory problems in the hordes which their butter and cream-laden dietaries insist they should. Building on this, he set out to drive a gleeful truck through many other dietetic pieties. Taste his demolition of scientific justifications for salt's stigma; enjoy his exposé of 'Salad, the silent killer'.[55] All heresy, but all deeply enlightening.

With food panics rooted in intensified capitalist production methods – the 'mad cow' BSE/vCJD scare is only the most dramatic of these[56] – sweeping the industrialised world, and with contention over food issues leaking between expert and lay constituencies – highly convoluted debates about genetically modified food provide one excellent example – issue after issue strains food science's boundaries. For Thomas Kuhn these circumstances suggest that normal science is about to flip into some new paradigm. We cannot tell what this new paradigm will look like. It might never emerge; nutritional science might roll gently toward the end of its particular history. Centuries of experience suggests otherwise. With hindsight's benefit our grandchildren may be astounded by our impercipience, berating us for not seeing what lay maturing so clearly in time's womb.

Making fun of rich confusions in and around food science is a bit like shooting fish in a barrel. Explaining that confusion is more challenging. This is where sociology should come in. We have no space here for a full analysis, but one factor appears critical: difficulties in converting *nutrition*, a laboratory science sitting on the cusp between physiology and biochemistry, into *dietetics* (*nutrition education* in North American usage), a professional practice rooted historically in hospital food management. At the heart of this difficulty lies something familiar to sociologists – *operationalisation*, the process of turning theoretical ideas into researchable investigations. In food science's domain, operationalisation means quitting near certainties in laboratory experiments for field settings where results emerge as low(ish) correlations among variables muddied by teeming personal, social and cultural factors. This, too, is familiar for us. Viewed from a food science perspective, dietetics looks like applied nutrition. Viewed from a sociological perspective, diatetics looks like social science. But this social science emerged under ruthless medical domination. Disparaging their expertise, male New Zealand medical panjandrums – modern society's higher clergy – turned a small group of female nutritionists and dieticians into docile under-labourers. [57] When respect could not be withheld, worthy women became honorary men: for two Otago University medical deans, doughty Dr Muriel Bell, this country's most important food scientist, was 'Physiologist, researcher, nutritionist, sometime Lecturer in the Department of Physiology, Professor Malcolm's right hand man.'[58] Through cowed female dietitians, male medical discourse sought to control all New Zealand women as they went about their daily chore of preparing family meals. Given this grimly gendered hegemony, we might expect dieticians to seek freedom through collaboration with social scientists. Their mundane practice would not change, but medical condescension's deadening weight might be eased.

Some dieticians have reached this conclusion, but not many.[59] More have followed another path. By following it we return to issues raised earlier in this chapter. In 1973 almost all New Zealand dieticians worked in hospitals, or in the Ministry of Health.[60] Twenty years later, many had escaped these enclosures. Significant numbers now worked for commercial food manufacturers, joining nutritional scientists who had deserted their discipline's stagnant normal science for more profitable (in money terms, if not in intellectual stimulation) pastures in applied food science.[61] By a roundabout route, decoding dietetic advice in the *Edmonds Sure to Rise Cookery Book* returns us to the urgent need for a rounded analysis of New Zealand's provisioning system's political economy.

Eating Out

Consumption presupposes production: we cannot eat food which we, or other people, have not grown or made. Production entails consumption: foodstuffs must be eaten before they rot. More clearly, perhaps, than any other branch of our discipline, the sociology of food forces us to appreciate that analytical distinctions between production and consumption reveal *and* conceal. A full understanding of food's significance requires us to watch these partners interlace, delighted and intrigued by the patterns they weave. This could be done in many places, but one prime location is the restaurant. As sociologists, we know remarkably little about these interesting places. Gary Alan Fine's nuanced account of American chefs' 'kitchen work' opens the way for somebody to mount a systematic study of interaction among New Zealand chefs, waiters and diners, perhaps using Talcott Parsons' analysis of role-governed interaction among doctors, nurses and patients for its model.[62]

What little else we think we know about restaurants has more to do with metaphor than sociological investigation. George Ritzer's McDonaldisation thesis[63] made this fast-food chain stand as emblem and harbinger for social rationalisation, for corporate rape, for worldwide cultural impoverishment. Centred on the notion of 'uncivilised civility', Joanne Finkelstein's social theoretical study turned restaurant patrons into cultural dopes, crudely manipulated by profit-hungry restauranteurs.[64] Recent critiques urge that structuralist accounts like these must be humanised by taking consumption seriously, and by taking actors' definitions seriously. Applying the now-familiar argument that globalising pressures educe localised responses, critics urge that Ritzer's thesis is over-drawn: that the manner in which patrons use McDonald's restaurants in different locations asserts, sustains and inflects local particularity.[65] Ray Krok's golden-arched imperialism[66] has not turned this wonderfully varied world into a wasteland levelled by, and made safe for, American values. Any sociology which assumes that Krok succeeded is stunted. Similarly, Alan Warde and Lydia Martens' research denies Finkelstein's 'diners as dupes' argument. They show that restaurant eating in Preston is patterned by class, that classic productivist category; but they urge that to stop analysis at this point ignores the meanings which inform diners' actions. 'Sensuous delight' infuses dining experiences, whether at a ritzy silver service joint or at McDonald's.[67] This point should be generalised beyond the restaurant's walls. As a New Zealand sociologist told local dieticians recently, 'eating is usually associated with pleasure and a sense of wellbeing. Its preparation provides opportunity for creativity and artistic expression. When eating is reduced to an act of survival, a dimension of the quality we all seek in life is absent.'[68] Three cheers for that!

For far too long, sociologists have been a grim-faced bunch. Taking consumption seriously forces us to lighten up. Reading sociology of food through an interest in consumption liberates research topics which productivist assumptions dismiss as frivolous: connections between food and sensuality (euphemism for sex) in New Zealand's and other countries' fiction,[69] or how food drives plots in movies ranging from delicious *Tampico* (Japan) and *Babette's Feast* (France) to that gruesome British slog *The Cook, the Thief, his Wife and her Lover*. Beyond appreciating that El Matador, this country's first licensed restaurant, opened in Auckland's Symonds Street as recently as 1959, and that major cities' (and many smaller settlements') street frontages were transformed when new BYO licences sparked a restaurant revolution from the 1970s,[70] we know precisely nothing about the sociology of New Zealand dining. Research opportunities tumble over each other here. How and why did our current café culture emerge? What does quaffing latte in one place rather than another mean for the quaffer? How did chefs turn into culture heroes, culinary rock stars? Was Ivan's, that ancient relic in Ponsonby Road's 'munchie mile', *really* mourned when its doors closed?[71] What lay behind struggles between two yuppie groups over Newmarket's White Lady pie cart? Did dimly recalled late-night student roistering at the pie cart really inspire one lot (the Chimes at Midnight faction, we might call them) to deny a Wall Street faction's fears that greasy smells dropped property values?

Lots of research to do, then, if we are to cook up a rich sociological stew in New Zealand. As elsewhere, a host of interesting and important issues about everyday life pivot on food. At the moment, almost nobody studies them. Bring a plate, and get stuck in!

Endnotes

[1]   Curtis, B. (1996) 'Producers, processors and markets: A study of the export meat industry in New Zealand', Unpublished PhD Thesis, Canterbury University, and Mabbett, J. (1998) 'Sociological aspects of the development and current structure of the New Zealand wine industry', Unpublished PhD Thesis, Auckland University provide examples.

[2]   Oakley, A. (1974) *The Sociology of Housework*, London: Robertson.

[3]   See Beardsworth, A. and Keil, T. (1997) *Sociology on the Menu: An Invitation to the Study of Food and Society*, London: Routledge, for a solid survey.

[4]   Germov, J. and Williams, L. (eds) (1999) *A Sociology of Food and Nutrition: The Social Appetite*, Melbourne: Oxford University Press. p. v.

[5]   Burnett, J. (1979) *Plenty and Want: A Social History of Diet in England from 1815 to the Present Day*, revised edition, London: Scholar Press; Levenstein, H. (1988) *Revolution at the Table: The Transformation of the American Diet*, New York: Oxford University Press; Symons, M. (1982) *One Continuous Picnic: A History of Eating in Australia*, Adelaide: Duck Press.

[6]   Fine, B., Heasman, M. and Wright, J. (1996) *Consumption in the Age of Affluence: The World of Food*, London: Routledge.

[7]   Tansey, G. and Worsley, P. (1995) *The Food System: A Guide*, London: Earthscan.

[8]   Burton, D. (1983) *Two Hundred Years of New Zealand Food and Cookery*, Wellington: Reed; Simpson, T. (1999) *A Distant Feast: The Origins of New Zealand's Cuisine*, Auckland: Godwit; Bailey, R. and Earle, M. (1993) *Home Cooking to Takeaways: Changes in Food Consumption in New Zealand During 1880–1990*, Palmerston North: Massey University Department of Food Science.

9   Te Rangi Hiroa (Buck, P.) (1950) *The Coming of the Maori*, second edition, Wellington: Maori Purposes Fund Board, pp. 85–112.

10   Burnett, *Plenty and Want*, p. 73.

11   Fairburn, M. (1989) *The Ideal Society and its Enemies: The Foundations of Modern New Zealand Society, 1850–1900*, Auckland: Auckland University Press.

12   Denoon, D. (1983) *Settler Capitalism: The Dynamics of Dependent Development in the Southern Hemisphere*, Oxford: Clarendon Press.

13   Simpson, *Distant Feast*, pp. 148–56.

14   Bailey and Earle, *Home Cooking to Takeaways*.

15   Sinclair, K. (1980) *A History of New Zealand*, revised edition, Harmondsworth: Penguin, p. 232.

16   Pugsley, C. (1991) *On the Fringe of Hell: New Zealanders and Military Discipline in the First World War*, Auckland: Hodder and Stoughton, p. 250.

17   Carter, I. and Perry, N. (1987) 'Rembrandt in gumboots', in Phillips, J. (ed.), *Te Whenua, Te Iwi: The Land and the People*, Wellington: Allen and Unwin, pp. 61–72.

18   Conly, G. (1984) *Wattie's: The First Fifty Years*, Hastings: J. Wattie Canneries Ltd, pp. 42–3.

19   Jesson, B. (1987) *Behind the Mirror Glass: The Growth of Wealth and Power in New Zealand in the Eighties*, Auckland: Penguin, pp. 156–7.

20   Curtis, 'Producers, processors and markets'.

21   Levenstein, H. (1993) *Paradox of Plenty: A Social History of Eating in Modern America*, New York: Oxford University Press, pp. 11, 237–45.

22   Kedgley, S. (1999) *Eating Safely in a Toxic World: What **Really** is in the Food we Eat*, Auckland: Penguin.

23   Levenstein, *Paradox of Plenty*, pp. 178–94.

24   Jesson, *Behind the Mirror Glass*; Sargent, S. (1985) *The Foodmakers*, Ringwood: Penguin.

25   Wrigley, N. (1998) 'How British retailers have shaped food choice', in Murcott, A. (ed.) (1998), *The Nation's Diet: The Social Science of Food Choice*, London: Longman, pp. 112–28 provides a model.

26   Bailey and Earle, *Home Cooking to Takeaways*, pp. 35–49.

27   Mennell, S. (1985) *All Manners of Food: Eating and Taste in England and France from the Middle Ages to the Present*, Oxford: Blackwell.

28   Bailey and Earle, *Home Cooking to Takeaways*, pp. 52, 283–8 counted 600 cookbooks published in the century after 1890, augmented through recipe slots in local newspapers' women's pages.

29   Edmonds (1999) *Edmonds Sure to Rise Cookery Book*, 46th de luxe edition, Auckland: Bluebird Foods.

30   Somerset, H.C.D. (1938) *Littledene: A New Zealand Rural Community*, Wellington: New Zealand Council for Educational Research, pp. 22–4.

31   Levenstein, *Revolution at the Table*, pp. 19–21.

32 Goodman, D. and Redclift, M. (1991) *Refashioning Nature: Food, Ecology and Culture*, London: Routledge, pp. 1–46.

33 Mintz, S. W. (1986) *Sweetness and Power: The Place of Sugar in Modern History*, New York: Viking, pp. 130–1; Walton, J. K. (1992) *Fish and Chips and the British Working Class, 1870–1940*, Leicester: Leicester University Press.

34 Levenstein, *Paradox of Plenty*, pp. 227–36.

35 Douglas, M. (1975) 'Deciphering a meal', *Daedalus* no. 101, pp. 61–81; Murcott, A. (1982) 'On the social significance of the 'cooked dinner' in south Wales', *Social Science Information* vol. 21, pp. 677–696; Charles, N. and Kerr, M. (1988) *Women, Food and Families*, Manchester: Manchester University Press.

36 Park, J. *et al.* (1991), *Ladies a Plate: Change and Continuity in the Lives of New Zealand Women*, Auckland: Auckland University Press.

37 Russell, D., Parnell, W. and Wilson, N. (1999) *NZ Food: NZ People. Key Results of the 1997 National Nutrition Survey*, Dunedin: Otago University, LINZ Activity and Health Research Unit. pp. 92–7.

38 Abraham, J. (1991) *Food and Development: The Political Economy of Hunger and the Modern Diet*, London: Kogan Page.

39 New Zealand Network Against Food Poverty (1999) *Hidden Hunger: Food and Low Income in New Zealand*, Wellington: New Zealand Network Against Food Poverty; Parnell, W.R. (1996) 'Poverty in developed countries: What are the nutritional consequences?' *Proceedings of the Nutritional Society of New Zealand* vol. 21, pp. 9–14.

40 Russell, Parnell and Wilson, *NZ Food: NZ People*, p. 163.

41 Boston Women's Health Book Collective (1998) *Our Bodies, Ourselves for the New Century: A Book by and for Women*, New York: Simon and Schuster.

42 Edmonds, *Edmonds Cookery Book*, p. 15.

43 New Zealand Nutrition Taskforce (1991) *Food for Health*, Wellington: Department of Health, p. vi.

44 Levenstein, *Paradox of Plenty*, p. vii.

45 Drummond, J. and Wilbraham, A. (1957) *The Englishman's Food: Five Centuries of English Diet*, new edition, London: Cape, pp. 357–9.

46 Bell, M. (1962) 'Nutrition in New Zealand,' *Supplement to the Journal of the New Zealand Association of Home Science Alumnae*, vol. 31, pp. 1–30; Russell, Parnell and Wilson, *NZ Food: NZ People*, pp. 26–69.

47 Kuhn, T. (1996) *The Structure of Scientific Revolutions*, 3rd edition, Chicago: Chicago University Press.

48 League of Nations (1936) *The Problem of Nutrition. Volume 2: Report on the Physiological Basis of Nutrition*, Geneva: League of Nations, pp. 13–27.

49 Bell, M., Gregory, E., Wilson, E. C.G. and Malcolm, J. (1940) *Good Nutrition: Principles and Menus*, Wellington: Department of Health, p. 24.

50 Plimmer, R.H.A. and Plimmer, V. G. (1935) *Food, Health, Vitamins*, seventh

edition, London: Longmans Green, p. 24.

[51] Sizer, F. S. and Whitney, E. N. (1994) *Nutrition: Concepts and Controversies*, 6th edition, Minneapolis/St Paul: West, p. xiii.

[52] Pennington, J.A.T. (1999) 'Many faces of the food pyramid', *Journal of Nutrition Education*, vol. 31, p. 133.

[53] Coory, D. (1988) *NZ Nutrition and Your Health*, Tauranga: Coory; Kedgley, *Eating Safely in a Toxic World*.

[54] Elkington, J. and Hailes, J. (1999) *The New Foods Guide: What's Here, What's Coming, What it Means for Us*, London: Gollancz; Shorland, F.S. (1989) 'Human nutrition is an ass', *Proceedings of the Nutrition Society of New Zealand*, vol. 14, pp. 180–2; Tansey and Worsley, *The Food System*.

[55] Steingarten, J. (1997) *The Man Who Ate Everything*, New York: Vintage, pp. 177–86, 196–204.

[56] Lacey, R. (1999) 'Mad cows and Englishmen', in Griffiths, S. and Wallace, J. (eds), *Consuming Passions: Food in the Age of Anxiety*, Manchester: Mandolin, pp. 34–40.

[57] Mein Smith, P. (1998) 'Bell, Muriel Emma, 1898–1974', in *Dictionary of New Zealand Biography: Volume 4, 1921–1940*, Auckland: Auckland University Press, p. 48.

[58] Hercus, C. and Bell, G. (1964) *The Otago Medical School under the First Three Deans*, Edinburgh: Livingstone, p. 163.

[59] Clancy, K. (1999) 'Reclaiming the social and environmental roots of nutrition education', *Journal of Nutrition Education*, vol. 31, pp. 191–4.

[60] New Zealand Committee on the Dietetic Profession (1973) *Report*, Wellington: Board of Health.

[61] Crooks, D. (1993) *Dieticians: 50 Years of Achievement and Challenge*, Wellington: New Zealand Dietetic Association. For research findings from New Zealand nutritionists and dieticians working for food corporations and non-governmental foundations, see *Proceedings of the Nutritional Society of New Zealand*, 1991, vol. 16, pp. 136–52, 178–80. Of course, some folk continued to work in academic settings, notably at Otago, Auckland and Massey (Palmerston North) Universities.

[62] Fine, G. A. (1996) *Kitchen: The Culture of Restaurant Work*, Berkeley: University of California Press; Parsons, T. (1951) 'Illness and the role of the physician: A sociological perspective', *American Journal of Orthopsychiatry*, vol. 31, pp. 452–60; Parsons, T. (1975) 'The sick role and the role of the physician reconsidered', *Millbank Memorial Fund Quarterly*, vol. 53, pp. 257–78.

[63] Ritzer, G. (1996) *The McDonaldisation of Society: An Investigation into the Changing Character of Contemporary Social Life*, revised edition, Thousand Oaks: Pine Forge.

[64] Finkelstein, J. (1989) *Dining Out: A Sociology of Modern Manners*, Cambridge: Polity.

108 —————— Sociology of Everyday Life in New Zealand

65   Alfino, M., Caputo, J. S. and Wynyard, R. (eds) (1998) *McDonalisation Revisited: Critical Essays on Consumer Culture*, Westport: Praeger; Smart, B. (ed.) (1999) *Resisting McDonaldisation*, London: Sage; Watson, J. L. (1997) *Golden Arches East: McDonald's in East Asia*, Stanford: Stanford University Press.

66   Love, J. F. (1995) *McDonald's: Behind the Golden Arches*, revised edition, New York: Bantam.

67   Warde, A. and Martens, L. (2000) *Eating Out: Social Differentiation, Consumption, and Pleasure,* Cambridge: Cambridge University Press

68   Stephens, A. (1997) 'Food, diet and gender in the 21st century', *Journal of the New Zealand Dietetic Association*, vol. 51, pp. 51–4.

69   Allen, B. (ed.) (1994) *Food*, Oxford: Oxford Univerity Press; pp. 389–400; Gifkins, M. (ed.) (1994) *Tart and Juicy: Food Stories from Australian and New Zealand Writers*, Auckland: Vintage.

70   Bailey and Earle, *Home Cooking to Takeaways*, pp. 263–5; Kirkpatrick, R. (1999) *The Bateman Atlas of Contemporary New Zealand*, Auckland: Bateman, plate 39.

71   Smith, N. (1995) 'Last orders for diners at Ivan's', *New Zealand Herald*, 25 May.

Bibliography

Abraham, J. (1991) *Food and Development: The Political Economy of Hunger and the Modern Diet*, London: Kogan Page.

Alfino, M., Caputo, J.S. and Wynyard, R. (eds) (1998) *McDonaldisation Revisited: Critical Essays on Consumer Culture*, Westport: Praeger.

Allen, B. (ed.) (1994) *Food*, Oxford: Oxford University Press,

Bailey, R. and Earle, M. (1993) *Home Cooking to Takeaways: Changes in Food Consumption in New Zealand During 1880–1990*, Palmerston North: Massey University Department of Food Science.

Beardsworth, A. and Keil, T. (1997) *Sociology on the Menu: An Invitation to the Study of Food and Society*, London: Routledge.

Bell, M. (1962) 'Nutrition in New Zealand', *Supplement to the Journal of the New Zealand Association of Home Science Alumni*, vol. 31, pp. 1–30.

Bell, M., Gregory, E., Wilson, C.G. and Malcolm, J. (1940) *Good Nutrition: Principles and Menus*, Wellington: Department of Health.

Boston Women's Health Book Collective (1998) *Our Bodies, Ourselves for the New Century: A Book by and for Women*, New York: Simon and Schuster.

Burnett, J. (1979) *Plenty and Want: A Social History of Diet in England from 1815 to the Present Day*, revised edition, London: Scholar Press.

Burton, D. (1983) *Two Hundred Years of New Zealand Food and Cookery*, Wellington: Reed.

Carter, I. and Perry, N. (1987) 'Rembrandt in gumboots', in Phillips, J. (ed.), *Te Whenua Te Iwi: The Land and the People*, Wellington: Allen and Unwin, pp. 61–72.

Charles, N. and Kerr, M. (1988) *Women, Food and Families*, Manchester: Manchester University Press.

Clancy, K. (1999) 'Reclaiming the social and environmental roots of nutrition education', *Journal of Nutrition Education*, vol. 31, pp. 191–4.

Conly, G. (1984) *Wattie's: The First Fifty Years*, Hastings: J. Wattie Canneries Ltd.

Coory, D. (1988) *NZ Nutrition and Your Health*, Tauranga: Coory.

Crooks. D. (1993) *Dieticians: 50 Years of Achievement and Challenge*, Wellington: New Zealand Dietetic Association.

Curtis, B. (1996) 'Producers, processors and markets: A study of the export meat industry in New Zealand', Unpublished PhD thesis: Canterbury University.

Denoon, D. (1983) *Settler Capitalism: The Dynamics of Dependent Development in the Southern Hemisphere*, Oxford: Clarendon Press.

Douglas, M. (1975) 'Deciphering a meal', *Daedalus*, no. 101, pp. 61–81.

Drummond, J. and Wilbraham, A. (1957) *The Englishman's Food: Five Centuries of English Diet*, new edition, London: Cape.

Edmonds (1999) *Edmonds Sure to Rise Cookery Book*, 46th de luxe edition, Auckland: Bluebird Foods.

Elkington, J. and Hailes, J. (1999) *The New Foods Guide: What's Here, What's Coming, What it Means for Us*, London: Gollancz.

Fairburn, M. (1989) *The Ideal Society and its Enemies: The Foundations of Modern New Zealand Society, 1850–1900*, Auckland: Auckland University Press.

Fine, B., Heasman, M. and Wright, J. (1996) *Consumption in the Age of Affluence: The World of Food*, London: Routledge.

Fine, G.A. (1996) *Kitchen: The Culture of Restaurant Work*, Berkeley: University of California Press.

Finkelstein, J. (1989) *Dining Out: A Sociology of Modern Manners*, Cambridge: Polity.

Germov, J. and Williams, L. (eds) (1999) *A Sociology of Food and Nutrition: The Social Appetite*, Melbourne: Oxford University Press.

Gifkins, M. (ed.) (1994) *Tart and Juicy: Food Stories from Australian and New Zealand Writers*, Auckland: Vintage.

Goodman, D. and Redclift, M. (1991) *Refashioning Nature: Food, Ecology and Culture*, London: Routledge.

Hercus, C. and Bell, G. (1964) *The Otago Medical School under the First Three Deans*, Edinburgh: Livingstone.

Jesson, B. (1987) *Behind the Mirror Glass: The Growth of Wealth and Power in New Zealand in the Eighties*, Auckland: Penguin.

Kedgley, S. (1999) *Eating Safely in a Toxic World: What **Really** is in the Food we Eat*, Auckland: Penguin.

Kirkpatrick, R. (1999) *The Bateman Atlas of Contemporary New Zealand*, Auckland: Bateman.

Kuhn, T. (1996) *The Structure of Scientific Revolutions*, 3rd edition, Chicago: University of Chicago Press.

Lacey, R. 'Mad cows and Englishmen', in Griffiths, S. and Wallace, J. (eds), *Consuming Passions: Food in the Age of Anxiety*, Manchester: Mandolin.

League of Nations (1936) *The Problem of Nutrition. Volume 2: Report on the Physiological Basis of Nutrition*, Geneva: League of Nations.

Levenstein, H. (1988) *Revolution at the Table: The Transformation of the American Diet*, New York: Oxford University Press.

Levenstein, H. (1993) *Paradox of Plenty: A Social History of Eating in Modern America*, New York: Oxford University Press.

Love, J.F. (1995) *McDonald's: Behind the Golden Arches*, revised edition, New York: Bantam.

Mabbett, J. (1998) 'Sociological aspects of the development and current structure of the New Zealand wine industry', Unpublished PhD thesis: Auckland University.

Mein Smith, P. (1998) 'Bell, Muriel Emma', in *Dictionary of New Zealand Biography: Volume 4, 1921–1940*, Auckland: Auckland University Press.

Mennell, S. (1985) *All Manners of Food: Eating and Taste in England and France from the Middle Ages to the Present*, Oxford: Blackwell.

Mintz, S. (1986) *Sweetness and Power: The Place of Sugar in Modern History*, New York: Viking.

Murcott, A. (1982) 'On the social significance of the 'cooked dinner' in South Wales', *Social Science Information*, vol. 21, pp. 677–696.

New Zealand Committee on the Dietetic Profession (1973) *Report*, Wellington: Board of Health.

New Zealand Network Against Food Poverty (1999) *Hidden Hunger: Food and Low Income in New Zealand*, Wellington: New Zealand Network Against Food Poverty.

New Zealand Nutrition Taskforce (1991) *Food for Health*, Wellington: Department of Health.

Oakley, A. (1974) *The Sociology of Housework*, London: Robertson.

Park, J. *et al.* (1991) *Ladies a Plate: Change and Continuity in the Lives of New Zealand Women*, Auckland: Auckland University Press.

Parnell, W. (1996) 'Poverty in developed countries: What are the nutritional consequences?' *Proceedings of the Nutritional Society of New Zealand*, vol. 21, pp. 9–14.

Parsons, T. (1951) 'Illness and the role of the physician: A sociological perspective', *American Journal of Orthopsychiatry*, vol. 31, pp 452–60.

Parsons. T. (1975) 'The sick role and the role of the physician reconsidered', *Millbank Memorial Fund Quarterly*, vol. 53, pp. 257–78.

Pennington, J.A.T. (1999) 'Many faces of the food pyramid', *Journal of Nutrition Education*, vol. 31, p. 133.

Plimmer, R.H.A. and Plimmer, V.G. (1935) *Food, Health, Vitamins*, 7th edition, London: Longmans Green.

Pugsley, C. (1991) *On the Fringe of Hell: New Zealanders and Military Discipline in the First World War*, Auckland: Hodder and Stoughton.

Ritzer, G. (1996) *The McDonaldisation of Society: An Investigation into the Changing Character of Contemporary Social Life*, revised edition, Thousand Oaks: Pine Forge.

Russell, D., Parnell, W. and Wilson, N. (1999) *New Zealand Food: New Zealand People. Key Results of the 1997 National Nutrition Survey*, Dunedin: Otago University, LINZ Activity and Health Research Unit.

Sargent, S. (1985) *The Foodmakers*, Ringwood: Penguin.

Shorland, F.S. (1989) 'Human nutrition is an ass', *Proceedings of the Nutrition Society of New Zealand*, vol. 14, pp. 180–2.

Simpson, T. (1999) *A Distant Feast: The Origins of New Zealand's Cuisine*, Auckland: Godwit.

Sinclair, K. (1980) *A History of New Zealand*, revised edition, Harmondsworth: Penguin.

Sizer, F.S. and Whitney, E.N. (1994) *Nutrition: Concepts and Controversies*, 6th edition, Minneapolis/St Paul: West.

Smart, B. (ed.) (1999) *Resisting McDonaldisation*, London: Sage.

Smith, N. (1995) 'Last orders for diners at Ivan's', *New Zealand Herald*, 25 May.

Somerset, H.C.D. (1938) *Littledene: A New Zealand Rural Community*, Wellington: New Zealand Council for Educational Research.

Steingarten, J. (1997) *The Man Who Ate Everything*, New York: Vintage.

Stephens, A. (1997) 'Food, diet and gender in the 21st century', *Journal of the New Zealand Dietetic Association*, vol. 51, pp. 51–4.

Symons, M. (1982) *One Continuous Picnic: A History of Eating in Australia*, Adelaide: Duck Press.

112

Tansey, G. and Worsley, P. (1995) *The Food System: A Guide*, London: Earthscan.

Te Rangi Hiroa (Buck, P.) (1950) *The Coming of the Maori*, second edition, Wellington: Maori Purposes Fund Board.

Walton, J.K. (1992) *Fish and Chips and the British Working Class, 1870–1940*, Leicester: Leicester University Press.

Warde, A. and Martens, L. (2000) *Eating Out: Social Differentiation, Consumption, and Pleasure*, Cambridge: Cambridge University Press.

Watson, J.L. (1997) *Golden Arches East: McDonald's in East Asia*, Stanford: Stanford University Press.

Wrigley, N (1998) 'How British retailers have shaped food choice,' in Murcott, A. (ed.) *The Nation's Diet: The Social Science of Food Choice*, London: Longmans, pp. 112–128.

6

Current Work Issues

Martin Tolich

Karl Marx's future of work (circa 1860):
Hunt in the morning, fish in the afternoon, rear cattle in the evening, criticize after dinner.

Auckland, 140 years later:
Cath cleans office blocks from 3 am to 6.30 am, delivers fed kids to school 8.45 am, minds neighbour's child voluntarily 9 am to 11 am, reskills at Unitec from 1 pm to 3 pm, teaches piano after school, and manages the Burger King drive-through until 8 pm, or 9 pm if it's busy. Listens to criticism on Radio Pacific talkback radio as she commutes the Auckland motorway to make a living. But is it living?

Whereas Waitangi Day and Anzac Day are New Zealand public holidays undergoing a revival of interest from the general population, Labour Day, first celebrated in New Zealand in 1899, has lost its meaning. Labour Day is not even protected in the Shop Trading Hours Repeal Act 1990. Waitangi Day, Good Friday, Christmas Day and Anzac Day (before 1 pm) are protected no-shopping days, [1] but not Labour Day. Most New Zealanders celebrate the late October holiday more as the gateway to summer. They do not link Labour Day to the eight-hour day act of 1899 or to the trade union movement that secured it. Labour Day seems an anachronism: the notion of eight hours each for sleep, play and toil is a luxury few workers enjoy. The forty-hour week is another anachronism. Only a third of the New Zealand workforce toils eight hours, five days per week. The majority of New Zealanders are employed in part-time work or for upwards of fifty to seventy hours per week. In the last decade those working part time (less than 30 hours) have increased by the epidemic proportions of forty-two per cent; many people working two or three jobs. These figures do not include those underemployed: those doing paid work at a level below their capability and/or willingness to do more.[2] This chapter explores the lives of New Zealanders working beyond and below the forty-hour week in insecure, poorly paid, non-unionised jobs. The chapter begins by trying to define work before explaining the rise and ramifications of part-time work in New Zealand society.

Defining Work

Getting one's head around the concept of work is similar to trying to hold jelly. The jelly is rather loose and likely to spill over with any attempt at containment. One person's work may be another's leisure. Gardeners, for example, may toil all day tending others' lawns but in the evening take great pleasure in mowing their own. The Hillary Commission ranks gardening as the leading form of recreation for New Zealanders. In this latter sense gardening may be an example of leisure. A definition of work seems elusive because the definition may not be found in the nature of the task but within its context.[3] Here the definition of work may become so personal that it loses its utility as a concept. McLennan, Ryan and Spoonley[4] provide an even less illuminating definition of work: 'work can be defined as virtually anything'.

The founding fathers of sociology, Karl Marx (1818–1883), Max Weber (1864–1924) and Emile Durkheim (1858–1917), do not give much help in nailing down a definition of work. They each studied the Industrial Revolution that took place in Britain between 1760 and 1830, but they did so in widely differing ways. Durkheim [6] focused on how the new occupations created by the Industrial Revolution produced a division of labour that integrated the population, each occupation mutually dependent on the other. Among other things, Weber[7] focused on the end of traditional authority (nepotism) and the beginnings of legal rational authority. Marx's [8] foci were many, all coalescing around the struggle of those forced off their land and into cities to work in the satanic textile mills.

Within the founding fathers' diverse outcomes there is a unity of sorts; a sense that sociology's roots are in the workplace and its effect on human beings. That in itself is a useful starting place: work and society. By understanding the workplace a researcher may define the spirit of a society.

A most useful definition of work is found not in the examination of the formal economy but within Anne Else's *False Economy*. Her observation is: 'No matter what happens to the jobs, there will be no shortage of work.'[9] Such eloquence needs unpacking. The work that Else is referring to is unpaid work; that is, household chores and childcare. Unpaid and paid work are not separate arenas to be defined but are inseparable. Even when robots have taken all the paying jobs there will still be unpaid work in the home. Most of that work is now invisible, at least in terms of calculating the Gross Domestic Product. Thus it is impossible to discuss the contemporary face of work without acknowledging that for most women, unpaid work and paid work are inextricably linked.[10]

A Service Economy for Whom?

Linear thinking pervades New Zealand society. That we are born, live and die, in that order, is somewhat guaranteed. The notion that a society always progresses *positively* through time is not so guaranteed. Until recently this has been a constant expectation of all New Zealanders, and for good reason. At one time New Zealand had one of the highest standards of living in the world, some of the best race relations, and was considered 'Godzone'.

Prior to 1976 New Zealand's international trade was dominated by exports to Britain. New Zealand was known as Britain's farmyard. The relationship was a good one and secured New Zealand a 'top three' standard of living. Most of the downturn in New Zealand's economic fortune stems from Britain joining the European Economic Community (now called the EU) in 1973. With its guaranteed international market gone, New Zealand could no longer sustain its high standard of living. New Zealand needed to diversify its types of jobs.

This diversity of jobs can be seen in changes in the percentage of those employed in the three sectors of the economy. A low 9.5 per cent of the population work in primary production: agriculture, fishing and forestry. Manufacturing, construction and mining employ 24.6 per cent of the workforce. The service economy employs 66 per cent. These service-sector jobs include a diverse grouping of those employed in transport and communication, business and financial services, social and personal services, wholesale and retail trade. More recently parts of the service sector have been known as the 'knowledge economy', where workers are defined as "symbolic analysts" manipulating symbols rather than machines.[11] An assumption underlining these labels is that they represent a sense of progress. This is not the case. After two decades of rising prosperity, real wages have declined since 1976,[12] with a debilitating effect on both work and society. It is now necessary for most New Zealand families to have two incomes.[13]

One other debilitating effect on real wages was the introduction of the Employment Contracts Act in 1991. The Employment Contracts Act is the most significant piece of labour legislation in New Zealand in the twentieth century. It ended a ninety-year period of social experiment in New Zealand industrial relations. The 1894 Industrial Conciliation and Arbitration Act had previously protected and encouraged unions by giving them the right to form and to strike. Under the old Industrial Conciliation and Arbitration Act, national wage settlements were paid to all workers. The pay settlement was known as an award.

The Employment Contracts Act was a radical departure from state protection of industrial relations, ushering in a new non-regulated relationship between employers and workers. [14] Within the new Act there was little recognition of the role of trade unions and new philosophy, purportedly providing a level playing field. The Employment Contracts Act outlawed sympathy strikes and compulsory unionism was revoked.[15] As important, the Act created the concept of enterprise bargaining, ending the historic practice known as award wages. Under the Employment Contracts Act workers at each work site needed to negotiate their own award. Logistically it is harder for union organisers to visit more sites with fewer, more part-time, workers. As a consequence union resources were overstretched and unions weakened. Trade union membership dropped in the decade from 1985 to 1996 from 683,006 workers in 259 unions to 339,327 workers in 83 unions. As a total of all workers, the density of unions has declined from 43.5 per cent to 19.9 per cent.[16]

What kind of society have these economic and organisational changes created in New Zealand? McLennan describes it in the following way:

> The baby boomers have been privileged in their employment experiences especially as they had access to free education and health care as they grew up in a buoyant labour market which paid well, offered careers and a choice of jobs. But even middle class baby boomers have faced redundancies as industry was restructured and downsized. Their children are confronted with greatly increased educational costs and a much more competitive job market. Since the 1980s, many have also faced major difficulties in getting employment.[17]

Anne Else [18] characterises these economic changes as one of the biggest upheavals in New Zealand's recent history. The change can be seen in the mix of paid-time and extra-time work. The economic change can equally be seen in figures documenting youth suicide, hospital waiting lists and infant mortality. In each list there is a sense of society's progress having ground to a halt.

Casual Jobs

Women's participation in the labour force is a significant feature of the post-World War II labour market. Women represent forty-five per cent of the labour force, up from forty-two per cent a decade ago. On one hand this is positive, in terms of emancipation of gender. Women are experiencing a greater right to employment participation. New Zealand women now hold many premier positions, such as Prime Minister, Leader of the Opposition, Chief Justice, (the next) Governor General, the Attorney General and the Chief Executive Officers of Telecom and WINZ. The irony of this success for women is that it does not remotely reflect the work experiences of most women in New Zealand.

The emancipation of women has real economic costs. Women are pushed into the workforce by the need for dual-income families. In the workforce women confront low wages within a narrow band of jobs in service-sector occupations where females predominate on a part-time basis.[19] All this, without any significant change in the household division of labour.[20] Ann Else's distinction between jobs and work is once again relevant. Being burdened by unpaid work responsibilities lessens women's job opportunities,[21] thus employment gains for women have been more likely in part-time work rather than in full-time jobs. In 1996, women made up 37.9 per cent of the full-time workforce, but accounted for 70.5 per cent of all those working part time.

Whether women choose to work part time or are forced into it, they don't choose the employment conditions that accompany it. Davidson and Bray state those conditions are:

> ... commonly associated with comparatively low rates of pay, reduced employment conditions and limited employment security. Furthermore, part-time workers command few fringe benefits, have fewer opportunities for further training or advancement, are also less likely to belong to a trade union or professional organization [22].

Austrin terms these less-skilled jobs, as jobs without careers, without 'sick pay, maternity pay, paid holidays or superannuation'.[23]

'Marginalised' and 'casualised' are terms used to describe the working conditions of part-time workers. 'Portfolio workers' is a novel term used by Ann Else to describe a range of paid and unpaid tasks performed by the women featured in *False Economy*.[24] Cath, the frantic motorway commuter featured at the beginning of this chapter, has a portfolio of tasks: from two part-time jobs, both in the service sector, teaching music, unpaid household and family tasks, and time spent voluntarily helping her neighbour. When Marx predicted the future of work (see beginning of the chapter), it is unlikely he foresaw portfolio workers.

Another term for casualised workers is 'temps' or temporary workers. Internationally, temporary workers are part of a growth trend in employment. In the United States the numbers of temp workers are growing at five times the rate of the general labour force.[25] The temp agency Manpower is now the single largest employer in the United States, with 560,000 workers.[26] The increasing demand for temps is employer-driven. Temps provide a cheap and disposable form of labour. Rogers found that temps are

> ... paid less, have fewer fringe, health, and retirement benefits, are unlikely to be unionised, have little or no long-term security, have a more difficult time qualifying for unemployment and workers compensation, and often slip through the cracks with regard labour legislation.[27]

Rogers also found temp jobs alienating for the employees.[28] Employees lack control of their employment conditions on a daily basis. For example, clerical workers may be given tasks like typing but have little idea of how the tasks fit into the larger scheme. Little of the employer's time is given in instructing or training temps. Most temps report doing the 'grunge' jobs, the tasks none of the more permanent staff would contemplate doing. Moreover, temps do not develop relations with fellow employees. A 'Cinderella' phenomenon occurs as the other staff go off to the Christmas party, for example, leaving the temp at home to mind the fort. This too is a form of alienation. There is also emotional alienation, given that the temp cannot complain, but is expected to grin and bear it. One solution is to leave, but to walk out of a temp assignment may soil the relationship both with the employer and with the temp agency. Thus Rogers asks rhetorically, 'What are the human costs of flexibility and who bears those costs?'[29]

Temp jobs are traditionally thought of as being outsourced via a Temporary Agency. Yet temporary work is endemic to the New Zealand workforce, given that a great deal of casualised part-time work should be classified as temping. Rather than working 10 am to 2.30 pm Monday to Friday, temp work hours are market driven, disposable and on demand. Hours vary from week to week, and workers may have no guarantee of minimum hours.[30] Davidson and Bray provide an example of supermarket employers in a low socio-economic area using temps on high-volume-benefit days.[31] 'Disposable' may be a better word for this type of employment. In the restaurant trade, for example, casual workers are called in on an as-needed basis to staff peak flows.[32] 'Subservient' workers may also be an apt description . The labour budget – the availability of hours – acts as a motivation whip for temps when extra hours are dished out by managers to their best and most subservient workers.[33]

The term 'temp' has become something of an oxymoron in the last decade. Perhaps 'semi-permanent temps' captures the contradiction. Gone are the days when temps in New Zealand were employed for a day or two to fill in for a sick employee. Now clients want 'staff for three, six months or sometimes twelve months'.[34] And temps are more than filling in for a missing typist. Temps may be executives. Light explains:

> Executive contracting is particularly suited to fixed-term projects such as new systems development and installation, financial restructure and review, backlog management, project management, product launch and to cover while corporate restructuring takes place. ... [Executive Temps] are expected to perform from day one and provide immediate results .... They accept that there is no longer a 'job for life' and that the responsibility for their livelihood no longer rests with the company but with them individually.[35]

Embedded in the growth of executive temps in the late 1990s has been the increase in the number of New Zealanders classed as self-employed, now twelve per cent of the workforce.[36] Those self-employed describe themselves in a variety of ways: consultants, between jobs, or their own bosses. Often the title 'self-employed' can be a euphemism for middle-class male unemployment or underemployment.[37] Among the self-employed, men outnumber women three to one and many of these self-employed end up stuffing letterboxes with offers of anything from garden work to computer repair. [38]

Employers use executive temps the same way they use casuals, it being cheaper to outsource. The self-employed further lower costs, given that there are so many self-employed consultants scrambling for business.[39] The self-employed absorb costs associated with health, unpredictability and equipment:

- Health costs are absorbed as people think they can work a bit longer, with fewer breaks ... and it catches up with them.
- Self-employed do all right in the good times but not so well in the seasonal downturns.
- The money may be good, but costs are high in terms of equipment replacement.

Other hidden costs are social. Those working outside traditional employment find it difficult to do normal things like securing a home mortgage.[40]

Self-employment is not a passing phase but a trend likely to be prolonged. David Thompson predicts that 'within the next 10 years a third of men and even more women will be without substantial paid work from their later forties on and half by their mid-fifties'.[39] In other words, the expectation of lifelong employment within one company is not realistic. Nor is the expectation of lifelong employment with a range of companies.[42] There are many reasons for this situation. Older workers are seen by employers as being expensive and expendable. For example, older workers are more likely to be resistant to innovation at work (such as new computer software), to have higher salaries and, perhaps more importantly, to be tied to an expensive superannuation scheme.

It is one thing to write about these issues in a detached academic manner. It is another to live them. I too fall within Thompson's trends. As I write this paragraph I too face redundancy and self-employment. My Pro-Vice Chancellor has written to me and my colleagues. The second paragraph stated the following:

> I am therefore able to advise that you would be eligible for reconfirmation. However, as there is more than one employee eligible for the same position, reconfirmation would be subject to a selection process in accordance with clause 9.4.3 of the University's Academic and General Staff Collective Employment Contract. If you are successful in the selection process, you would be reconfirmed in the position .... If you are unsuccessful, then the redeployment and surplus staff provisions of the University's Academic and General Staff Collective Employment Contract would apply.'

Currently this reconfirmation is held up by a union-manoeuvered court injunction, but inevitably I will need to dust off my c.v. and compete with my colleagues who are also required to reapply for their jobs. I doubt it will be the last time I do so. In this new environment working until sixty-five may be unusual rather than the normal.

The advice given to people who have been made redundant or who face redundancy is not soothing. Sullivan suggests workers in this situation go back to school every five to ten years to reskill.[43] Other advice is to plan for career changes. For instance, some people in marketing might consider teaching as an option, rather than moving from one marketing position to another. Inkson's suggestions focus on a renewed self-management.[44] By this Inkson means unemployed persons need to have the ability to motivate themselves, to be mobile and to get out there and improvise. He also says the notion of good qualifications ensuring a person a lifetime of employment no longer holds true. Rather than one qualification, an employee needs flexibility around a self-designed career path, treating employers as temporary partners, not permanent bosses. In other words, do unto others as they (the employers) have done unto you. Individualistic responses like these are unlikely to solve the problems of any of the 111,000 people currently registered unemployed.

Profile

What follows is something novel, the world turned upside-down. In the business section of any Saturday edition of the *New Zealand Herald* there is a column in which a successful businessperson describes a typical day. Here is an edited interview where Tim, an unemployed person, was asked the same standard questions. Tim was a former accountant and had been unemployed for eight years.

1. What makes your day at work?
   I am a househusband. And the time I have been unemployed I've done some accounting work and furniture restoration. So what makes my day at work? I think to arrive at the end of each day with a sense of having accomplished something. Because the work itself is fairly fragmented between housework and the furniture ... to just achieve something among those activities each day, or some focus.
   Simply making progress, on a piece of furniture for example. Or just keeping the house tidy as well. I guess what I'm saying is that I don't have to complete a task. I don't have to finish one big job.

2. How did you get to where you are today?
   It was quite easy. I think becoming older contributes significantly. But also I chose to have a change of direction in terms of the work that I was doing. I previously had accounting and administration work continuously

from the time I left school and I chose to try and get into some sort of social service situation, where I could use accounting plus work with people. And to that end I went to university and did some appropriate study, but at the completion of that it tied in with us moving to a smaller town and then to find that maybe that kind of qualification in a smaller town was not as helpful as had we gone to Auckland or Wellington or a place where I could have got a job with a government department.

3. Who is your most important mentor in your current situation?
   Well, I guess a personal faith would be what I would be thinking of .... Yes, a religious faith, if you can think of a biblical teaching as a mentor.

4. What is the biggest challenge to being a househusband?
   Well there was a time where I had to come to terms with not going out to work. And with my wife going out to work full time, and she was happy doing that, but there was an initial acceptance, or coming to terms with the fact that, you know, I wasn't the main breadwinner. It's just a case of accepting the present situation. But not seeing it as a permanent one for the rest of your working life, but to accept it as okay, this is how it is at this time.

5. How do you relax?
   I think something we can call our place is important. And be it at the moment to take the dog for a walk into the country, the school up the back road from where we live. Music is good for me. Yes, and then I guess you know on another level, well prayer would be, you know at times as well, but just to be in a quiet environment I think occasionally is good, and to hear your own thoughts.

6. What skills would you like to have?
   I feel that you can lose that edge but you haven't when you're limited of course and you can almost become you know deskilled. Or you feel that, you know the sense of worthlessness can come and be it real or imagined but, for example, I made the mistake first time but still I wouldn't know how to use EFTPOS. And maybe some other computer developments that I haven't kept pace with. Yes, it's scary in a sense, trying to keep up to date.

This interview was hurriedly taken the day before Tim left New Zealand for Australia along with the 40,000 other New Zealanders in 2000 who, like

Tim, hope for better jobs and a higher standard of living.[45] His children are prospering there.

Jobs and the Future

Can New Zealanders find something to celebrate in Labour Day? Or are all New Zealand holidays problematic? Given the unclosed gaps between Maori and Pakeha, celebrating Waitangi Day is not without difficulty. Anzac Day commemorates a disaster, lest we forget. The material in this chapter indicates that as a nation we are taking backward steps. The promise that each generation will leave its country better off is dwindling. The only certainty is that even when the jobs are all gone there will still be much work left to do.

The future of jobs is the future of New Zealand society. At present this future looks bleak. On the one side there are those in jobs, working either too few or too many hours; and on the other are those outside of formal employment. And there are those in casualised part-time jobs, subject to regular and often disruptive changes.[46] McLennan, Ryan and Spoonley sum up the inclusion/exclusion from society as:

> Access to paid work, especially full time, well-paid work, is fundamental to economic well-being. It is one of the most significant determinants in deciding who has access to credit and goods, including quality housing, health and education. It contributes to self-esteem and good health, and provides human and financial resources that then sustain future generations. Conversely, those who do not have access to paid employment, either because they cannot work, are reliant on a benefit or can only get part-time, poorly paid employment face substantial social and economic difficulties. [47]

Perhaps the enactment of the Employment Relations Act in October 2000 will promote a more level, state-supported playing field in industrial relations. The Act returns to the spirit of an earlier period, between 1894 and 1991, when the state's Industrial Conciliation and Arbitration Act 1894 openly nurtured trade unions as integral to the democratisation of New Zealand society. This nurturing state changed dramatically between 1991 and 2000 when the National Government introduced the Employment Contracts Act, creating enterprise bargaining and ending compulsory unionism. It was symbolic that the words 'trade unions' were not mentioned in the Employment Contracts Act.

Under the new Employment Relations Act (2000) trade unions are once again nurtured: unions are recognised as being the employees' only legitimate bargaining agent; the Act ends single enterprise bargaining allowing for multi-employer contracts; it allows unions reasonable access to workplaces to meet and recruit workers; it promotes employer-funded trade-union education; and perhaps most optimistically there is an expectation that 'good faith' bargaining will take place. In other words, negotiations will be conducted with mutual respect and confidence between employers, employees, and their unions. Time will tell. At least within the spirit of the Employment Relations Act there are signs of support for unions, providing the possibility of collective responses to private problems.

Endnotes

[1] Davidson, Carl and Marianne Bray (1995) *Women and Part time work in New Zealand*, Christchurch: Brookhouse Publishing, p. 40.

[2] McLennan, Gregor, Allanah Ryan, Paul Spoonley (2000) *Exploring Society: Sociology for New Zealand Students*, Auckland: Longman, p. 126.

[3] Grint, Keith (1991) *The Sociology of Work: An Introduction*, U.K: Oxford: Polity Press.

[4] McLennan, Ryan and Spoonley, op. cit., p. 117.

[5] Tausky, Curt (1984) *Work and Society: An Introduction to Industrial Society,* Itasca Illinois: Peacock Publishers, p. 31.

[6] Durkheim, Emile (1964) *The Division of Labour in Society*, New York: Free Press.

[7] Weber, Max (1977) *The Protestant Ethic and the Spirit of Capitalism*, New York: Macmillan.

[8] Marx, Karl (1965) *Manifesto of the Communist Party*, San Francisco: China Books.

[9] Else, Anne (1996) *False economy: New Zealanders face the conflict between paid and unpaid work*, New Zealand, North Shore City: Tandem Press, p. 147.

[10] Davidson and Bray, op. cit., p. 49.

[11] Ministry of Economic Development (1999) *What is the knowledge economy?* http://www.med.govt.nz/pbt/infotech/knwledge_economy/knowledge_economy-o4.html#P55_12865

[12] Welch 1999.

[13] Haine 1989, cited in Davidson 1995, p. 28.

[14] Deeks, John, Jane Parker and Rose Ryan (1998) *Labour and Employment Relations in New Zealand*, Auckland: Longman.

[15] Boxall, Peter (1993) 'Management Strategy and the Employment Contracts Act 1991', in Raymond Harbridge (ed.) *Employment Contracts: New Zealand Experiences*, New Zealand: Victoria University Press.

[16] Statistics New Zealand (1998) Auckland, p. 323.
[17] McLennan, Ryan and Spoonley, op. cit., pp. 132–3.
[18] Else 1996, op. cit., p. 60.
[19] Davidson and Bray, op. cit., p. 25.
[20] Davidson and Bray, ibid., p. 29.
[21] McLennan, Ryan and Spoonley, p. 122.
[22] Davidson and Bray, ibid., p. 70.
[23] Austrin, Terry (1994) 'Work', in Paul Spoonley, David Pearson and Ian Shirley (eds) *New Zealand Society: A Sociological Introduction*, Palmerston North: Dunmore Press, p. 246.
[24] Else op. cit., p. 146.
[25] Light, Elizabeth (1997) 'A temporary trend: Leased executives and contractors are part of the move to outsourcing', *New Zealand Business*, October.
[26] Else op. cit., p. 63.
[27] Rogers, Jackie (1995) 'Just a Temp: Experience and Structure of Alienation in Temporary Clerical Employment', *Work and Occupations* 22:2; pp. 137–166.
[28] Ibid.
[29] Ibid.
[30] Else op. cit., p. 63.
[31] Davidson and Bray, p. 40.
[32] Sullivan, Margie (1995) 'Redefining Work: Why the job is under threat', *New Zealand Business*, August, p. 22.
[33] Leidner, Robin (1993) *Fast Food, Fast Talk: Service Work and the Routinization of Everyday Life*, Berkeley: University of California Press.
[34] Sullivan, op. cit., p. 18.
[35] Light, op. cit., pp. 30–2.
[36] Ibid., p. 29.
[37] Else, op. cit., p. 71.
[38] Ibid., p. 69.
[39] Sullivan, p. 114.
[40] Ibid., p. 22.
[41] Thompson, David cited in Bruce Ansley (1999) 'The Future of Work', *New Zealand Listener*, September 4, p. 14–19.
[42] Sullivan, op. cit., p. 23.
[43] (http://www.immigration.govt.nz/research_and_information)
[44] McLennan, Ryan and Spoonley, p. 135.
[45] Ibid., pp. 130–1.

Bibliography

Ansley, Bruce (1999) 'The Future of Work' *Listener*, September 4, 14–19.

Austrin, Terry (1994) 'Work', in Spoonley, P., Pearson, D. and Shirley, I.

(eds) *New Zealand Society: A Sociological Introduction*, Palmerston North: Dunmore Press.

Boxall, Peter (1993) 'Management Strategy and the Employment Contracts Act 1991', in Harbridge, R. (ed.) *Employment Contracts: New Zealand Experiences*, Wellington: Victoria University Press.

Davidson, Carl and Bray, Marianne (1995) *Women and Part Time Work in New Zealand*, Chrischurch: Brookhouse Publishing.

Deeks, John, Parker, Jane and Ryan, Rose (1998) *Labour and Employment Relations in New Zealand*, Auckland: Longman.

Durkheim, Emile (1964) *The Division of Labour in Society*, New York: Free Press.

Else, Anne (1996) *False economy: New Zealanders face the conflict between paid and unpaid work*, North Shore City: Tandem Press.

Grint, Keith (1991) *The Sociology of Work: An Introduction*, Oxford: Polity Press.

Leidner, Robin (1993) *Fast Food, Fast Talk: Service Work and the Routinization of Everyday Life*, Berkeley: University of California Press.

Light, Elizabeth (1997) 'A Temporary trend: Leased executives and contractors are part of the move to outsourcing', *NZ Business*, October.

Marx, Karl (1965) *Manifesto of the Communist Party*, San Francisco: China Books.

——(1977) *Capital: A Critique of Political Economy* Vol. 1, New York: Random House.

Massey News (2000) 'Career fulfillment and success in the new millennium',

McLennan, Gregor, Ryan, Allanah and Spoonley, Paul (2000) *Exploring Society: Sociology for New Zealand Students*, Auckland: Longman, p. 126.

Ministry of Economic Development (1999) *What is the Knowledge Economy?* http://www.med.govt.nz/pbt/infotech/knowledge_economy/knowledge_economy-04.html#P55_12865

Rogers, Jackie (1995) 'Just a Temp: Experience and Structure of Alienation in Temporary Clerical Employment', *Work and Occupations* 22:2:137–166.

Statistics New Zealand (1998) New Zealand Official Yearbook, Wellington: GP Publications.

Sullivan, Margie (1995) 'Redefining Work: Why the job is under threat', *NZ Business*, August.

Tausky, Curt (1984) *Work and Society: An Introduction to Industrial Society*, Itasca, Illinois: Peacock Publishers.

Weber, Max (1977) *The Protestant Ethic and the Spirit of Capitalism*, New York: Macmillan.

7

Media, Advertising and Everyday Life

Wayne Hope and Rosser Johnson

Introduction

Advertising and the media have shaped everyday life since the emergence of mass circulation daily newspapers. Historically, this occurred within regional or national territories. Now, the globalisation of capitalism and mass communication has allowed major advertisers to reconstruct the contours of everyday life. In this context, New Zealand is arguably the world's most commercially saturated society. This chapter will explain why this is so by delineating the changing interconnections between the media, advertising and everyday life. We begin with some concepts and definitions. This will enable us to critique media constructions of consumer culture in the context of New Zealand history and global capitalism.

Concepts and Definitions

Everyday Life and the Media

The notion of everyday life appears quite straightforward. The *Oxford Dictionary* defines everyday as 'occurring daily, worn or used on ordinary days, commonplace'.[1] Everyday life, therefore, refers to the unremarkable – eating, sleeping, walking, working, sitting around, going out. Yet this kind of definition explains very little. The dictionary leads us toward the truism that everyday life is comprised of everyday activities. This begs a central and controversial question: what is the significance of these activities?

Everyday life does not exist in isolation. It has a societal dimension which is constituted by the flows and networks of media communication. The usage of newspapers, magazines, telephones, radio, television and the new digital technologies forms the communicative infrastructure of civil society. In practice, communicative infrastructures reflect the cultural location and social density of human settlement. In a small town or village, the weekly newspaper, religious publications, school and sports club newsletters are forums of local influence, identity and solidarity. In modern Western societies, small-town residents may also listen to regional or national radio stations, watch regional, national or satellite television, and converse via telephone, email, or websites. In large urban settings, these habits of media coverage are inseparable from everyday routines of work, leisure and domesticity. The triangulation of everyday life, mediated communication and civil society has been aptly summarised by Jeffrey Alexander and Ronald Jacobs:

> Media texts provide a certain flow of cultural material from producers to audiences who in turn use them in their lifeworld settings to construct a meaningful world and to maintain a common cultural framework through which intersubjectivity becomes possible even among those who may never come into contact with each other.[2]

In the sense described here, mediated intersubjectivity can generate feelings of class, cultural, local and regional solidarity. Mass-media institutions may also coordinate a shared imaginary of nationhood and national history. The consecutive, daily nature of newspapers and news broadcasts combines with weekly and monthly magazines to form the temporal architecture of everyday life. This temporal architecture enables citizens to imagine themselves as part of a nation moving calendrically through time.[3] The everyday and the national are publicly conjoined by live media events, such as sporting contests, dramatic political announcements, and major disasters. These become plot points for updating the ongoing narratives of civil society and nation.

However, one cannot automatically assume a functional mass-mediated relationship between the microworld of everyday life and the macroworld of society. In a primary sense, everyday life is conditioned and riven by structural relations of power. In a class-polarised society, the lifeworlds of the rich are structurally and spatially separated from the lifeworlds of impoverishment. The 'squeezed' middle classes are torn between bourgeois aspirations and the fear of downward mobility. In these circumstances, the mass media does not necessarily provide 'a common cultural framework' for intersubjectivity and public understanding.[4] Instead, the media may serve to amplify the ideals of individualism, consumer choice and private acquisition. If this occurs, the social solidarities of everyday life will be endangered.

Everyday Life and Advertising

In a critical discussion of advertising the most fundamental concept is that of the commodity. This commodity has two distinct components of value. The first is use value, which derives from the actual properties and functions of the commodity itself. The second is exchange value, which is less concrete and requires an agency (typically money) through which to function. Importantly, both types of value are required for an object to become a commodity. An individual's production of some 'thing' may fulfil a need and use value, but it is not a commodity. That status can only be reached when there is use value for another person. Then ownership can be transferred through a medium of exchange (usually money), which demonstrates the exchange value. It is at this point that the 'thing' becomes a commodity.[5]

The long-term legitimacy of capitalism depends on its ability to offer material benefits to the majority of the population. This requires the inculcation of consumer lifestyles and the promotion of affluence as a societal accomplishment.[6] A form of indirect coercion is involved here; people believe they will be penalised or embarrassed for not trying to 'keep up with the Jones's'. In this context, the idea of status competition among consumers is clearly located within the discourse of advertising.

Broadly speaking, the sociology of consumption can be traced back as far as the 1500s.[7] However, before the 1880s, advertising was mostly used as a tool for announcing and promoting novelties and fringe products. The subsequent penetration of advertising discourse into the everyday lifeworld of the bourgeoisie reflected underlying changes in the dynamics of capitalism. The paradigm of the mass which constituted the formation of modern society was critical in the development of advertising. It allowed for the modern mass-marketing model (in which costs are decreased through increasing sales) to evolve. Correspondingly, conditions of 'massness' were vital in creating the standardised desires that were needed to fuel a consumer economy.

Everyday Life, Advertising and the Media

By the 1920s in North America and Western Europe advertising had merged with everyday life. Advertiser-supported consumerism had succeeded in alleviating much of the working-class resistance to capitalism that had developed in the later 1800s. Once this had been achieved, the opportunity existed to further integrate the commercial system into everyday working-class life. This was not, however, seen as an easy process. Advertising had to break down the 'barriers of individual habits'[8] that stood against a more mass-mediated paradigm of consumption. Corporate capital required mass advertising to alter social, economic and psychological life in favour of demand creation.[9] To this end, advertising furthered an 'ideology of consumption [that] responded both to the issue of social control and the need for goods distribution.'[10] Simply put, the purpose of advertising was to manufacture consumers and, therein, create their demand.

Obviously, this necessitated further re-constructions of everyday life. In the first instance, demand creation required the household to be more fully integrated into the system of consumption. The family had to be weaned away from a purely wage–salary–work orientation. In addition, saving and spending needed to be driven by the desire to accumulate consumer objects and pleasures. This, in turn, required the establishment of taste and lifestyle cultures largely centred around youth.[11] Meanwhile, the creation of hire purchase and credit-card-based patterns of consumption reshaped financial management within households.[12]

Advertising was also structurally central to the economic system itself. It helped break down opposition to the imposition of scientific management in workplaces. Advertising revealed the consumption-based benefits that the new workplace system would bring. The line was 'work hard and these consumer items can be yours'. In order to integrate advertising further with everyday life, products became associated with feelings and universal values. The underlying assumption was that people could not live normal lives without the products advertised. The needs and wants of people could not be satisfied without the purchase of ever more goods and services. Indeed, the notion of customer satisfaction was produced by the continual whetting of appetites and provoking of desires.

This implies a world in which individuals need not adapt to prevailing moral norms. Instead of the individual adapting to society, consumption is predicated on society adapting to the individual. The stress on the individuated product or service illustrates this trend. This kind of advertising psychologically reinforces and naturalises the habit of consumption. The French sociologist Jean Baudrillard emphasises how the external object provides validation for the individual human subject. These objects function to authenticate existence – just as the 'abundance of products puts an end to scarcity; the abundance of advertising puts an end to insecurity.'[13] What advertising also provides is a code which is based on 'status'. This allocates and systematises personalities into a hierarchical dynamic. Most importantly, Baudrillard argues that the nature of this code is not transparent. It functions to obscure the real social relationships of production. Individuals can perceive hierarchies of status, but only within the status of the code itself. This allows the dominant in society to maintain and extend their supremacy.

According to Baudrillard, advertising 'speaks' to the consumer in symbolic form. The specifics of the message transferred and the visible aims of the medium are not significant issues. Baudrillard is more concerned with how advertising works in and of itself:

> ... i.e. as an object referring not to real objects, not to a real world or a referential dimension, but from one sign to the other, from one object to the other, from one consumer to the other.[14]

This implies that advertising is not predicated on 'the lie' (to whatever degree this lie might be evidenced). Rather, the aim of advertising is to construct and perpetuate a system which is based on statements that are neither true nor false. It generates a mode of feeling and being which is self-fulfilling. In short, advertising works primarily because consumers (and advertisers) believe it will. This analysis can also be applied to the products advertised – their perceived efficacy depends on the advertising discourse itself.

Advertising promises hope rather than understanding. To this end, the object advertised facilitates a pseudo-event, which becomes a real event only when the consumer buys the product and naturalises the discourse. Moreover, this discourse is self-referential; it has no external reality. Every manifestation of advertising is a metaphor for the brand. Thus, advertising depends on the willingness of individuals and companies to enter a world that can only be validated in the act of purchase. At one level this is obvious. Without the buying of advertised products the system would fail. However, it is the process through which this occurs which is the important point here. Advertising can be validated without the need for proof or efficacy.

However, advertising also operates within socially constructed frameworks of meaning, whether individuals are conscious of these or not. One central framework is that of the 'free gift'. Underlying every advertisement is the assumption that the consumer is getting something for nothing (even if this is only the informational content). When one has the feeling of getting 'something for nothing', the underlying logic of commodity exchange is obscured. In these circumstances individuals do not reflect on the relations of power that are manifest in everyday life. This, rather than the promotion of products for commercial purposes, is the ultimate goal of the advertising system. Advertising is based on the 'understanding' that it is a social service in which 'all products are presented as services, all real economic processes are staged and reinterpreted socially as effects of giving, of personal allegiance and affective relations'.[15] If this is the case, then advertising can be seen as the grammar of capitalist society. Advertising symbols pervade everyday life yet they relate only to themselves. This serves to obscure the structural relations of power behind a façade of choice and the 'freedom' of the gift.

Media, Advertising and Everyday Life under Globalisation

Globalisation and New Zealand Society

By the mid 1990s, New Zealand was no longer a nationally constituted economy. Domestic business activity was incorporated within the flows and networks of global capitalism. In the four years following the October 1987 stockmarket crash, the number of New Zealand listed companies fell from 288 to 111.[16] From 1989 to 1994, foreign stock exchange shareholdings jumped from 19 to 51 per cent. [17] By 1995, the ratio of foreign investment stock to GDP had reached 46.7 per cent (compared to Australia 22.2 per cent, Canada 20.5 per cent). And of firms employing 100 workers or more, 32.9 per cent were overseas based (up from 22.8 per cent in 1989).[18]

The global dynamics of finance and production intermesh with the global dynamics of media communication. The deregulation of national broadcasting systems, combined with new communication technologies, has allowed major conglomerates to develop worldwide production and distribution networks. The global commercial media system is now dominated by General Electric, AT&T / Liberty Media, Disney, Time-Warner, Sony, News Corporation, Viacom, Seagram and Bertelesmann.[19] Their holdings incorporate print media, film and television production, book publishing, recorded music, telecommunications infrastructures, and Internet providers. Global media threatens the viability of nationally constructed media systems. Yet, successive New Zealand governments have actively abetted global media business strategies. Four pivotal events illustrate this process: the deregulation of broadcasting (1989); the entry of TV3 and pay television (1989); the sale of Telecom; and the lifting of restrictions on foreign media ownership (1991). The net result has been a further contraction and commercialisation of public media. In 1996, for example, the National-led coalition government sold the

41 commercial stations of state-owned Radio New Zealand, the Radio Bureau (an advertising production studio), and Radio New Zealand Sport to the New Zealand Radio Network Ltd for $89 million. The buyer was equally owned by Wilson and Horton (100 per cent owned by Tony O'Reilly's Independent Newspapers Group – INP), Australian Provincial Newspapers (over 42 per cent INP owned), and Clear Channel Communications. Also in 1996 the Radio Network Ltd bought the Prospect radio network, giving it control of 53 stations and 60 per cent of radio advertising in New Zealand. With its new stable, the company declined to renew its supply contract with Radio New Zealand's news service in April 1997.[20]

Although Television New Zealand remains state-owned, it is run as a predominantly commercial enterprise. In most countries, public broadcasters are legally required to promote national identity and culture. New Zealand relies on competitive bidding by programme makers through New Zealand On Air. A survey of 11 OECD countries in 1999 showed New Zealand had the lowest local content on television, with 24 per cent; the most comparable country, Ireland, had 41 per cent.[21] The privately-owned TV3 is controlled by CanWest Global Communications Corporation, a part-owner of the Ten Network in Australia and with links in Chile and the UK. Pay television broadcaster Sky Network Television Ltd is 41 per cent owned by the News Corporation-controlled Independent Newspapers Ltd (INL).

Media and Advertising

Since the mid 1980s many local advertising agencies have become part of global empires. Thirty years ago 80 per cent of New Zealand advertising was booked with locally owned agencies. By the early 1990s, almost 75 per cent was booked with subsidiaries of overseas-owned firms.[22] Additionally, the overall advertising 'market' has fragmented. By the mid 1990s, there were approximately 175 radio stations and 21 national and regional television channels.[23] When new technologies (primarily the Internet) are added, it is clear there has been an enormous increase in both advertising time and media competition.[24] This is illustrated by the growing significance of the 18–29 age group (the almost mythical 'Generation X'). Such people are the earliest adopters of new technology.[25]

With sharpening competition for markets and market niches, total advertising expenditure has increased. In 1990, $997 million was spent across all media. By 1999 this figure had risen to $1.4 billion.[26] The percentage breakdown was as follows:

Advertising share by medium, 1999[27]	
Television	34.3 per cent
Newspapers	32.6 per cent
Radio	12.6 per cent
Magazines	11.2 per cent
Community newspapers	7.3 per cent
Outdoor advertising (e.g. billboards)	1.2 per cent
Cinema	0.8 per cent

The 1990s saw a significant shift in the share of expenditure between the two most dominant media. In 1990 newspaper advertising accounted for 40.7 per cent of all advertising spending. In 1999, this figure had fallen to 32.6 per cent (see table). Therefore, although television's share of total advertising fell from 35.2 per cent to 34.3 per cent[28] over the same period, this medium became the greatest beneficiary of advertising spending. This reflects television's growing centrality to everyday life; it is the most consumed of all mass media. For this reason, television encapsulates the social changes wrought by advertising over the last decade and a half.

Prior to 1984, there was a statutory maximum amount of advertising per hour. This was removed with broadcasting deregulation in the face of competition. Networks also increased on-air self-promotion. More significantly, advertising has been insinuated into programmes themselves. By the late 1990s, TVNZ was scheduling advertorials: paid 'editorial' segments within normal programmes. For example, the 1990s magazine show *Good Morning* did not initially feature advertisement breaks. Rather, the show was structured around four-minute advertorials. Advertisers were also able to sponsor information segments, with a supermarket chain buying the naming rights to a weekly review of meat and produce.[29] This influence has abated somewhat in more recent years, with the re-introduction of advertisement breaks. The advertorial, however, remains. Significantly, there was little viewer resistance to its presence. Advertorial has increasingly been seen as an acceptable funding mechanism and even as a distinctive programme genre.

In February 1989 TVNZ significantly relaxed its rules concerning the sponsorship of programmes and established a unit to manage sponsorship deals. Sponsors contributed to the production of promos for the programme and helped develop a marketing strategy around their brand.[30] TVNZ even went so far as to produce a booklet and video ('Television Sponsorship – the Ultimate Guide') which it sent to various companies and advertising agencies.[31] The strategy was remarkably successful. Sponsorship revenue for TVNZ doubled in 1992 and approached the global average of four per cent of total revenue for the channel. Examples included *Countrywide Bank Grandstand* on TV1 and 'brought to you by' deals for *The Simpsons* (Coca-Cola) and *Wheel of Fortune* (Unilever) on Channel Two. TV3 was also actively seeking sponsors at this time. Examples include *Mobil Sport* and *Wynne's Sport*.[32]

Increasing levels of sponsorship were a response to tightening advertising budgets coupled with media and audience fragmentation. This is because sponsorship 'can target psychographics through active participation, better than advertising targets demographics through passive means'.[33] Companies look to match their product with the tone or substance of a programme; this is called 'affinity'. Examples are Air New Zealand with travel shows and State Insurance with *Crimewatch*. By contrast, companies will tend not to sponsor programmes that do not fit their image. The ASB Bank, for example, had a policy of not being associated with high-risk activities (such as gambling or motorsport).[34]

By the mid-1990s, sponsorship had become a routine feature of New Zealand television. No genre was immune. In April 1998 Nissan started sponsorship of *Holmes*, the main current affairs show on TVNZ's Channel One. The deal was arranged by Nissan's advertising agency, Whybin TBWA.[35] Magazine-style current affairs shows such as *Sixty Minutes* and *20/20* are also sponsored. Little public debate has ensued from such developments. So far, most comments have focused on the potential conflict of interest between an investigative programme and the concerns of the sponsor. When TVNZ actively sought sponsorship for the breakfast news show, the general manager of sales and marketing for TVNZ discounted the notion that a sponsor could influence editorial content. Interestingly, more controversy surrounded attempts to introduce advertising and/or sponsorship to the publicly owned Radio New Zealand. The non-commercial orientation of this network sharpened the reactions of both staff and public.[36]

As market-oriented formats dominate media schedules, the purchasing power of audience members assumes greater significance. There are two dimensions to this. In the first instance, customers must have sufficient resources to buy goods and services or the access to them. Secondly, advertisers' interests are served best by targeting the more affluent in society.

Advertisers will lean towards programming which caters for certain kinds of economic and social values. Advertising, therefore, promotes ideas and ways of life compatible with corporate interests. This marginalises working-class media, radical political alternatives and non-consumerist principles. Indeed, any media system that focuses on market criteria is biased in favour of the political and economic status quo. The role of advertising is crucial here as it provides material support and ideological legitimacy for the commercial system.

The current system of capitalism seems to require a redefinition of free speech. The citizen's right to free speech through elected representative bodies and the corporate market's right to commercial speech are in direct conflict. If commercialism intrudes into the private and public sphere then corporate culture will be the dominant ideological discourse.[37] Social awareness of this tendency is obscured by the assumption that consumer choice is identical to an individual's freedom of expression. The move from 'citizen' to 'consumer' means that people can only evaluate themselves as commercial actors.[38]

Advertising and Everyday Life

Reconstructing everyday life to fit consumer values is an obvious aim of the advertising industry. The promotion of global brands is central to this process. Since the mid-1980s, advertisers have increased the visibility of major brands. The aim was to extend the traditional association between branded products and positive experiences into everyday life. Therefore, instead of just having a television commercial feature children drinking Coke, the aim is for children to devise an advertising campaign for Coke in class. As Naomi Klein writes:

> The effect, if not always the original intent, of advanced branding is to nudge the hosting culture into the background and make the brand the star. It is not to sponsor culture but to be the culture.[39]

The corporate chain store also integrates commercial imperatives into everyday life. These are global outlets with completely standardised production and selling techniques. The choreography of a chain store is replicated worldwide. The most obvious example is McDonalds. McDonalds has rationalised the production and distribution of fast food to such an extent that the brand itself serves as a metaphor for social and economic change. Think of the connotation of the phrase 'McJob'. After the highly publicised

'McLibel' trial in the United Kingdom, the Chief Justice adjudged 'that McDonalds pays its workers low wages, helping to depress wages for workers in the catering trade in Britain'.[40] McDonalds is so sensitive about 'McJob' that it has threatened to sue the *Oxford Dictionary*, among others, for using the term. The typical McDonalds restaurant also shows the extent to which commercial realities have shaped the 'product'. Consider the manner in which the food is assembled:

> ... the food ... arrives at the restaurant preformed, precut, presliced, and 'pre-prepared', often by nonhuman technologies ... there is no need for them to form the burgers, cut the potatoes, slice the rolls, or prepare the apple pie. All they need to do is, where necessary, cook or often merely reheat the food and pass it on to the customer.[41]

The rationalisation process continues after the meals have been eaten. Diners are supposed to dispose of their own waste. This further reduces the costs for McDonalds – the template of the production line incorporates the customers themselves. Of course, McDonalds' advertising obscures this factor. The cartoon figure Ronald McDonald encourages children to pick up litter. Meanwhile, television advertisements emphasise the convenience of the meals and promote each restaurant as a family fun 'experience'.

This phenomenon is not limited to McDonalds or, for that matter, to fast food. More recently, Starbucks and Borders have launched chain stores which focus on coffee and books respectively. Starbucks is a multinational chain with enormous resources at its disposal. Yet its stores are deliberately designed to disguise this fact. In its own newsletters, Starbucks is promoted as a haven where sophisticated people can enjoy the lifestyle benefits that accrue from branded coffee products. Borders adopts a similar approach to book retailing. Its stores promote an individual and personalised 'experience' (in contrast to the standardised corporate reality). However, commercial goals are paramount. *En route* to an in-store reading of his recent book, the alternative filmmaker Michael Moore confronted a picket line of striking workers. He refused to continue unless the staff could air their views. The staff were allowed to speak but Moore was censored; his future readings at Borders were cancelled.[42] Stores such as Borders represent an intensification of consumer culture. It is easy to see how chain stores like McDonalds associate certain lifestyles with their branded products. The chain-store branding of The Gap, Ikea, Borders, Starbucks and The Body Shop is harder to deconstruct. These stores actively disseminate the view that they project atmosphere and lifestyle rather than product. As Naomi Klein puts it:

> This isn't dreck for the masses, it's intelligent furniture, it's cosmetics
> as political activism, it's the bookstore as 'old-world library,' it's the
> coffee shop that wants to stare deep into your eyes and 'connect'.[43]

This is the most pernicious intrusion of advertising into everyday life. Advertising strategies and campaigns are deliberately constructed to make normal lived existence indistinguishable from commercial brands and culture.

Although global corporations drive the branding process, local developments have also commercialised the broader horizons of everyday life. The most striking example concerns the commodification of 'New Zealandness' and its history. One of the latest Toyota New Zealand television campaigns was simply a collage of magic moments from advertisements of the past twenty years. A similar approach was adopted by Telecom to promote its millionth mobile phone customer. Sporting 'products' are also framed in this manner. America's Cup advertisements focused on the 'Kiwi-ness' of the enterprise – the nation was shown pulling together for the team. The Adidas-sponsored All Blacks have incorporated the haka in an advertising campaign. In all of these cases, cultural life and collective memory are resold to audiences as commodified nostalgia.

Corporate commercial interests also construct spectacles of consumption. In Auckland's Village Entertainment Centre multiplex movie theatres, a food hall, bars, a theme restaurant, games parlours, a cyber café, a bookstore, and the city's information centre architecturally form a giant maze. The effect is to create a space entirely devoted to the consumption of various complementary products and experiences. Such constructions are increasingly replacing public spaces as preferred meeting and recreation venues. In this way, everyday life is subtly but definitively recast as a consumer experience.

The mass media also project spectacles of consumption. One recent example was the launch of the Global Plus credit card. In a masterstroke of marketing, the new card was conjoined with a 'world record' bungee jump off Auckland's Sky Tower. The presenters of the show wore Global Plus logos, viewers were constantly told that the event was brought to them by Global Plus, and an advertising campaign was built around the bungee jump and the new 'record' holder – A. J. Hackett. Connecting an event with a product in this way does more than raise its profile. The advertising rationale that underpins the entire spectacle situates the contrast between ordinary life and extraordinary events within a commercial context. The subtext is that such events can only be experienced and consumed with advertiser or sponsor support.

Politics has also been reshaped by commercial imperatives. Advertisements have always been identifiable features of the political landscape. However, since 1984, governments and government departments have used advertising seamlessly. Under the fourth Labour Government a social welfare initiative, GST, and income-tax reform were sold to the public like consumer products.[44] By the late 1990s, this strategy had spread to government departments. For example, the 1999 WINZ series of advertisements featured Api the caseworker. In doing this, the department was open to criticism that it regarded self-promotion as more important than work assistance. When politics, policies and government departments are treated as 'products', corporate and public life appear indistinguishable.

Corporate-driven consumerism also shapes biophysical aspects of everyday life. The direct marketing of drugs via television exemplifies this. The most notorious example is the promotion of Xenical, beginning in May 1998.[45] Although this drug has obvious health benefits, the advertising campaign focused on lifestyle improvements associated with its use. Advertisements have featured people who want to swim with their families or watch their children's sporting activities. The most overt association between Xenical use and lifestyle improvement features a woman who lists the qualities of a highly adventurous life (this includes, among other things, 'making love to a stranger'). She culminates the advertisement with the statement 'but first I'd like to tie my own shoes'. This sequence implies that overweight women will experience an adventurous lifestyle after using the drug.

Despite some controversy (such as the advertisements that featured Father Christmas over the 1998/1999 summer season[46]), the Xenical campaign has been remarkably successful. The manufacturer, Roche, claimed that over 65 per cent of doctors had prescribed the drug in the first four weeks.[47] By August 1998 it was reported that nearly 10, 000 people were using Xenical.[48] In the following ten months, this figure increased to approximately 30, 000. Over the same period 89 per cent of General Practitioners prescribed the drug.[49] The monetary results were equally impressive. In its first year, Xenical earned $12 million in retail sales,[50] with $3 million in July 1999 alone.[51] This success has been entirely driven by a television advertising campaign which implicitly claims that losing weight is a lifestyle issue. This is not to argue that the drug has no benefits. However, pharmacists reported a large number of non-obese people enquiring about the drug the month after the campaign started.[52] Doctors also reported that patients without weight problems were demanding the drug.[53]

The infomercial and related programmes merge advertising logics with everyday life. This is not a new development. In the USA fifteen and thirty-minute commercials were scheduled as programmes during the 1940s and early 1950s. Stricter advertising and programme sponsorship regulations subsequently removed infomercials from the networks after the late 1950s. In 1984 the Federal Communications Commission (FCC) removed statutory time limits on the amount of advertising per hour.[54] At the same time, credit cards enabled people to order products from television and the number of cable channels increased. These channels often needed programming in marginal times, so timeslots were available at reasonable rates.[55] These slots were filled by infomercials. If they are to work, viewers need to believe that they are watching a genuine programme, such that the information content drives the commercial message (rather than vice versa). The characteristic features of the infomercial are set out below:

Textual Features of the Infomercial	
Information	Which focuses on the quality and value of the product and is meaningful even if the product is not bought.
Problem/Solution structure	This introduces a problem and solves it through using the product.
Toll-free number	This ought to be visible for at least 30 seconds in every 'commercial' segment.
Structure	This needs to mimic commercial television, i.e. there ought to be identifiable 'editorial' and 'advertisement' sections.

One hybrid of the infomercial is the revenue enhanced programme (REP). An REP is part entertainment, part educational and part infomercial; it aims to generate both sales and ratings. Therefore, the REP has to look like normal commercial television without discouraging direct responses from the audience.[56]

In New Zealand, imported infomercials played in 1993[57] and local versions appeared the following year.[58] As in the United States, this trend was facilitated by the liberalisation of advertising rules. For TVNZ, this source of revenue became more important as new players entered the recession-hit television market. In these circumstances, TVNZ felt compelled to introduce twenty-four-hour programming. Initially, mainstream advertisers favoured the shorter form of direct response television (DRTV) – two-minute commercials. These were quickly absorbed to become part of the normal television schedule. *The Ford Report*, for example, enabled the company to deliver 'maximum bangs for their diminished advertising bucks'.[59] Other short DRTV segments include the Food in a Minute, the Glad Wrap, and Jif series of commercials. AGB McNair figures show that television advertising featuring an 0800 number was worth over NZ$100 million in 1995 (an increase of 31 per cent over 1994).[60] These figures suggest significant advantages for business. The Korean car company Daewoo, for example, has benefited immensely from DRTV exposure. Their sales for the 1997–98 year increased 84 per cent in a market that contracted by eight per cent.[61]

The long form of DRTV has recently become more visible. TV2, TV3, TV4 and Prime Television all feature infomercials on weekday mornings, while TV1 has its own advertorial programme *Good Morning*. In July 1999, TV4 announced it would screen infomercials for an extra two hours a day; this was a more profitable revenue source than conventional advertising.[62] The two main local DRTV companies (Prestige Marketing – now Quantum Prestige – and L.V. Martin & Son) have both produced their own infomercials. The 'Reading Master' series, for example, is now in its third incarnation.

Infomercials have also reconfigured the 'light entertainment' genre. This can be understood as a dual process. First, in a practical, televisual sense, the infomercial and the revenue enhanced programme (REP) share common features with the primetime sponsored programme (PSP).[63] Second, in an ideological (or marketing) sense, the infomercial and the PSP process information in the same way. In other words, every PSP is infomercialised. This process is identifiable by the presence of at least one 'call to action' (CTA) along with a pervasive advertising orientation within the informational segments. According to the marketing literature, these two factors alone would allow any programme to be classed as DRTV. In this context, one can rank individual programmes on a scale of infomercialisation. For example, *Arnotts' Dreams Come True* scores at the low end of the scale since it does not have a 'call to action' within the programme. At the other extreme are *Unichem Medical File* and *Woolworths' Ready Steady Cook*. These programmes continually promote low-cost consumer products and so are extremely infomercialised. Lifestyle-oriented programmes (such as *Bayley's Home Front* and *Corban's Taste New Zealand*) cannot focus on specific products to the same extent. Consequently, they are at the mid-point of the scale. However, these programmes remain significantly influenced by the infomercial model. The salient point is that such programmes have a clearly identifiable sales orientation to the information they present. This reveals a breakdown of the traditional split between editorial and advertising content.[64]

As we have mentioned previously, globalisation radically separates the lifeworlds of rich and poor. Primetime sponsored programmes (PSPs) subtly reinforce this process. One clear example is *United Travel Getaway*. This programme offers a lifestyle that is derived from both the holidays themselves and from the connotations of affluence and consumption that accompany the 'person who travels'. The importance of aspiring to this doubly coded lifestyle can be seen in the opening voiceover, which sets the tone for the entire programme. It welcomes the viewer with the invitation to 'follow your dreams with *United Travel Getaway* as tonight we journey to [insert the names of the three destinations].' The presenter introduces the show in a similar vein:

> We're going to take you to the places you've always wanted to visit. The hot spots. The cool things to do. From the divinely decadent to the cheap and cheerful.

These announcements suggest that the programme (also) acts as a surrogate for those who cannot travel. The information it presents does not just provide practical advice about the travelling lifestyle; it also provides an alternative for those who cannot attain travel status. Even if viewers cannot afford any of the advertised holidays, they can learn about a foreign country and 'see the sights' on their television screens. By comparison, those viewers who *can* afford one of the special deals are uniquely privileged – they can experience in person what they see on their screen (for a special price). Indeed, the programme is primarily aimed at those who can actually take up a travelling lifestyle on a (relatively) low budget.

However, the secondary audience (those who cannot afford the deals) are not ignored. For them, *United Travel Getaway* provides the safety valve of surrogate, armchair travel. This is vital to the success of the programme. It is unlikely that the majority of viewers could afford the holidays advertised. In order to keep ratings high, these viewers must be satisfied. However, the main aim of the show is simply to sell travel deals. Thus, the larger secondary audience can be seen as vehicles. Their viewership (in sufficient numbers) keeps the programme viable for more affluent viewers who can find out about the special deals.

Mitre 10 Dream Home revealed another dual-viewership strategy. The programme features two families who could not afford to own their own homes. They represented viewers from the same socio-economic background, but they also represented the dream of homeownership for the poor. Such viewers could entertain the prospect of homeownership. The two families also did some home renovation with sponsored and branded products. This implied that some people (those of lower socio-economic status) cannot aspire to a higher status without the intervention of advertising and sponsorship.

Conclusion

In New Zealand, advertising has become central to social and economic life. This is because it 'drives' contemporary capitalism. Without advertising, the capitalist system literally could not function; there would be no method of creating and managing demand. However, advertising messages won't work if they cannot be received. Therefore, advertising cannot function without access to the mass media. Correspondingly, the main function of the media is to transmit advertising messages. Media texts *also* inform, entertain (or even educate), but these functions are ancillary to commercial imperatives. The audience 'completes the circuit' by purchasing the goods and services advertised.

It is essential to appreciate what advertising *does* through the media. In our view, advertising's 'commercial speech' promotes a commodified understanding of the world and of social relationships. The products promoted in advertisements are imbued with personal qualities, and this encourages people to regard them in a personal, subjective manner. Indeed, lifestyles deriving from the possession of advertised goods appear to promise more happiness than personal relationships can provide.

Crucially, however, the infiltration of advertising into everyday life is experienced unequally. The global media system (to which New Zealand belongs) primarily caters for audiences with a middle or upper-middle-class horizon of consumption. Those who cannot enter this material world are positioned as inadequate consumers. In practice, this condemns the rural and urban poor to a second-class existence. They are confronted by consumer lifestyles which they cannot legally acquire.

The television infomercial and the primetime sponsored programme (PSP) represent the apogee of consumerism. The audience is constructed as consumers and *only* as consumers. Infomercials and PSPs show that advertising logic has so permeated mainstream media that its presence appears unremarkable. The traditional distinction between programmes and advertisements is disappearing without public realisation or resistance. This is a highly disturbing development. Most New Zealanders experience no discernible difference between media content, advertising and everyday life.

Endnotes

1   *Oxford Illustrated Dictionary* (1979) Oxford: Clarendon Press.
2   J. C. Alexander and R. N. Jacobs, 'Mass Communication, Ritual, and Civil Society', in T. Liebes and J. Curran (eds) (1998) *Media Ritual and Identity*, London: Routledge, p. 27.
3   See especially B. Anderson, *Imagined Communities: Reflections on the Origin and Spread of Nationalism*, London: Verso, 1983.
4   Alexander and Jacobs, 1998, p. 27.
5   K. Marx, *Capital Volume I*, Harmondsworth: Penguin, 1976, p. 125.
6   D. Strinati, *An Introduction to Theories of Popular Culture*, New York: Routledge, 1995, pp. 58–9.
7   See G. McCracken, *Culture and Consumption – New Approaches to the Symbolic Character of Consumer Goods and Activities*, Bloomington & Indianapolis: Indiana University Press, 1990, especially the introduction.
8   H. W. Hess 'History and Present Status of the "Truth-in-Advertising" Movement as Carried on by the Vigilance Committee of the Associated Advertising Clubs of the World', *Annals of the American Academy of Political and Social Science*, CI May, 1922, p. 211 cited in S. Ewen, *Captains of Consciousness: Advertising and the Social Roots of Consumer Culture*, New York: McGraw Hill, 1976, p. 19.
9   D. Smythe, *Dependency Road: Communication, Capitalism, Consciousness and Canada*, Norwood, New Jersey: Ablex Publishing, 1981, p. 89.
10   Ewen, *Captains of Consciousness*, p. 19.
11   A. Werwick, *Promotional Culture: Advertising and Ideology in Late Capitalism*, Guildford: Biddles, 1991, p. 24.
12   J. Ford and K. Rowlingson, 'Producing consumption: Women and the making of credit markets', in S. Edgell *et al.* (eds) *Consumption Matters,* Oxford, Basil Blackwell, 1996, p. 110. This article shows how lower socio-economic classes remain prime targets for credit-based consumption and the highly gendered patterns that are involved.
13   J. Baudrillard, *The System of Objects*, London: Verso, 1996, p. 171.
14   Ibid., p. 125.
15   J. Baudrillard, *The Consumer Society: Myths and Structures*, London: Sage, 1998, p. 165.
16   B. Gaynor, *New Zealand Herald,* October 14 1997, p. A11.

17   R. Le Heron and E. Pawson, *Changing Places: New Zealand in the Nineties*, Auckland: Longman Paul, 1996, pp. 34–36.
18   Rosenberg, 1989, pp. 30–33.
19   R. McChesney, *Rich Media, Poor Democracy*, Urbana and Chicago: University of Illinois Press, 1999, pp. 78–118.
20   J. Kelsey, *Reclaiming the Future: New Zealand and the Global Economy*, Wellington: Bridget Williams, 1999, p. 197.
21   *New Zealand Herald*, July 1 1999, p. 3.
22   M. Perry, 'Some Implications of the Internationalisation of Commercial Capital for New Zealand', *New Zealand Geographer*, Volume 46, Number 2, 1990, p. 28.
23   *AdMedia*, September 1995, p. 24.
24   J. Farnsworth, 'New Zealand Advertising Agencies: Professionalisation and Cultural Production', *Continuum, The Australian Journal of Media & Culture*, Volume 10, Number 1, 1996.
25   R. Hillgrove, 'The NeXt Generation', in T. Agee (ed.) *NZ Marketing Resource and Case Studies Book*, Auckland: Mintys Media, 1996.
26   *National Business Review*, May 26 2000, p. 39.
27   These figures are taken from *Fastline*, May 25 2000.
28   These figures are from the *National Business Review*, May 26 2000, p. 39.
29   Anonymous, 'Good morning, can we interest you in…', *The Independent*, March 8 1996.
30   M. Slade, 'TVNZ Targets Sponsorship in Revenue Drive', *National Business Review*, February 1 1989.
31   P. Teutenberg, 'Sponsors: Old Masters in a New Frame', *Marketing*, February 1994.
32   E. Scott, 'Without whom…', *AdMedia*, March 1991.
33   K. Lawrence, 'Finding the Perfect Partner', *Marketing*, March 1999.
34   Teutenberg, 'Sponsors: Old Masters in a New Frame'.
35   *Fastline*, April 23 1998.
36   See D. Welch, 'Free To Air?' *New Zealand Listener*, March 21 1998.
37   A. Mattelart, *Advertising International: The Privatisation of Public Space*, London: Routledge, 1991, p. 87.
38   S. Ewen, 'From Citizen to Consumer?', *Intermedia*, Volume 20, Number 3, 1992, p. 23.
39   N. Klein, *No Logo: Taking Aim at the Brand Bullies*, London: Flamingo, 2000, p. 30.
40   Ibid., p. 237.
41   G. Ritzer, *The McDonaldization of Society: An Investigation into the Changing Character of Contemporary Social Life* (rev. edn.), Thousand Oaks, California: Pine Forge Press, 1996, p. 103.
42   Klein, p. 183.
43   Ibid., p. 136.

44 B. Harvey 'Advertising', *Metro*, October 1989.
45 *The Dominion*, May 28 1998. Xenical is manufactured by Roche, a global pharmaceutical company.
46 *Pharmacy Today*, November 1998.
47 *The Independent*, July 15 1998.
48 *New Zealand Herald*, August 20 1998.
49 *Pharmacy Today*, June 1999.
50 *National Business Review*, July 9 1999.
51 *Pharmacy Today*, September 1999.
52 *The Dominion*, June 5 1998.
53 *New Zealand Herald*, July 9 1999.
54 J. Sivulka, *Soap, Sex and Cigarettes: A Cultural History of American Advertising*, Belmont, California: Wadsworth, 1998, p. 409.
55 H. Blumenthal and O. Goodenough, *This Business of Television*, New York: Billboard Books, 2nd Edition, 1998, p. 277.
56 A. Miller, 'The next generation of direct response television', *Direct Marketing*, Garden City, August 1997.
57 *The Independent*, May 28 1993.
58 *Marketing*, July 1994.
59 P. Teutenberg, 'Ford's Affordable Campaign', *Marketing*, June 1994.
60 R. Firebrace, 'Targeting Through TV', *Marketing*, June 1997.
61 K. Lawrence, 'Direct Response Television Advertising: Call 0800 Hardsell', *Marketing*, March 1999.
62 *Fastline*, July 29 1999.
63 The programmes investigated were all broadcast on commercial television in New Zealand in 1999. There were nine programmes in that year which had the minimum criteria necessary to be classed as a Primetime Sponsored Programme (PSP); they were broadcast in weeknight primetime slots and had sponsorship that extended, at the very least, to naming rights. These programmes were *Arnotts Dreams Come True, Bayleys Home Front, Corbans Taste New Zealand, Firth Ground Force, Mitre 10 Changing Rooms, Mitre 10 Dream Home, Unichem Medical File, United Travel Getaway,* and *Woolworths Ready Steady Cook.*
64 For an assessment of these programmes on a scale of infomercialisation, see R. Johnson, *But Wait There's More! The infiltration of the infomercial into mainstream primetime television*, Unpublished MA Thesis, Auckland University of Technology, 2000, Chapter 4.

Bibliography

AdMedia, September 1995.
Agee, T. (n.d.) 'Order now, our operators are standing by...' unpublished report, Dept of Marketing, University of Auckland.

Alexander, J. C. and Jacobs, R. N. (1998) 'Mass Communication, Ritual, and Civil Society', in Liebes, T. and Curran, J. (eds) *Media Ritual and Identity*, London: Routledge.

Anderson, B. (1983) *Imagined Communities: Reflections on the Origin and Spread of Nationalism*, London: Verso.

Anonymous, (1996) 'Good morning, can we interest you in...', *The Independent*, March 8.

Anonymous (1998) 'The top ten grossing infomercials in 1997', *MC Technology Marketing Intelligence*, New York.

Baudrillard, J. (1996) *The System of Objects*, London: Verso.

Baudrillard, J. (1998) *The Consumer Society: Myths and Structures*, London: Sage.

Blumenthal, H. and Goodenough, O. (1998) *This Business of Television*, New York: Billboard Books, 2nd edition.

Davidson, D. (1999) 'The Emergence of DRTV into Traditional Brand Marketing', *Direct Marketing*, Garden City, May.

The Dominion, May 28 1998.

The Dominion, June 5 1998.

Eicoff, A. (1988) *Direct Marketing through Broadcast Media*, Chicago: NTC Publishing Group.

Ewen, S. (1976) *Captains of Consciousness: Advertising and the Social Roots of Consumer Culture*, New York: McGraw Hill.

Ewen, S. (1992) 'From Citizen to Consumer?' *Intermedia*, Volume 20, Number 3.

Farnsworth, J. (1996) 'New Zealand Advertising Agencies: Professionalisation and Cultural Production', *Continuum, The Australian Journal of Media & Culture*, Volume 10, Number 1.

Fastline, April 23 1998.

Fastline, July 29 1999.

Fastline, May 25 2000.

Firebrace, R. (1997) 'Targeting Through TV', *Marketing*, June.

Ford, J. and Rowlingson, K. (1996) 'Producing consumption: Women and the making of credit markets', in S. Edgell *et al.* (eds) *Consumption Matters*, Oxford: Basil Blackwell.

Gaynor, B. (1997) *New Zealand Herald*, October 14.

Harvey B. (1989) 'Advertising', *Metro*, October.

Hawthorne, T. (1998) 'Opening doors to retail stores', *Direct Marketing*, Garden City, January.

Hawthorne, T. (1998) 'When and why to consider infomercials', *Target Marketing*, Philadelphia, February.

Hillgrove, R. (1996) 'The NeXt Generation', in Agee, T. (ed.) *NZ Marketing Resource and Case Studies Book*, Mintys Media: Auckland.

The Independent May 28 1993.

The Independent July 15 1998.

Johnson, R. (2000) *But Wait There's More! The infiltration of the infomercial into mainstream primetime television*, Unpublished MA Thesis, Auckland University of Technology.

Kelsey, J. (1999) *Reclaiming the Future: New Zealand and the Global Economy*, Wellington, Bridget Williams.

Klein, N. (2000) *No Logo: Taking Aim at the Brand Bullies*, London: Flamingo.

Lawrence, K. (1999) 'Direct Response Television Advertising: Call 0800 Hardsell,' *Marketing*, March.

Lawrence, K. (1999) 'Finding the Perfect Partner', *Marketing*, March.

Le Heron, R. and Pawson, E. (1996) *Changing Places: New Zealand in the Nineties*, Auckland: Longman Paul.

Lewis, H. (1995) 'I'll quote you ... if you've said something useful', *Direct Marketing*, Garden City, September 1995.

Lewis, H. (1995) 'Information on infomercials', *Direct Marketing*, Garden City, March 1995.

Marketing July 1994.

Marx, K. (1976) *Capital Volume I*, Harmondsworth: Penguin.

Masko, M. (1997) 'What every brand manager needs to know about direct response television', *Brandweek*, New York.

Mattelart, A. (1991) *Advertising International: The Privatisation of Public Space*, London: Routledge.

McChesney, R. (1999) *Rich Media, Poor Democracy*, Urbana and Chicago: University of Illinois Press.

McCracken, G. (1990) *Culture and Consumption – New Approaches to the Symbolic Character of Consumer Goods and Activities*, Bloomington & Indianapolis: Indiana University Press.

McLaughlin, R. (1998) 'The three acts of an infomercial', *Target Marketing*, Philadelphia, September.

Miller, A. (1997) 'The next generation of direct response television', *Direct Marketing*, Garden City, August.

National Business Review, July 9 1999.

National Business Review, May 26 2000.

New Zealand Herald, August 20 1998.

New Zealand Herald, July 1 1999.

New Zealand Herald, July 9 1999.

Oxford Illustrated Dictionary (1989) Oxford: Clarendon Press.

Perry, M. (1990) 'Some Implications of the Internationalisation of Commercial Capital for New Zealand', *New Zealand Geographer*, Volume 46, Number 2.

Pharmacy Today, November 1998.

Pharmacy Today, June 1999.

Pharmacy Today, September 1999.

Ray, D. (1996) '"Infomercial King" Mike Levey discusses success secrets', *Direct Marketing*, Garden City, October 1996.

Ritzer, G. (1996) *The McDonaldization of Society: An Investigation into the Changing Character of Contemporary Social Life* (rev. edn.), Thousand Oaks, California: Pine Forge Press.

Scott, E. (1991) 'Without whom…', *AdMedia*, March.

Silverman, G. (1995) 'Planning and using infomercial campaigns effectively', *Direct Marketing*, Garden City, September.

Silverman, G. (1996) 'Infomercials: Analyzing what went wrong (and how to make it work!)', *Direct Marketing*, Garden City, July.

Sivulka, J. (1998) *Soap, Sex and Cigarettes. A Cultural History of American Advertising*, Belmont, California: Wadsworth.

Slade, M. (1989) 'TVNZ Targets Sponsorship in Revenue Drive', *National Business Review*, February 1.

Smythe, D. (1981) *Dependency Road: Communication, Capitalism, Consciousness and Canada*, Norwood, New Jersey: Ablex Publishing.

Strinati, D. (1995) *An Introduction to Theories of Popular Culture*, New York: Routledge

Teutenberg, P. (1994) 'Ford's Affordable Campaign', *Marketing*, June.

Teutenberg, P. (1994) 'Sponsors: Old Masters in a New Frame', *Marketing*, February 1994.

Welch, D. (1998) 'Free To Air?', *New Zealand Listener*, March 21.

Werwick, A. (1991) *Promotional Culture: Advertising and Ideology in Late Capitalism*, Guildford: Biddles.

8

Aesthetic Leisure

Claudia Bell and John Lyall

'Leisure' is a term usually expressed in opposition to work. Leisure may
be summed up as the absence of work, or the time outside work
commitments, or the treats and rewards of non-working time. Yet our type
of work is what is generally used as a short-cut definition of ourselves and
others. For instance, newspaper reports of accident victims or criminals
usually mention name, age and occupation (referring to public domain
experience). However, it is leisure time (private domain experience) that
is usually perceived as when we express ourselves, when we can be our
'real' selves. Self-actualisation may be a powerful personal reward, as,
through leisure activities participants develop specialised skills, talents
and knowledge, along with the sheer pleasure and self-gratification of
engaging in the activity itself.[1]

Participation in arts activities is a popular use of leisure by New
Zealanders. In this chapter we explore the idea that New Zealand has long
been a nation of creative people. Indeed, we suggest that this could be claimed
as part of our national character. A recent major New Zealand survey explored
'arts participation' in the population, and discovered that this is a regular
feature of life for nearly all New Zealanders. We look at the increased
aestheticisation of a range of activities that are engaged in as enjoyable
leisure, observing that some forms of consumption might now be regarded
as arts participation. If this is so, then the rate of arts participation by New
Zealanders may be even higher than the recent Creative New Zealand study
indicates.

Arts Participation

Arts Every Day

Arts Every Day Mahi Toi Ia Ra is a study of arts participation by New Zealand adults, published by Creative New Zealand in May 1999.[2] The research for this report was carried out in partnership by Creative New Zealand and the Hillary Commission. Creative New Zealand's 1994 Act defines the arts as 'all forms of creative and interpretive expression'. Hence *Arts Every Day* projects an inclusive understanding of the arts. It embraces 'the full spectrum of arts activities in New Zealand, ranging from the grassroots to the professional'. It also includes 'both the creative process and participation as an audience member, reader or listener'.[3]

The findings of the study showed that the arts (according to the definitions above) are integral to the daily lives of New Zealanders. [4] The findings 'challenge some major misconceptions about the average Kiwi lifestyle and demonstrate the pervasiveness of arts in our daily lives'. They show that 93 per cent of New Zealand adults (2.45 million) took part in an average of five different types of arts activity a year. Ninety per cent (2.37 million) took part in an average of 3.7 arts activities over a four-week period. The figures indicate that those who do not participate in any form of arts activity are a small minority. There were no significant differences in participation levels according to income group, age, gender, ethnicity or region. For those with tertiary qualifications, 96 per cent took part in 4.6 arts activities in the four-week period. It seems that age, education and income have far more influence in the choice of arts activities than in the level of participation in the arts.

The traditional idea of the arts as the territory of the wealthy and better educated sectors of the population is disproved in the report by its broader definitions of what constitutes arts participation. The élitist view narrows arts to such genres as opera, ballet, classical music, fine art and theatre; and participation to visiting galleries or attending a concert, the ballet or the theatre. While these particular activities are engaged in more often by those in higher income groups and with tertiary education, the study shows that cost is not a defining variable in attendance; people on lower incomes are often enthusiastic and frequent supporters of these arts areas.

Some findings of this study:

- Women (97 per cent) participate more than men (90 per cent).

- Reading (fiction 59 per cent, non-fiction 63 per cent) was the most popular arts activity.
- The second most popular activity was listening to rock / pop music (43 per cent).
- Over a four-week period, 205,000 people read poetry and 149,800 engaged in creative writing.
- Over one year, more than half of those participating in Maori arts activities were non-Maori.

The list below shows the ten most popular general arts activities (of 69 identified by the researchers) for all adults (as performer or audience) over a four-week period:

- Reading non-fiction
- Reading fiction
- Rock/pop music
- Classical/chamber music
- Story-telling
- Country/folk music
- Singing
- Knitting
- Design arts
- Band music.

The ways of participating were mostly 'as a hobby' (84 per cent). Thirty per cent also participated as teachers or students. The main reasons given for participation were enjoyment, entertainment, personal growth and development, as a means of expression, for stress reduction, and to upskill. This suggests that arts activities are an important contribution to the general wellbeing of a large number of New Zealanders.

For those who did not participate in any way at all (7 per cent of the total surveyed), some said they didn't have time (42 per cent); were not interested (33 per cent); or preferred other activities (20 per cent).

Seventy-seven per cent agreed that 'arts and cultural activities help define who we are as New Zealanders'. While the report makes no overt linkage, this seems a valid claim. Surely the 'kiwi ingenuity' tradition rests on an inherent ability to express, in very practical terms, creative responses to everyday practical problems?

From Élite Arts to DIY

During the European Renaissance artists were honoured by the Church and state; they were patronised by the élite. In an hierarchy of the arts, what we refer to as 'fine arts' or 'high arts' (painting and sculpture) had – and still have – high status. The creations of amateur practitioners were much lower in the hierarchy. In most discourse on the arts, amateurs' work has stayed in this inferior position. Hence the products and activities of amateurs have received relatively little social or official interest. Perhaps part of the appeal to participants has been their private-domain status.

A major social change of industrialism was the clear separation of work from leisure. The fluidity of pre-industrial time was replaced with distinct blocks of commodified time which could be sold to an employer, or kept as leisure. Guardians of public morals were afraid that the non-work time might mean time to get into trouble. In the nineteenth century benign pastimes were vigorously encouraged. The ideology of the productive workplace invaded the home as productive leisure. [5]

Industrialism brought new wealth to the middle classes, which led to the concept of 'hobbies'. Some joined the élite in collecting art and fine objects. The less wealthy became collectors of more affordable items; many of the products of the age became collectable because they would soon be obsolete. The act of collecting therefore transcended class; status lay in the value of the objects being collected.

In the late nineteenth century fretworking became a craze for both working and middle-class men: a creative pastime using low-tech tools to make decorative household objects. This led to the 'arts and crafts movement', a significant period in design history. The fad for fretwork was also significant historically because the new 'domestic masculinity' in the middle classes began the trend that is still present in DIY: a combination of hobby and chore. Much of its appeal lay in the valorisation of physical engagement in leisure by those whose daily occupations had long since lost any manual labour component; and the scope for individual decisions in decoration and design.

The Domestic Aesthetic Tradition in New Zealand

If we accept the definition of 'arts', in the *Arts Every Day* document – which includes knitting, embroidery and cake decorating – then we can extrapolate from this and include any and all home-made crafts. This means we can probably quite comfortably redefine New Zealand's history as one in which the population was essentially an art-making one.

Early inhabitants of Aotearoa had to rely on their own resources and skills of innovation. Maori adapted to this environment through their ability to improvise. Driven by necessity they made a rich array of cultural artefacts for use and decoration. Early-nineteenth-century scholar Elsdon Best noted, for instance, the ability of Maori to find ways of working greenstone to create versions of objects previously made of other materials.[6]

The origins of Pakeha handmade craft objects can be traced back to the recycling practices of the whalers, who used whale vertebrae for chairs and stools, and whale teeth for scrimshaw. For the earliest European settlers, from about the 1830s, processes of retrieval ad hocism, creating hybrid objects from materials to hand, boldly resolved needs for practical tools and objects. Redundant materials were not discarded, because they might 'come in handy' one day. The new objects created from these resources embodied ingenuity while symbolising the remoteness of the makers, geographically and economically, from purchasable commodities.

Once the settlers had permanent shelter they could turn their energies to creating home comforts: hearth rugs from rags, kauri bread boards and modest accessories for everyday use. Abundant raw materials enabled a huge range of crafts to develop. Many of these objects were made from timber off-cuts or left-over wool and cloth. The rag rug was particularly popular. These rugs followed the English cottage style, but were localised by the inclusion of cut-up bush singlets and old farm jerseys. [7] In the 1880s and 1890s when commercial patterns became available, there was a craze for making tea cosies. In Northland kauri gum (New Zealand amber) was a material for craft-making.

Unlike cottage industries, this craft-making was not about creating saleable articles, but about making objects for creative pleasure, and for the usefulness and decorativeness of the final product. Values and folk-wisdom of the time also encouraged active hands and domestic busyness. Parents, teachers and other adults in authority promoted productive leisure as an antidote to other, possibly destructive pastimes.[8]

Even while at war, leisure was used constructively. Soldiers in the New Zealand Wars of the 1860s spent their spare time carving their own rifle butts. A category of objects called 'trench art', from World War I, may be seen at the Army National Memorial Museum at Waiouru. Trench art includes matchbox holders and cigarette lighters made from used cartridge shells, knives from bullets, and trinkets from army buttons and foreign coins.[9]

In New Zealand, as elsewhere, a generation survived the 1930s Depression by fashioning basic needs out of whatever materials were available: adult garments cut down for children; clothing from cotton flour sacks (often dyed pink by soaking in water with the pink covers of the popular *Weekly News)*; floral garments from colourful tea towels; furniture from fruit and vegetable boxes and kerosene cans; farm gadgets from oddments of wood and wire.

This form of practical creativity was lauded in a society with just a small part of the population committed to fine arts. Practical skills were respected far more than the aesthetic arts. In the predominantly rural society imbued with a firm Protestant ethic, design was about functional problem-solving, not about fashion, or style, and certainly not about ostentatious display. The term 'kiwi ingenuity' came to sum up meeting practical needs with limited resources; a remnant of pioneer inventiveness and respect for the ability to improvise. Kiwi ingenuity is a powerful reference to creativity as a readily recognised national attribute.

Transforming artisans still had their place after World War I. Making things from retrieved materials was still a popular activity for the farmer, home-maker and hobbyist. Farmers improvised and solved problems through recycling oddments. Like the home-makers and hobbyists, their creations explored potentials never envisioned by the original manufacturers. For the hobbyist, simple, useful domestic objects such as trays and coffee tables were made from spent matchsticks; sea shells became ashtrays or decorations on picture frames and boxes; and creative sewing fashioned old garments into new. The iconic lampshade of wooden TT2 (ice-block) sticks and the matchstick model cathedral [10] are ironic commentary on the industrial age; factories manufactured the components that the artisan recycled by the most low-tech transformative process of all: hand labour. Handicraft competitions were extremely popular in New Zealand exhibitions and at annual agriculture and produce shows. The range of categories was dazzling, including one for that most quintessential of kitchen arts – edible fruit, bottled in decorative patterns. [11]

Post-depression there was still a general caution about frivolous expenditure. 'More money than sense' was a popular adage of parents of the postwar baby-boom generation, a proverbial critique of silly spenders. After the war farm women still had one best dress; children wore home-made hand-me-downs; few men owned suits. Certainly there was very little evidence of the overseas cult of consumerism in New Zealand households. Shining new household appliances demonstrated by high-heeled, shirt-waisted women were seen in a few American magazines; but that was foreign territory indeed. Meanwhile, the English womens' magazines that were popular in New Zealand (such as the *English Women's Weekly* and *Woman)* still relied heavily on knitting patterns and recipes to ensure sales. Locally produced magazines followed the English model, with the emphasis on housewives' home work, rather than extravagant consumption and glamorous escapism.

Clarke and Crichter refer to the 'Protestant leisure ethic': the desire to avoid laziness or idleness, and to seek pleasure in work-like leisure such as hobbies. They suggest that people with a strong work ethic are also likely to have a strong leisure ethic, their leisure productivity rewarding their perseverance, creativity and skill.[12] This appears to have been part of the cultural style for New Zealand. The need for unattainable objects, combined with socially approved ways of spending leisure, have meant that time has been given to making things. We have, therefore, always been a nation of creative people.

Participation By Consuming

Aestheticising Everyday Life

There has been a shift in New Zealand culture from the ethos of frugality and thriftiness that came with the 1930s Depression and the War. In this present age of the global mass-consumption of manufactured goods, the ability to 'make something out of nothing' as a fundamental recycling and conservation ethic in domestic economy is a diminishing part of everyday life. Well before credit-card culture small indulgences were saved for, little spending was just for fun, and leisure spending was not on credit. Now, value is constantly created and destroyed; what was once admired is later discarded and despised.[13] For us, here and now, one of the creative impulses of everyday culture is the drive to satisfy pleasure.

Baudrilliard writes of consumption as 'social labour'. In his analysis, individuals are urged by late capitalism to 'work' at consumption, much as they were urged to work at production.[14] The economy needs people to consume. Some people lose jobs or can no longer work, but they are still encouraged to participate in consumer culture. Consumption has become central to the shaping of personal identity, reified in purchasing lifestyle.

Consumerism has resulted in the accelerated aestheticisation of commodities used in everyday life. Through the purchase of goods that have a high level of design, for instance a Phillipe Stark toilet brush, or a Karen Walker garment, or a sleek new piece of furniture, is one not also participating in the arts – as a consumer? These objects fit Creative New Zealand's category of participation 'Design Arts – fashion, graphic, landscape, architecture, furniture, interior design'. If arts participation includes 'participation as an audience member', then does *seeing* or *buying* fashion, or architecture, or interior design mean one is to be included as an arts participant? An advantage of such participation is that one requires no special knowledge, in contrast to the appreciation of 'high culture'. The items are accessible purely through the ability to pay.

For the manufacturers and retailers of new products, adding value via aesthetic and functional considerations – whether to toilet brushes, bicycles – increases their profits. Indeed, in the case of bicycles (and any other sports gear) a whole range of aesthetic accessories is available. For those making the purchase, the greater aesthetic value of the item adds cachet – promoting the item to a higher niche, underlining its desirability and status – and hence greater consumer satisfaction. In the contemporary era, the consumer is (at least some of the time) a hedonist; and hedonism is necessary in a modern economic system. The growth of hedonism is attributed to the rise and valorisation of the middle-class consumer.

Willis uses the term 'grounded aesthetics' to explain the processes of commodification which underpin a 'common culture' in the consuming practices of various groups, for instance young people. Rather than the commodity carrying its own inherent meaning, meaning and value reside in its usage, which might include peer group acceptance and status. In terms of the everyday, many consumer items are controlled by transnational capitalist corporations, laden by advertisers with signifiers to assert status and desirability; but the meanings are finally constructed by the consumers (who may embrace or reject any product).[15]

For consumers, purchases are statements of income and discretionary spending. Much of that spending goes on things that convey 'style'. Michel Maffesoli suggests that style serves a purpose in contemporary society: it is 'played' for others, and in front of others, and this forms a reciprocal relationship with others.[16] Erving Goffman explains that goods people buy or own 'take on the properties of status symbols if the purchase of them is indicative of membership in a particular status group'.[17] When goods are primarily appropriated as status symbols, the items one must buy keep changing, because there is an endless flow of status symbols and tastes. It is in the makers' and sellers' interests to keep these changing styles flowing through the retail outlets. It is in the purchasers' interests to keep changing styles, because constant requirements to buy the new commodity restricts membership to those with the same level of discretionary income. Hence the evolving nature of fashion, and of what is fashionable. Fashion constructs self-image and perception of status relative to others.

This is a new phase in Western history: one in which people are less valued for their commitment to the work ethic, but can impress others by their skills as consumers. One can show skills as a 'talented consumer'. In turn, the respect for consumption (people aren't embarrassed by stating they have credit-card debt, for instance) has the economic role of increasing consumer demand for merchandise and services. Hard-headed money-makers can create a fortune from people's fantasies about desirable items.

However, many people are disadvantaged by capitalism and consumer society, and are unable to express much in the way of personal taste through the purchase of domestic consumer items. An outlet for expression of aesthetic desire may be through watching other people consume on television: the glorious houses and fabulous clothes of characters in soap operas; consumption-for-display in house and garden programmes; and every possible consumer item promoted in advertisements. As Noeline's daughter-in-law Dione – the young housewife in *Sylvania Waters* – said as she looked at advertisements for (unaffordable) refrigerators: 'I'm allowed to dream, aren't I?'

Changing Rooms

Television aids and abets everyday dreaming. One of the most popular television programmes in 2000 was *Changing Rooms*. During its season it rates in the top ten programmes in New Zealand every week. This local programme (based very faithfully on a British series) is about the styling of domestic spaces – 'a site for material expression unparalleled elsewhere'.[18] *Changing Rooms* demonstrates how fantasies or dreams can become achievable reality. The processes shown are made to look accessible: each redecorating project is budgeted at less than $2,000. By adapting some of the ideas, a viewer might manage a transformation for less. *Changing Rooms* links to a magazine which shows how to make or decorate particular items shown on the programme; such as a coffee table or a mosaic bench top, using fairly basic tools.

What are the reasons for this programme's popularity?

- Is it because with rising interest rates, enhancing one's home is a way of adding to property value? In a culture which still has a high (but currently decreasing) rate of home-ownership, one's home is considered a long-term, positive financial investment.

- Is it because people have become so alienated in their work environments that self-expression at home has taken on higher pleasure/leisure value?

- Is it because of the strong national mythology of do-it-yourself, of ingenuity, of practical skills? (Painting the living room a new colour is not too challenging if one is low on technical expertise.)

- Is it because of media saturation of messages that this is the current fad? Home and garden magazines are riding an all-time sales high in New Zealand at present.

- Is it because of the heavy local sponsorships of these *advertorial*-type TV programmes, packaged so they become about 'us'? If we are told and shown enough times, the persuaders might get their message through; and 'we' can enhance 'our' spaces.

- Is it because there is some status attached to having an impressive home? This might (a) reflect one's status elsewhere (e.g. in the workplace); or (b) make up for one's lack of status elsewhere (e.g. in the workplace).

- Or does it just illustrate a popular fantasy (a stylish interior), and show how to realise it?

- Or is it a mixture of all of the above reasons?

Beautiful Gardens

The television garden design programmes also hold a strong place in television ratings. The New Zealand suburban backyard was not a style inherited from the British terraced house tradition or from European cities, where houses did not have space around them. Rather it was a celebration of having 'space to move', to grow vegetables, to have hens, and of some measure of self-sufficiency in the domestic economy of earlier New Zealand. In many suburbs the backyard, including a straight concrete path articulating a direct route to the ubiquitous Hills Hoist clothes line, has evolved to stylish 'out-door living' and entertaining areas.

The barbecue as at-home entertaining has been around for a long time, and is proudly claimed as a positive 'lifestyle' feature (certainly in comparison with Britain, where barbecues are less often possible). Current attention to designing elegant outdoor rooms is a new phase of outdoor living. Television advertorials urge hard pavers for lower maintenance, and low-skill gardening for greatest visual effect: for instance, single easy-care specimens in large pots (some cycads are so expensive that they have computer chips embedded in them to track them if they are stolen). Add some lightweight outdoor furniture, and one has created an exterior social space. Television can show a complete transformation in a matter of minutes. Essentially, this is exterior decorating.

Commodification of the outdoor aesthetic implies available leisure to enjoy these newly created spaces. Like the glossy house-and-garden magazines, these programmes are referred to as 'aspirational', a comment on viewers' dreams of locating themselves further up the social hierarchy through their talents as consumers. This redesign and decoration of the home and garden is a site to reify success; the home symbolises the achievement of material security. Indeed, grand décor may contradict ordinary reality, hinting at a past that includes a gentility and class origin that are blatant fiction.[19]

Homes and gardens are but two examples of sites for aestheticising leisure and practical, artistic self-expression. Consumption for aesthetic pleasure is now an important form of social participation. Is this also arts participation? *Looking* for aesthetic pleasure combines leisure, participation and consumption. The boundaries are blurred.

Digital Creativity and Computer Games

New digital technology – such as scanners, digital cameras and video cameras – and a greater use of desk-top publishing mean that more and more people are designing their own invitations, gift cards and websites. Consequently there is more involvement in authoring and production. Any generic computer now comes with the software needed to be an author/graphic designer. This means an inevitable increase in 'arts participation' as people generate at home what was previously a commercial-quality product. For instance, a modest electronic keyboard costing (perhaps $300) can now generate sound files directly to the family computer, and a CD can be created. Thus people can not only participate in the writing and playing of music, but also become sound recordists and CD producers.

We identify several strands in this collective upskilling:

(a)   Rapidly increasing involvement in these activities as more people own computers. This, coupled with increasingly sophisticated software, means there is potential for the product to be a lot better than before (i.e. technically competent, visually more appealing, produced on higher quality output devices).

(b)   Participating in the Internet, chat rooms and email, and putting leisure activities on a personal website (anything from topiary to poetry to collecting) upskills the user, and adds to the design and aestheticisation of these leisure activities.

(c)   Inevitably this new set of resources and skills raises both the technological literacy and, significantly, the 'arts participation' of leisure.

From the first video games like *Frogger, Space Invaders* or *Pong* some twenty-five years ago, to the completely immersive multi-player universes inhabited by a wide range of game players today, we have the development of one of the biggest industries on the planet: computer games.

The increased band-width and speed of computers has enormously enhanced the entire aesthetic potential of the interface, and of the engagement with the game. Game visuals have more appeal – the animations more seamless, the game-play depth more immersive – and there is now five-channel surround sound with cushion or backpack to vibrate you as you play. Games are now played for significant numbers of hours per day by many individuals. The computer gaming industry supports a small group of super players who can earn large prizes in global competitions.

The increased power of the family desk-top computer allows the player to customise roles. Where once the players played the generic global game such as Monopoly, one can now play Civilization as the New Zealand tribe or Maori nation, and build the great pyramids of Rotorua, and the labyrinth of Wellington, the great library of Auckland. Everyday histories wilfully proliferate. This new incarnation of game-playing as a standard leisure activity is totally aestheticised: effectively an interactive 'home theatre'.

Aspirations

An Australian survey in the mid-1990s of people's everyday cultural practices included material on artistic pursuits.[20] A theme of the study was the making of cultural choices, in every dimension of daily life. What channels people into these taste categories? Individuals think they make choices of their own volition; but are their choices predictable? In other words, how are symbols used for social differentiation?

The research showed that differences are not random; that regularities or patterns correspond to other dimensions of human activity and of social structure. Social class, age, gender, education and ethnicity are crucial in distributing cultural interests and abilities across the population. At the same time, social and cultural power play a large part in determining taste preference, used to mark social position. So 'taste' and what people consume, that which is visible to others, sorts into an hierarchy. Every day, people and objects are assessed. The key issue is 'positioning'. If culture identifies people and groups in the sense of setting them apart, and in the sense of placing them on an hierarchy (some more important than others), then it follows that we are not just referring to social difference, but also to inequity. The 'aspirational' are those wanting to move to (or appear to be part of) what they perceive as a higher social position than the one they currently occupy.

This may take place through arts participation; or, we argue, via consumption: through the purchase of highly aestheticised objects, rather than through a taste for those traditional markers of the élite – opera, theatre, art and music. In this debate, the boundaries between 'participation' and 'consumption' are difficult to determine. For instance, is the person watching the opera an arts participant, or the consumer of a marketed opera experience, or both?

Arts Participation and National Identity

Arts Every Day shows a high level of arts participation in New Zealand. The tradition of recycling available materials into new creations, and Kiwi ingenuity as a claimed national characteristic, indicate this has long been true. However, we also suggest that some forms of consumption might be considered an everyday way of participating in the arts. The advantages of this to the consumer are that no special arts skills or education are required. There is plenty of guidance on what is desirable to consume, for instance in magazines, advertising, and television 'lifestyle' shows. If we add the rapid growth in home desk-top publishing using digital aesthetics, then we can count ourselves even more creative.

The question is, given that our level of arts participation is high, why has this not been adopted as a major feature of the national identity of New Zealanders? Why is this major preoccupation of New Zealanders not proportionately represented in the media? While kiwi ingenuity has long been a national claim, it best fits the 'good keen man' and 'No 8 fencing wire' realm of national mythmaking: the pioneering spirit, rather than the present everyday social and creative processes of unsung practitioners. The public status of artists and of hobbyists has remained modest.

Arts participation by that 93 per cent identified in the Creative New Zealand report is largely a private-domain activity, undertaken not at a public or competitive level, in contrast to sport. The traditionally gendered nature of national identity constructs has also given priority to public activities of males in war, sport, occupations and politics, rather than to private activities enjoyed mostly by women. While that 93 per cent of New Zealanders identified as arts participants obviously includes men, it is predominantly the private part of men's lives that resides within those figures.

Nevertheless, if we accept Creative New Zealand's definition of arts participation as 'all forms of creative and interpretive expression', then our conclusion has to be that we are a nation of very creative people indeed; and one where much of the arts participation is actively evolving to embrace digital technology.

Endnotes

1   Stebbins, Robert A. (1992) *Amateurs, professionals and serious leisure*, Montreal: McGill University Press, p. 123.

2   Creative New Zealand (1999) *Arts Every Day Mahi Toi Ia Ra*, Wellington: Arts Council of New Zealand, Creative New Zealand.

3   Ibid., p. 5.

4   The Creative New Zealand / Hillary Commission study is not directly comparable with any overseas studies. We therefore cannot be certain that this high level of 'arts participation' is unique to New Zealand.

5   Gelber, Stevan M. (1999), *Hobbies*, U.S.A.: Columbia University Press.

6   Riley, Bob (1995) *Kiwi Ingenuity – A Book of New Zealand Ideas and Inventions*, Auckland: AIT Press, p. 2.

7   Wolfe, Richard (1997) *All Our Own Work*, New Zealand, Auckland: Viking, p. 51.

8   Gelber, op. cit., p. 1.

9   Wolfe, op. cit., p. 97.

10   Photographs of these can be seen in *All Our Own Work, New Zealand's Folk Art*, by Richard Wolfe, Viking New Zealand, 1997; p. 71 and p. 84.

11   For instance, the Official Programme of the *34th Annual Spring Show* organised by the Stratford A and P Association in 1943 lists 113 Home Industries sections in which one could enter items. This excluded the usual Cooking Section: 'As a War Effort and to avoid wastage, this section has been deleted from the 1943 Show'. However, here is a selection of sections one could enter: stencilled cushion or article; prettiest frock for child under 5 years; novelty tea cosy; rug made from waste; article made from sugar bag; hand-knitted homespun pullover; any model in fretwork; woodwork model; decorated wooden article (not poker work); Text: first verse of the N.Z. National Anthem; any garment from two skeins of wool; Boys: article from scrap. For adults there were 25 sections for Sewing and Fancy Work, and 17 in the Woollen Section. The Juvenile section had 17 Sewing and Fancy Work sections to enter, and 16

Metal Work and Woodwork sections.

The Schedule of Classes at the *1954 New Zealand Easter Show* in Auckland has most of the same needlework categories, as well as hot water bag cover knitted, tatted work, dressed doll, and article costing not more than 2/6. It provided more opportunities for model makers: aeroplane, yacht, steamer, old-time vessel, stationary petrol or steam engine, boiler, locomotive with or without rolling stock, machinery not necessarily a working model.

[12] Gelber, op. cit., p. 11.
[13] Thompson, Michael (1979) *Rubbish Theory*, U.K.: Oxford University Press.
[14] Braudrilliard, Jean (1998) *The Consumer Society*, London: Sage, p. 84.
[15] Barber, Chris (2000) *Cultural Studies – Theory and Practice*, London: Sage, p. 288.
[16] Maffesoli, Michel (1996) *The Time of the Tribes*, London: Sage.
[17] Gronow, Jukka (1997) *The Sociology of Taste*, London: Routledge, p. 33.
[18] Dant, Tim (1999) *Material Culture in the Social World*, Buckingham, Phildelphia: Open University Press, p. 70.
[19] Bell, Claudia (1996) *Inventing New Zealand*, Auckland: Penguin, p. 167.
[20] Bennett, Tony, Michael Emmison and John Frow, *Accounting for Tastes,* Cambridgeshire: Cambridge University Press, 1999.

Bibliography

Barber, Chris (2000) *Cultural Studies – Theory and Practice*, London: Sage.
Bell, Claudia (1996) *Inventing New Zealand*, Auckland: Penguin.
⨯ Bennett, Tony, Emmison, Michael and Frow, John (1999) *Accounting for Tastes,* Cambridge: Cambridge University Press.
Braudrilliard, Jean (1998) *The Consumer Society*, London: Sage.
Creative New Zealand (1999) *Arts Every Day Mahi Toi Ia Ra,* Wellington: Arts Council of New Zealand, Creative New Zealand.
Dant, Tim (1999) *Material Culture in the Social World*, Buckingham, Phildelphia: Open University Press.
Gelber, Stevan M. (1999) *Hobbies*, U.S.A.: Columbia University Press.
Gronow, Jukka (1997) *The Sociology of Taste*, London and New York: Routledge.
Maffesoli, Michel (1993) *The Time of the Tribes*, London: Sage.
Riley, Bob (1995) *Kiwi Ingenuity – A Book of New Zealand Ideas and Inventions*, Auckland: AIT Press.
Stebbins, Robert A. (1992) *Amateurs, Professionals and Serious Leisure*, Montreal: McGill University Press.
Thompson, Michael (1979) *Rubbish Theory*, U.K.: Oxford University Press.
Wolfe, Richard (1997) *All Our Own Work,* New Zealand: Viking.

From Embankments to Corporate Boxes: Watching Sports

9

Camilla Obel

This chapter considers the changes to the largest outdoor sports stadiums in New Zealand, focusing on the staging of rugby union matches. Sports facility managers, sports administrators, academics and politicians worldwide are debating how to provide facilities for the 'public' attending live sports events. Public interest in this matter has forced these 'key actors' to address questions including: who should pay for the upgrade or renovation of stadiums and who benefits? Should cities compete with other cities for the right to stage a popular sports event by improving a local sports facility? Why do new or renovated stadiums look the same? Can they prevent 'hooliganism' among spectators? How many corporate boxes are enough?

Sports-spectating brings together two aspects of academic interest: the popular spectator involvement in sports that generates excitement; and questions of who controls, designs, manages and pays for stadiums' 'bricks and mortar'. In this chapter I combine an analysis of the popular enjoyment of sports-spectating with a critical investigation into the political economy of the current stadium development in New Zealand. Overall, this chapter presents a sociological account of how sports-spectating in New Zealand has changed dramatically over the last decade. Attendance at live sporting events involves several social groups, including spectators and athletes, and indirectly local, national and international/global sports organisations, governments, and business interests. Changes affecting this network of actors are theorised using ideas about place, space and spectacles. This discussion of changes to the design of sports stadiums, and aspects of sports-spectating, highlights future issues that might influence the social interaction in, and the construction and design of, stadiums.

The Consumption of Spectacle

One of my favourite pastimes is watching sports. Most of this is done in front of the television, and over the last couple of decades I have been able to watch an increasing number of sports and events from around the world. These developments are not unique to the New Zealand context; they clearly follow a global trend[1]. The introduction of television to New Zealand in 1960 and satellite link-up from the early 1970s revolutionised our visual access to events from around the world. We now had live coverage of sports events that we could not attend in person and previously could access only through radio broadcasting. The use of television to broadcast sports events encouraged us to regard the two-dimensional visual images it provided as a good substitute for being present at the sports event, if not better. Statistical data suggests that the majority of New Zealanders regard television viewing as one of their favourite pastimes. *Life in New Zealand,* which surveyed over 4,000 individuals over the age of 14 in 1990–91, revealed that 42 per cent rated watching television and videos among their favourite leisure activities. Only reading, which 48 per cent rated among their favourite leisure activities, was more popular[2]. On average more men (47 per cent) rated television and video viewing as a favourite leisure activity than women (37 per cent). Forty-five per cent of Maori men ranked television and video viewing among their favourite leisure activities, compared to only 30 per cent of Maori women. By contrast, more Maori women enjoyed visiting friends (46 per cent), listening to music (43 per cent) and reading (38 per cent) than watching television and videos (ibid.)[3].

Fifteen per cent of New Zealanders listed taking part in organised sports as a favourite leisure activity. By contrast, only 11 per cent listed watching sports and taking part in informal sports as their favourite activity. Gender differences with respect to watching sports were considerable.[4] Only 6 per cent of the surveyed women indicated that watching sports was one of their favourite activities compared with 17 per cent of the men. Twenty-two per cent of Maori men listed watching sports and 20 per cent taking part in organised sports (20 per cent) among their favourite leisure activities, while only 16 per cent of non-Maori listed watching sports and taking part in organised sports (19 per cent) as their favourite activities. The comparative data for women revealed a greater ethnic difference. Nineteen per cent of Maori women ranked organised sports among their favourite leisure activities compared with only 10 per cent of non-Maori women. In addition, 8 per cent of Maori women rated watching sports compared with only 5 per cent of non-Maori women. However, 8 per cent of Maori and 7 per cent of non-Maori women enjoyed informal sports.[5]

These data provide us with information about which leisure activities were popular at the time the survey was conducted. However, they do not tell us why certain activities are more popular than others, nor what kinds of experiences we get from taking part in leisure activities. These questions are the focus of the first part of this chapter. Specifically I want to address what goes on at stadiums and what 'gets done' through sports spectating. The excitement that some sports fans speak about when they come 'face to face' with a sports star is clearly very different from the experience of watching your favourite sports performers on television on a Saturday afternoon. While some sports fans speak of a qualitative difference, new technologies are becoming available that will provide a 'three-dimensional' experience from my living room. As a 'virtual spectator' I have already experienced this in the televising of the America's Cup. The computer technology enabled me to follow the race accurately because a three-dimensional, computer-generated picture of the boats sailing on a sea of grid-lines provided a constant update of their progress. This computer technology is likely to be utilised in the television coverage of sports events which lack a clearly defined field of play, such as yachting and motor-sports as well as iron-man, cycling and golf events.[6]

New developments in the technology of television constitute the viewer as a more active participant who can manipulate selected images. Philips, advertise that with their new 'match-play' television set the viewer can freeze and replay the action from the sports field, breaking down the action into several images presented simultaneously on the screen. Perhaps in the future I will be able to replay a selected sequence of play, and rotate and change the angle to get a different view of the action. This will undoubtedly provide me, as a viewer at home, with an advantage over spectators at the stadium who can only watch the game from the angle of their allocated seats. Of course, spectators on embankments – soon to be a very small minority of spectators at outdoor sports events in New Zealand – can move to another position on the embankment to get a different perspective on the game. While predicting that the 'couch-potato' might have certain advantages over the attending spectator, I also know that stadium innovations in the future are likely to include individual television monitors at each seat, like those currently provided for coaching staff at some venues and, incidentally, on some airlines. This would not be a revolutionary innovation. Replay-screens have long been a prominent feature of sports stadiums (for example, those used in cricket in the late 1970s).[7]

What this discussion highlights is that the distinction between 'live' attendance at home and live attendance at the event is becoming blurred through technological innovations. However, personal experience reminds me that live attendance at a sports event can give me profoundly different experiences of spectating. These are embodied experiences of attending and watching athletes perform. Expectations of a unique 'atmosphere' (in this case unfulfilled) from attending a Rugby Super 12 match on the embankment is expressed in the following, from a Canterbury University student:

> Now I'm not much of a rugby fan, but I went along to the Crusaders v Blues, assured that the atmosphere on the embankment was second to none, and worth going along for on its own. Well, apart from the filth harassing those standing in the aisles (why?) and the odd drawn-out cry of Caanterburry, the most excitement came during a Mexican wave. Is this the best the crowd could come up with – pathetic! No wonder many rugby supporters are such renowned drinkers; it's to hide the boredom. I have heard more get up and go at cricket matches, supposedly the more refined cousin of New Zealand sport. Where was the singing and harassment of the opposing players and supporters? Nowhere. The walk to the ground was equally subdued; it was more like a funeral procession than a sporting fixture. That's not to say that there was not the support, many were decked out in red and black, but like that proverb of a child who should be seen and not heard, many took this literally. Surely someone could come up with something better than that long drawn out cry of Canterbury that resembles someone's last dying breath. Come on Christchurch, how about some enthusiasm? Write into Canta and let us know if you have any suggestions for songs or chants; maybe they could be portrayed onto the big screen at matches so everyone could learn them. How about it?[8] .

What do these expectations, and the suggestion that spectators should be more 'active' at sports events, tell us about sports spectating? Anthropologist John MacAloon has focused on the latter to explain a profound change in attitude by spectators towards attending the Olympic Games. MacAloon interviewed individuals who, prior to attending the opening ceremony at the 1984 Olympic Games, were sceptical of the values and ideals linked to the sports event. However, after attending, they expressed a sense of being caught up in the heightened emotions of the Games.[9] To explain these individuals' 'change of heart', MacAloon examined the Olympic Games through the 'spectacle' frame. To refer to major sports events as 'spectacles' initially conjures up a suspicion or scepticism that they are pointless or tasteless forms of entertainment or, in the case of major, international sports events, that they constitute ritualistic displays of patriotic loyalty. However, the idea of the spectacle enables us to explain why rugby tests, the European soccer cup or the Olympic Games are so popular and may appeal even to those profoundly sceptical of the nationalistic or 'idealistic' messages associated with them.

MacAloon argues that since the 1930s the Olympic Games have come to represent 'spectacles', through the desire to reach a mass audience and through the willingness to negotiate key principles (such as amateurism) in order to accommodate as many nations as possible and to ensure the quality of the performance.[10] Extending this argument to the staging of rugby games in New Zealand, it could be argued that since the mid-1980s, but especially following the broadcasting of matches to global audiences, they have increasingly come to represent 'spectacles'. Like the Olympic Games, which are public displays that attempt to appeal to the eye 'by their mass, proportion, color, or other dramatic quality',[11] rugby matches have increasingly attempted to attract spectators with displays and entertainment, including parades, fireworks, cheerleaders, live music, parachute jumps, horsemen and so on. These newer forms of entertainment, are not differentiated for those on the 'cheaper' seats and the 'corporates' in their luxury boxes. By contrast, the encouragement to consume hot dogs and beers in the stands and on the embankments, and three-course meals with wine in the corporate boxes, adds to the leisure/pleasure experience of spectator attendance with diffused forms of entertainment.

These developments have not gone uncriticised. In an interview with a member of the New Zealand Rugby Football Union conducted in 1996, the life-member suggested that 'very soon we'll be running rock concerts with rugby games as curtain raisers'. This entertainment to attract more spectators is likely to destroy the culture of rugby which, he claimed, is based on such ideals as participation and voluntary involvement.[12]

While members of the International Olympic committee have been keen to promote the Olympics as a celebration of human kind and joyfulness, they are constantly broken by the stuff of 'ordinary life'. Political, ideological and economic interests are repeatedly blamed for imposing constraints and forcing the Games to change. Drug scandals, commercial interests versus environmental concerns, and the hijacking of the Games for political or ideological purposes all threaten to disrupt the 'preferred' images and ideals of the Games and make us sceptical of the promises of joyfulness, shared humanity and equality. However, the presentation of the Olympics as spectacle has the ability to attract large (and heterogeneous) audiences. MacAloon suggests that the spectacle liberates 'individuals to *want* to, to be free to, do more than watch'.[13] He explains the process this way:

In cultures that already emphasize individuality, minimize the sense of obligation and responsibility for collective action, and inbreed hostility towards, for example, ritual, spectacle may have an unanticipated 'positive' effect. The spectacle frame erected around ritual may serve as a recruiting device, dissembling suspicion toward 'mere ritual' and luring the proudly uncommitted. Those who have come simply to watch and to be watched, to enjoy the spectacle or to profit from it, may find themselves suddenly caught up in actions of a different sort at levels of intensity and involvement they could not have foreseen and from which they would have retreated had such participation been directly required or requested of them.[14]

MacAloon's analysis suggests that spectacles appeal to spectators because they do not require participation in symbolic celebration of a collective identity but simply allow them to enjoy the event. If participation was expected or required as a civic obligation to support a local or national team, it would transform the event into a ritual with a deeper meaning. This would leave it open to a critical or sceptical assessment. Arguably this was experienced in New Zealand in the 1970s and 1980s when civil protest against continued rugby contact with South Africa encouraged a deeper criticism of the game and a profound scepticism towards its participatory and egalitarian ideals.[15] The promotion of rugby matches or the Olympic Games as spectacles, on the other hand, does not claim to provide deep, emotional experiences. Instead, spectacles invite spectators to 'admire but not to be deceived'[16]. They create possibilities for spectators to maintain a distance yet to experience heightened emotions.

The active participation in sports events by spectators can therefore be explained as a contradictory, double experience of being liberated from obligation or duty to celebrate certain values yet at the same time choosing to be caught up in the heightened emotions created by the event. Arguably, this encourages a larger and more heterogeneous audience. Thus, while major sports events are promoted as opportunities to take part in the celebration of national and international ideals, it is the spectacular and diffused image of such events that is capable of attracting the largest audiences. This engrossed participation is expressed as fans' 'noise', according to geographer John Bale. His argument about the active participation of spectators at soccer games links the design of stadiums with the desire of fans to make their presence felt. Fundamentally, Bale argues that 'space' is never neutral in social affairs. Like MacAloon, but pursuing a different argument, Bale argues that the experience of attending soccer games is contradictory.[17] 'Football places', he argues, are increasingly 'placeless': homogeneous concrete 'spaces' designed to eliminate the particularity of 'place' and avoid providing the home team with an advantage through knowledge of pitch irregularities. This development follows the objective of achievement sports and the requirements of the production of sports records. However, a crowd's 'noise' creates a place in otherwise sterile and indistinguishable surroundings and makes sports 'spaces' meaningful places to support *our* team.[18]

Research suggests that crowds are effective at this 'place creation'. The 'noise' from spectators' drums, horns, rattles, cheering and chants affects the outcome of games, according to research on 'home advantage'. In team sports involved in home-and-away competitions, playing at home in front of a home crowd statistically increases a team's chance of winning.[19] Players also perceive the 'home advantage' to have an effect on the outcome of matches, citing the sense of obligation and commitment to local fans and supporters as added pressure to perform. Coaches, likewise, regard playing at home as an advantage. They try to re-create the interaction between the team and supporters at away games by encouraging supporters to fax messages to the team, and by emphasising that the supporters are counting on the team to bring home a win[20]. Sports event managers are also interested in creating an atmosphere where fans can experience the excitement of supporting their team. However, this must not dominate the event to the extent that it might discourage visitors from attending. This is significant because visitors provide a direct economic boost to the local economy. The more visitors a sports event can attract, the greater the economic impact the events will have for the local economy.

'Spectacle' and 'place-making' are two concepts that explain the active involvement of spectators at sports events. The former highlights the liberating possibilities of experiencing sports events as spectacles, because this affords the spectator the freedom to merely watch and not to be deceived by illusions of greater meanings and values associated with the event. At the same time, the spectacle provides spectators with diffuse, unique and emotional experiences. This involvement in the event turns stadiums into places of significant emotional meaning and encourages the view of stadiums as sacred places of collective memory. In an analysis of the modern stadium which draws on Clifford Geertz's interpretation of the Balinese cockfight,[21] Niels Kayser Nielsen argues that the recollection of stadium events helps establish social communication and group relationships. He states:

> The stories of stadiums thus become, in the words of Clifford Geertz, (hi)story, told 'for one another'. At the same time, they are creators and interpreters of identity; a meta-social comment on being a citizen of a

city, which people exchange among themselves or read about in the city's newspaper on Monday mornings – after the weekend's occurrences at the stadium.[22]

In this view, the stadium performs as 'an inward identification for local users' whose identity may be affirmed through their knowledge and experience of significant stadium events. The significance of the stadium as an 'archive of material of remembrance' also works outwardly towards inhabitants in other cities as a tourist attraction. This has not gone unnoticed by commercial and political actors eager to cash in on these popular and potentially lucrative events.

Stadiums and Sports Events

Over the last decade there have been significant changes to both outdoor and indoor sports spectating and playing facilities in New Zealand. Until the introduction of television in 1960 in New Zealand, stadiums showcased sporting competitions mostly to local spectators. Since then, the potential to reach national and global audiences has encouraged businesses and local governments to sponsor stadium developments. It is the opportunity for cities to be showcased and teams or competition sponsors' logos and advertising signs to be broadcast to viewers nationally and internationally that has encouraged this development. In turn, the cost of new stadiums has meant that their design needs to generate increased income. These changes parallel trends worldwide, where new stadiums have been built to accommodate sports teams and to encourage a more affluent group of spectators. However, the political economy of stadium developments is contingent upon the particular history of sports and their playing and spectating facilities, as described in the following comparison between stadium developments in the USA and New Zealand.

The shift in New Zealand towards developing stadiums which can generate increasing revenue through the sale of corporate boxes, and membership seats, and through improved catering facilities, follows the trend in the USA and Canada. Baade and Sanderson, who have researched the relationship between major league franchise teams and cities in the USA, have characterised the change to stadiums this way: 'As affluence has spread, fans have moved from the outfield grass to hard-back bleacher seats to individual seats with armrests to luxury loges.'[23] This development can be explained by looking at changes to the relationship between major league teams, cities and stadiums. In the USA, the relationship between sports teams

and stadiums was, until the 1950s, characterised by professional teams playing in privately built stadiums. Cities then began to publicly finance stadiums to attract or hold onto major league teams. Stadiums became key negotiating points for any team thinking of moving from one city to another.

This intensified by the 1970s when major league teams began sharing their major source of income – gate revenue, sale of broadcasting rights and sponsorship – while changes to taxation and labour market regulations meant that players' salaries escalated.[24] As a result, team owners' income grew, but so did their expenses. As a consequence owners sought new ways to increase their income. It is in this context that stadiums have gained in significance. Owners began bargaining with cities to build a new or improved playing facility or risk losing the team to another city. The owners' position was strengthened by the cartel structure of the major leagues, which limited the number of teams allowed in each league. This agreement ensured team owners a monopoly in their local market and weakened the local government's negotiating position when confronted with a major league team's demand for a new publicly funded stadium. As a further enticement to teams to stay, local governments and stadium developers offered owners of major league teams the income from corporate boxes, stadium advertising, parking and concessions. This unequal relationship has been described in the quote below:

A fundamental fact of life concerning stadiums and arenas is that once they are built, they are fixed in place, while teams that use them are potentially mobile. This puts an enormous bargaining advantage in the hands of teams playing in publicly owned stadiums. Teams can exploit the threat of leaving a city to wring out of the manager of the stadium rental agreements that leave the city pretty much holding the bag.[25]

While the context in which publicly funded stadiums in the USA have emerged differs from the New Zealand context, the fundamental 'immobile fact' concerning stadiums still applies. In New Zealand, sports teams do not have a history of moving from one city to another in search of a better or more profitable stadium. However, the political economy of sports stadiums was, from the beginning of stadium establishments, characterised by disputes over the income that could be generated from charging spectators to attend events. From the 1840s sports grounds were enclosed to provide tracks and playing fields for races and team sports and to enable the charging of spectators who watched events mostly from a standing position on an embankment.[26] Since then various local interest groups have been involved in developing sports stadiums and venues and in seeking some of the financial benefits generated from staging sports events.

From the 1880s rugby union matches began to attract relatively large spectator crowds. By the turn of the century, key political figures in the country proclaimed that rugby union was *the* national sport and the All Black team of 1905 was heralded as the finest representation of the colony by Prime Minister Seddon.[27] Such a proclamation encouraged national rugby-union administrators to set ticket prices at two shillings for test matches involving visiting British and Australian teams in the first decade of the twentieth century. This level of pricing was strongly protested by local citizens and by the local rugby union administrations. The New Zealand Rugby Football Union was called 'greedy' and 'hypocritical' because of its staunch anti-commercialism and anti-professionalism policies that only allowed national representative players a payment of three shillings a day when on tour.[28]

While the NZRFU and the provincial unions argued over the ticket price for test matches, the provincial unions' financial position strengthened as a result of the popularity of the game. This was particularly the case for the provincial unions that were successful in Ranfurly Shield matches. From the 1920s sports journalists and radio commentators helped boost interest in the shield when they proclaimed that it generated 'fever' among local supporters. The teams which held on to the shield for several matches, and some for several years, attracted large crowds and generated significant income for their unions. Apart from funding the travel expenses of the representative teams, this income was used to improve the stadiums. In the late 1920s, after a period of successfully defending the shield, the Canterbury provincial unions provided a loan to the Victory Park board which managed Lancaster Park, for the development of a stand. In the period from the 1950s to the 1980s, the Canterbury provincial union, the Canterbury Cricket Association and the NZRFU provided the Victoria Park board with loans to extend the spectator facilities at Lancaster Park. The park's spectator capacity expanded to a peak of 58,500 by 1965.[29] Since the 1980s the capacity of stadiums has decreased as embankment areas have been turned into seated stands.

City Boosters and Stadiums as Gold Mines'

While embankment areas decreased in the 1980s, it was not until the 1990s that stadium designs changed radically, mirroring stadium developments in Europe and North America. This coincided with the establishment of the professional, transnational Rugby Super 12 competition, which was broadcast to viewers globally through Rupert Murdoch's media corporation.[30]

The new potential for global television exposure provides an opportunity to promote the city hosting the sports event as a unique or exciting tourist destination. This makes the stadium the central place for the presentation of the city and increases the importance of the events staged at the stadium. The ability to attract major sports events and the potential for global exposure has fuelled debates over the renovation and development of new stadiums in New Zealand. In 1997, the general manager of the Victory Park board, which managed Lancaster Park, commented on the debate in the *Press* by emphasising the increased television exposure of the stadium and thereby Christchurch city: 'This year Lancaster Park was seen on TV by more than 200 million people. In a city that prides itself on the quality of its parks, surely the one park that has such international exposure should be up to a standard befitting the reputation of the city with the best parks in the world?'.[31]

These comments followed an earlier statement by the NZRFU that the four rugby test stadiums in New Zealand were of such a poor standard that they faced losing major rugby matches. In November 1997, the CEO of the NZRFU, David Moffett, announced that the poor state of the rugby playing facilities in New Zealand was jeopardising New Zealand's bid to co-host the fifth Rugby World Cup in 2003:

> NZRFU chief executive officer, David Moffett, has a stark message to deliver to not only those in the game but also all of the local bodies and authorities administering the country's stadiums. Unless all of them, especially those in the main centres, undergo drastic refurbishing in the next few years, the joint bid New Zealand is launching with Australia to hold the 2003 World Cup will be weakened.[32]

While pressure was mounting on the NZRFU to improve facilities, the union threatened to withdraw the category A test-status from those stadiums that could not provide seating facilities for all spectators. The threat of losing international rugby matches encouraged provincial unions, stadium trusts, city councils and local businesses to devise plans to up-grade existing venues and, in the case of Wellington, to plan for a new, all-seated stadium.

The risk of losing test and Rugby Super 12 matches from stadiums has encouraged local governments to part-fund rugby stadium upgrades. City councils have been keen to invest in stadium improvements because these matches are capable of attracting large spectator numbers and visitors by 'show-casing' the city to global audiences. The upgrade of the four category A rugby-test venues (Eden Park, Wellington WestpacTrust Stadium, JADE

Stadium and Carisbrook) has been funded by local governments to a varying degree. The upgrade to Eden Park is exclusively privately funded while the new WestpacTrust Stadium in Wellington, which replaced the old Athletic Park in 1999, is almost one-third publicly-funded. In the South Island, a tenth of the cost of the upgrade to both Carisbrook and JADE Stadium is by direct public funding. The Otago Rugby Union provides the remaining funding to cover loan repayments for Carisbrook, while the Christchurch City Council guarantees the estimated $35 million loan to upgrade JADE Stadium. This use of local taxpayer funds has encouraged debate over the financial viability of the stadium renovations and developments and other such public investments, as expressed in the following comment:

> Common sense and commercial reality should say that New Zealand with a total population of about 3.5 million (similar to large overseas cities which have developed successful sports stadiums) should have only one national ground, a showpiece where all major rugby games could be played in front of large attendances capturing the huge financial returns that rugby is now capable of generating. But geography, rugby's traditions and New Zealand's idiosyncratic parochialism all play a part in the scramble that sees the four major cities, and others, striving to capture the rugby dollar.[33]

This statement neglects the fact that the NZRFU benefits from not owning a national stadium because it can use the threat of withdrawing a rugby test to force stadium trusts, local governments and local businesses to invest in upgrading stadiums. It also discounts the possibility that local actors who fund the upgrade of stadiums to secure allocation of tests and Rugby Super 12 matches may benefit through increased global exposure and more visitors. The latter view is presented by Campbell Prentice, General Manager of JADE Stadium, in an article in The *Press*:

> An economic impact survey taken in 1996 showed that a major international sporting fixture held at Lancaster Park generates between $15 million and $17 million to the city. Of this amount, $9 million is money that arrives in the pockets of visitors and the remaining is money spent by locals. Over the past 40 years this has amounted to more than $600 million in today's dollars.[34]

Such economic estimates are used to encourage public spending on sports stadiums. However, several academics researching the economic effect of staging major sports events have criticised such estimates as exaggerated.[35]

They highlight that estimates rarely take into account the 'expenditure substitutes' that occur as a result of individuals' decisions on spending discretionary income. For example, Quirk and Forte argue that 'fans have only limited amounts of money available to spend on recreational and leisure activities. Any money spent on attending a sports event means there is less available to spend on alternatives, such as movies, plays, concerts, VCR rentals, and the like'.[36] Researchers also highlight that increased economic transactions will appear greater the smaller the region considered, and question whether expenditure by local consumers constitutes economic growth.[37] Even with increased expenditure in a city or region, Molotch suggests that 'there is little evidence that growth eases problems of unemployment, high housing costs, or impoverished city budgets'.[38]

These criticisms highlight that only the ability to attract wealthy consumers and investors from *outside* the city or region will have a significant effect on local economies. Following this logic, the upgraded stadiums seek to cater for the more affluent spectators, who are targeted with the opportunity to rent corporate boxes and to sponsor new buildings. It has therefore been argued that the design of new or redeveloped stadiums is compromised by the need to provide for increased luxury seating and hospitality facilities.[39] This is reflected in the substantial amount of revenue needed to fund renovations and constructions of new sports facilities with expanded areas for corporate boxes and membership seats.

In May 1998 the Victory Park board sold the naming rights to Lancaster Park to JADE at a cost of $4 million over 10 years. Despite this income, and a $4 million injection from the Christchurch City Council, the general manager of JADE Stadium, Campbell Prentice, explained in an interview that the renovated stadium will need to generate more from all its income sources. The new JADE Stadium is expected to have 72 corporate boxes (each will seat up to 16 'corporates'). This is an increase of 43 corporate boxes to the existing 10 boxes in the No. 3 stand, established in 1988, and the 19 boxes in the Hadlee stand which was completed in 1993. To cover the cost of the upgrade, the new stadium will need to generate $1 million more in rental from rugby and cricket than it is currently receiving (an increase of approximately 150 per cent). It will also require an increase of $1 million from the sale of corporate boxes (an increase of approximately 100 per cent) and an increase in hospitality royalties of approximately $400,000, or 200 per cent.[40]

Like JADE Stadium, the three other upgraded rugby-test venues depend on the increased income generated from luxury seating. The $175 million private funding for renovating Eden Park is dependent on a substantial amount from the sale of corporate boxes and club seats. A total of 80 corporate suites were for sale in 1999 at a price between $160,000 and $200,000 for a ten-year licence and a ten-year right of renewal, excluding an annual rent of $52,000 (ticket inclusive).[41] The sale of 80 suites alone is likely to generate around $14 million initially, while 3,000 club seats priced from $1,250 to $1,750 will generate approximately $4 million a year. A quarter of the estimated revenue needed to cover the development costs for the new WestpacTrust Stadium in Wellington ($122 million) is expected to come from the sale of membership seats ($33 million). Approximately $22.8 million is to come from the sale of naming rights and corporate suites, and an estimated $33 million from the sale of 2,500 membership seats at $13,500 each.

While the financial viability of upgraded stadiums increasingly depends on the sale of luxury seating, the ability to sell corporate boxes relies on the allocation and staging of enough major events. Datacom Employer services', Wellington Chairman, John Gill, criticised the projected costing for the new Wellington WestpacTrust Stadium, noting that the reversal of the initial decision to privately fund the development meant that ratepayers would have to cover any drop in income for the stadium: 'With the project costing $121 million, the annual depreciation will be $3–$5 million, the capital charge will be $12–$24 million, and the cost to the ratepayer will be steep'.[42] Like others critical of the public funding of sports stadiums, Gill noted the drop in spectator attendance at Wellington events in the years 1996 and 1997. His concern is that the risk exposure on capital outlay such as for the Westpac Trust Stadium will remain intact throughout the extremely long break-even period.

Despite the attraction of major sports events, spectator attendance is unpredictable. In the past this meant that the stadium trusts' income from staging major events fluctuated. Increasingly, stadiums have negotiated fixed-rental agreements with local and national rugby and cricket bodies, in order to make their financial position less vulnerable to these fluctuations. In relative terms this has meant that revenue from the sale of corporate boxes, hospitality, signage and other sponsorship relations has increased, while revenue generated from sports events has declined. This means that the business of stadium trusts is increasingly separated from that of selling tickets.

These stadium developments increase the cost of attending sports events. Sports writer Barry Clarke noted in the *Sunday Star-Times* that to watch the All Blacks in the 2000 season would cost a small fortune. Premium seats at Eden Park for the test against the visiting Scottish team were priced at $100, while other stand seats cost between $45 and $80. Club members could get the cheapest terrace seats for $30. At Carisbrook, covered stand seats sold for between $60 and $70, while uncovered seats cost $45 and the terraces $25 for an adult ($15 for a child). At JADE Stadium stand tickets for the Tri-Nations test against South Africa cost between $45 and $75 for uncovered seats. Seating in the temporary stand cost $40, while entry to the embankments (for the last time) cost $30. The most expensive tickets to a rugby test in the 2000 season could be found in Wellington, where tickets for the Bledisloe Cup match at the WestpacTrust Stadium cost between $60 and $110. By comparison, Clarke noted that tickets to the Australian National Rugby League final at the new Stadium Australia built for the 2000 Olympics cost between $A36.50 and $A97, while the most expensive ticket to the State of Origin match cost $A66 in Sydney and $A88 in Brisbane. At an exchange rate of A80c to a New Zealand dollar, those prices translate to between $45 and $121 at Stadium Australia and $83 and $110 for the State of Origin matches. This makes these prices comparable to those charged at New Zealand stadiums.

Entertainment for the Privileged, and Community Celebration

This chapter has argued that sociological understandings of sports spectating need to take into account both the experiences spectators get from consuming major sports events, such as rugby matches and the Olympic Games, and the production of stadiums for the staging of such events. Combining an analysis of these two aspects of sports spectating presents an explanation for local tax-payers' support of the development of costly stadiums despite indications that such investments do not appear to generate economic growth and might, in fact, cost local tax-payers more in the long run. Despite the high cost of attending live rugby matches in New Zealand, spectator numbers at the most expensive new stadium, the WestpacTrust Stadium in Wellington, have remained high in 2000. However, since income from selling tickets to rugby matches generally fluctuates, the new stadiums in New Zealand include a large number of

corporate boxes. It is income from these facilities that constitutes the most significant and reliable income for stadium trusts. These developments are part of the changes to the way we watch sports today.

Records for live attendance at rugby matches were set in the period between the late 1950s and early 1970s, coinciding with the introduction of live television broadcasting. Since then, spectator numbers have declined due to renovations and new developments which have resulted in stadiums that can seat fewer spectators. At the same time, increased coverage has encouraged people to spend more time viewing sports on TV. Income from the sale of broadcasting rights along with marketing, sponsorship and merchandise sales has greatly overtaken the amount that can be generated from selling tickets to spectators. While sports increasingly rely on income associated with media dissemination, the exponential rise in income associated with the commodification and mediation of sports has been followed by a rise in income from stadiums. The introduction of corporate boxes at stadiums in the 1980s, the catering associated with these facilities, and the expansion of membership seating facilities, have all increased the income stadiums can generate from live attendance at sports events.

Today spectators are being charged higher prices for the opportunity to attend their favourite sports events. As highlighted in the discussion of ticket prices, a consequence of the upgrade and development of new stadiums is that, while they are part-funded by the broad base of local tax-payers, this group subsidises the develop-ment of leisure facilities for the more affluent local citizens and visitors. Those who have already paid to stage the matches through their taxes, but who cannot afford to attend the stadiums, have the option of watching 'their' team perform on either free-to-air television channels, which usually broad-cast matches after the event, or pay (for the second time) to watch their team perform live on a pay-TV channel, such as SKY Television Network.

This suggests that live sports spectating has changed from a mass experience to a privileged experience for fewer individuals. However, local tax-payers may encourage public investment in stadium developments because they see the retention of their team or a test match as an important representative icon. Hosting major sports events may help create a feeling of collective identity, community spirit and unity which local spectators may celebrate while attending. For those local supporters of stadium developments who can no longer afford to attend significant sporting events, the new stadium may still represent an important connection to the city and the community. The sense of local pride and identity experienced when *their* stadium is being broadcast to millions of viewers may serve as a reward for financial contribution and may soften the blow of not being able to afford to attend. Spectators are provided with more than sports when they attend. Rock bands, fireworks, cheerleaders, mascots, parachute jumps, hot dogs, beers and three-course meals are among the activities spectators are entertained with, lengthening the total event and diffusing the focus from the celebration of a collective identity towards a 'spectacle' designed to entertain the whole (corporate?) family.

Endnotes

1   The abundance of sports on television is in part a consequence of three interdependent developments involving technological innovation in broadcasting, de-regulating of broadcasting legislation and increasing competition between broadcasters for popular 'media-products'. Sports broadcasting, because of its popularity, its ability to fulfil local content quota and its relative inexpensive production cost, has been used to attract viewers to new or existing television networks. This development has encouraged academics studying sports to view the relationship between sports and the media as intricately intertwined (see David Rowe (1999), *Sport, Culture and the Media*, Buckingham, Philadelphia: Open University Press, p. 2). They argue that sports increasingly depend on income associated with their media dissemination to consumers rather than the 'traditional' source of gate income from attending spectators. At the same time, television networks' survival increasingly depend on their exclusive rights to broadcast popular sports.

2   Russell, D. and Wilson, N. (1991), *Life in New Zealand Survey*, Commission Report Executive Overview, Wellington: Hillary Commission, Table IV.1a.

3   The Life in New Zealand Survey tables only include two groups of New Zealanders, distinguished on the basis of their ethnic origin: 'NZ Maori' and 'Other NZers'. This is despite the fact that the survey forms the participants filled out include 'European', 'N.Z. Maori', 'Cook Island Maori', 'Samoan' and a space to write a different ethnic origin under the category 'Other' (*Life in New Zealand*, Appendix D, General Details). This means that the data is less useful in an analysis of the significance of ethnic origin for leisure participation.

4   This information did not distinguish between watching sports *live* and watching sports *on television*.

5   See Tony Veal, Bob Gidlow and Harvey Perkins (1998) 'Interpreting leisure participation in New Zealand', in Perkins, H. and Cushman, G. (eds), *Time*

Out? Leisure, Recreation and Tourism in New Zealand and Australia, Auckland: Longman, for a comparative discussion of leisure participation in New Zealand and Australia.

6   Dann, L. (2000) 'More events for virtual fans', *Sunday Star-Times*, July 23, p. A5.

7   See Ian Harriss (1990) 'Packer, Cricket and Postmodernism', in Rowe, D. and Lawrence, G. (eds), *Sport and Leisure: Trends in Australian Popular Culture*, Sydney: HBJ.

8   Button, J. (2000) 'Dying breath or footy chants?', *Canta*, Issue 4, p. 14.

9   MacAloon, J. (1984) 'Olympic Games and the Theory of Spectacle in Modern Societies', in MacAloon, J. (ed.), *Rite, Drama, Festival, Spectacle: Rehearsals Towards a Theory of Cultural Performance*, Philadelphia: ISHI Press.

10   MacAloon, op. cit., p. 263.

11   MacAloon, op. cit., p. 243.

12   Interview with NZRFU life-member, May 1996.

13   MacAloon, op. cit., p. 269.

14   Ibid.

15   See for example Shona Thompson (1988) 'Challenging the hegemony: New Zealand women's opposition to rugby and the reproduction of a capitalist patriarchy', *International Review for the Sociology of Sport*, vol. 23, no. 3, pp. 205-211, and Geoff Fougere (1989), 'Sport, Culture and Identity: The Case of Rugby Football', in Novitz, D. and Willmott, B. (eds), *Culture and Identity in New Zealand* (eds) Wellington: GP Books.

16   Bale, J. (1995) 'Virtual Fandoms: Futurescapes of football', in Brown, A. (ed.) *Fanatics! Power, Identity and Fandom in Football*, London: Routledge.

17   Bale, op. cit, pp. 271-272.

18   See for example B. Schwartz and S. F. Barsky (1977) 'Home Advantage', *Social Forces*, vol. 55, no. 3, pp. 641-661, M. S. Mizruch (1985), 'Local sport teams and the celebration of community: A comparative analysis of the home advance', *Sociological Quarterly*, vol. 26, pp. 507-518 and Eric Leifer, (1995), *Making the Majors: The Transformation of Team Sports in America*, Cambridge, Massachusetts: Harvard University Press.

19   Gibson, D. (1997), 'Crowd size and home advantage in Super 12 Rugby', Unpublished honours paper, Sociology Department, Canterbury University.

20   Geertz, C. (1973) 'Deep play: Notes on the Balinese cockfight', in *The Interpretation of Cultures*, New York: Basic Books.

21   Nielsen, N. K. (1995) 'The Stadium and the City: A Modern Story', in Bale, J. and Moen, O. (eds) *The Stadium and the City*, Keele: Keele University Press, p. 31.

22   Baade, R. and Sanderson, A. (1997) 'Cities under siege: How the changing financial structure of professional sports is putting cities at risk and what to do about it', in Hendricks, W. (ed.), *Advances in the Economics of Sport,* Vol.

2, Greenwich, Connecticut: JAI Press Inc., p. 82.

23 See M. F. Bernstein (1998) 'Sports stadium boondoggle', *The Public Interest*, no. 132, pp. 45-57.

24 Quirk, J. and Fort, R. (1992) *Pay Dirt: The Business of Professional Team Sport*, Princeton, N. J.: Princeton University Press, p. 145.

25 See for example David Grant, (1999), 'Clashes of Culture and Class: The Jockeys' strike of 1920', in Patterson, B. (ed.) *Sport, Society and Culture in New Zealand*, Stout Research Centre: Victoria University.

26 See Jock Phillips (1987) *A Man's Country?: The Image of the Pakeha Male – A History*, Auckland: Penguin Books.

27 See Geoff Vincent (1996) Practical Imperialism: The Anglo-Welsh Rugby Tour of New Zealand, 1908, Unpublished M.A. Thesis, History Department, Canterbury University, New Zealand, p. 78-88.

28 Palenski, R., Chester, R. and McMillan, N. (1998) *The Encyclopedia of New Zealand Rugby*, Singapore: Moa Hodder Beckett.

29 See Camilla Obel (1998) 'Local and Global Publics: shifting popularity in rugby union and rugby league', in Perkins, H. and Cushman, G. (eds), *Time Out? Leisure, Recreation and Tourism in New Zealand and Australia*, Auckland: Longman.

30 Prentice, C. (1997) 'Why Christchurch deserves a better park', *The Press*, Dec. 15, p. 5.

31 Lindsay Knight, 'Stand up... and be (dis)counted', *NZRugby*, 1997, Nov. no. 8, p. 50.

32 Reddington (1998) 'The mad scramble for a new stadium', *MG Business*, March 30, p. 23-24.

33 Prentice, op. cit.

34 See Quirk and Fort, op. cit., Baade and Sanderson, op.cit., Bernstein, op.cit. and Mules, (1998), 'Taxpayer Subsidies for Major Sporting Events', *Sport Management Review*, vol. 1, no.1, pp. 25-44.

35 Quirk and Fort, op. cit., p. 174.

36 Mules, op. cit., p. 31.

37 Ibid., p. 32.

38 See Baade and Sanderson, op. cit.

39 Interview with Campbell Prentice, Dec. 1998.

40 Bruce, M. (1998), 'Who will pay to do up Lancaster Park?', *The Press*, March 6, p. 5.

41 Gill, J. (1997), 'Ten Years On', *Chartered Accountants Journal*, Dec., p. 35.

42 This graph was created using the Victory Park Board's *Annual Financial Statements* (1981-1998). The category 'Total other rental' is rental income other than sports and events including squash club, Wilson Rd properties, CRFU office, referees room, etc.

Bibliography

Baade, R. and Sanderson, A. (1997) 'Cities under siege: How the changing financial structure of professional sports is putting cities at risk and what to do about it', in Hendricks, W. (ed.) *Advances in the Economics of Sport,* Vol. 2, Greenwich, Connecticut: JAI Press Inc.

Bale, J. (1995) 'Virtual Fandoms: Futurescapes of football', in Brown, A. (ed.) *Fanatics! Power, Identity and Fandom in Football,* London: Routledge.

Bernstein, M. F. (1998) 'Sports stadium boondoggle', *The Public Interest,* no. 132, pp. 45-57.

Bruce, M. (1998) 'Who will pay to do up Lancaster Park?', *The Press,* March 6, p. 5.

Button, J. (2000) 'Dying breath or footy chants?', *Canta,* Issue 4, p. 14.

Clarke, B. (2000) 'Rugby support comes at a price', *Sunday Star-Times,* June 18, p. A5.

Dann, L. (2000) 'More events for virtual fans', *Sunday Star-Times,* July 23, p. A5.

Fougere, G. (1989) 'Sport, Culture and Identity: The Case of Rugby Football', in Novitz, D. and Willmott, B. (eds) *Culture and Identity in New Zealand* (eds) Wellington: GP Books.

Geertz, C. (1973) 'Deep play: Notes on the Balinese cockfight', in *The Interpretation of Cultures,* New York: Basic Books.

Gibson, D. (1997) 'Crowd size and home advantage in Super 12 Rugby', unpublished honours paper, Sociology Department, Canterbury University.

Gill, J. (1997) 'Ten Years On', *Chartered Accountants Journal,* Dec., pp. 35-36.

Grant, D. (1999) 'Clashes of Culture and Class: The Jockeys' strike of 1920', in Patterson, B. (ed.) *Sport, Society and Culture in New Zealand,* Stout Research Centre: Victoria University.

Harriss, I. (1990) 'Packer, Cricket and Postmodernism', in Rowe, D. and Lawrence, G. (eds) *Sport and Leisure: Trends in Australian Popular Culture,* Sydney: HBJ.

Interview with Campbell Prentice, CEO Victory Park Board, 1998.

Interview with NZRFU life-member, May 1996.

Knight, L. (1997) 'Stand up...and be (dis)counted', *NZRugby,* no. 8, p. 50.

Leifer, E. (1995) *Making the Majors: The Transformation of Team Sports in America,* Cambridge, Massachusetts: Harvard University Press.

MacAloon, J. (1984) 'Olympic Games and the Theory of Spectacle in Modern Societies', in MacAloon, J. (ed.) *Rite, Drama, Festival, Spectacle: Rehearsals Towards a Theory of Cultural Performance*, Philadelphia: ISHI Press.

Mizruch, M. S. (1985) 'Local sport teams and the celebration of community: A comparative analysis of the home advance', *Sociological Quarterly*, vol. 26, pp. 507-518.

Mules, T. (1998) 'Taxpayer Subsidies for Major Sporting Events', *Sport Management Review*, vol. 1, no.1, pp. 25-44.

Nielsen, N. K. (1995) 'The Stadium and the City: A Modern Story', in Bale, J. and Moen, O. (eds), *The Stadium and the City*, Keele: Keele University Press.

Obel, C. (1998) 'Local and Global Publics: shifting popularity in rugby union and rugby league', in Perkins, H. and Cushman, G. (eds) *Time Out? Leisure, Recreation and Tourism in New Zealand and Australia*, Auckland: Longman.

Palenski, R., Chester, R. and McMillan, N. (1998) *The Encyclopedia of New Zealand Rugby*, Singapore: Moa Hodder Beckett.

Phillips, J. (1987) *A Man's Country?: The Image of the Pakeha Male – A History*, Auckland: Penguin Books.

Prentice, C. (1997) 'Why Christchurch deserves a better park', *The Press*, Dec. 15, p. 5.

Quirk, J. and Fort, R. (1992) *Pay Dirt: The Business of Professional Team Sport*, Princeton, N. J.: Princeton University Press.

Reddington, I. (1998) 'The mad scramble for a new stadium', *MG Business*, March 30, pp. 23-24.

✗ Rowe, D. (1999) *Sport, Culture and the Media*, Buckingham, Philadelphia: Open University Press.

Russell, D. and Wilson, N. (1991) *Life in New Zealand Survey*, Commission Report Executive Overview, Wellington: Hillary Commission.

Schwartz, B and Barsky, S. (1977) 'Home Advantage', *Social Forces*, vol. 55, no. 3, pp. 641-661.

Thompson, S. (1988) 'Challenging the hegemony: New Zealand women's opposition to rugby and the reproduction of a capitalist patriarchy', *International Review for the Sociology of Sport*, vol. 23, no. 3, pp. 205-211.

Veal, A., Gidlow, B. and Perkins, C. (1998) 'Interpreting leisure participation in New Zealand', in Perkins, H. and Cushman, G. (eds) *Time Out? Leisure, Recreation and Tourism in New Zealand and Australia*, Auckland: Longman.

Victory Park Board, *Annual Financial Statements*, 1981-1998.

Vincent, G. (1996) Practical Imperialism: The Anglo-Welsh Rugby Tour of New Zealand, 1908, Unpublished M.A. Thesis, History Department, Canterbury University, New Zealand.

10

Shopping!

Robin Kearns, Laurence Murphy and Wardlow Friesen

Introduction

At one level, shopping is such an ordinary part of daily life that it might easily be overlooked as a subject for serious academic study. We all shop. The purchase of goods ranging from the routine (groceries) to the occasional (cars, houses) becomes part of our everyday geographies, given that we invariably *go* shopping. At another level, shopping can engage us with spectacular aspects of urban life through the fact that the places we go to are frequently sites of carefully designed fantasy and illusion.[1]

Advertising has become a key method by which the meaning as well as the cost and availability of goods is conveyed to us. A recent newspaper advertisement for the Auckland Downtown Shopping Centre depicted a slim young woman carrying a shopping bag on which was emblazoned the slogan 'I shop therefore I am'. An interesting aspect of this advertisement is that the shopping centre is being advertised rather than a particular shop or product. The place is the object of marketing and the subject is a gendered consumer whom, it is implied, gains her identity through the act of shopping. Whimsically, and paraphrasing the philosopher René Descartes, the advertisers suggest not only that she will gain status through shopping at the mall, but also that she will come into her own (existence) through engaging in the act of shopping at that place.[2]

In this chapter, we explore some of the tensions inherent in everyday experiences of shopping in New Zealand. In this exploration, we are drawing on Frow and Morris's suggestion that familiar elements of everyday life such as shopping malls should be understood as carriers of complex and conflictual social processes.[3] Following these writers, we seek to incorporate into our reading of shopping both theoretical and vernacular (or folk) understandings of this otherwise banal activity which we all, to a greater or lesser extent, participate in. In effect, shopping practices can be viewed as texts, which can be read in a variety of ways: from the vantage point of both academic disciplines (economic, social cultural perspectives) and from non-academic viewpoints.

One tension we all confront in engaging in an ordinary activity is that we increasingly encounter extraordinary places. As social geographers, our underlying interest is in the theme of place. It is our view that the processes of consumption and our personal identities are connected through the places in which we shop. This connection is implied in the idea of sense of place, which can be seen as involving a mutually reinforcing relationship between the experience of actual places and our 'place-in-the-world', understood as status and identity ascribed by ourselves and others.[4]

We argue that there has been a rapid and profound shift in the style of consumption and retailing over the last 20 years in New Zealand. The corner store has, to a large extent, been displaced by the centralised and internalised mall containing a host of stores and other attractions. In turn, the idea of the mall has 'colonised' other places in the city. This shift has occurred at the same time as the act of retailing from home has been reinvigorated through technology such as the Internet.

We organise the chapter into six sections. First, we examine some of the material dimensions of shopping. Second, we sketch some ideas, drawn from the international literature on consumption, to assist our understanding of shopping. Third, we briefly survey the social history of shopping in New Zealand, leading up to mall developments. We consider the shopping centre as the primary site of contemporary consumption, moving into the mall to consider recent developments and diversification especially in Auckland. Fourth, we consider shopping in rural areas that are beyond easy reach of these 'cathedrals of consumption'. Section five considers various forms of participation in consumer behaviour that are shaped by age, social class, or avowed resistance to consumer culture. A short final section offers some concluding remarks.

Shopping is 'Real'

The changing nature of New Zealand's society and economy has been the subject of considerable academic scrutiny in the light of New Zealand's 'experimentation' with new forms of regulation and economic practices.[5] It is notable that throughout these analyses, attention is directed towards the 'real' economy of manufacturing industries, financial services, land-based production systems and government departments. Shopping seldom appears in these accounts of economic restructuring, changing employment relations, new technologies, and financial growth and decline. There are a number of reasons why shopping seldom appears in these accounts, not least of which is the degree to which shopping is conceived as a 'derivative' activity. People need to receive income (wages, salaries, benefit) in order to shop. Thus, sources of income figure prominently in our reviews of life in New Zealand. Yet the notion of shopping as a secondary or 'less real' activity is problematic. Shopping for food, clothing and shelter is a necessary dimension of our existence in capitalist/urbanised society. We often shop beyond our means as a consequence of credit systems. Shops are sources of employment for many thousands of workers, mainly female and casualised. Shops and shopping malls are valuable pieces of real estate. Shopping, therefore, has 'real' economic and social impacts. In this section, we provide an empirical collage of data on shopping in New Zealand as a backdrop to our discussion of the social and cultural dimensions of consumption.

Official monthly retail sales figures give a broad indication of the value of shopping in the economy. For the month of May 2000, total retail sales amounted to $3.6 billion. Total annual retail sales in 1999 amounted to over $41 billion.[6] Excluding motor-vehicle and motor-servicing expenditures, the major components of retail sales have consistently been food, footwear, clothes and soft-furnishings items. In March 1990, $560 million dollars was spent on food and by March 1999, this figure had risen to $797 million. Monthly expenditures on clothing and softgoods rose from $114 million to $119 million for the same period. More recent data indicates that the upward trend is continuing, with an expenditure of $121 million for May 2000. Retail sales per head of population increased from approximately $2,100 per month in 1991 to $2,700 per month in 2000. These figures offer an insight into the scale of retail expenditures in the economy and highlight the importance of ordinary, everyday purchases. Consumption is as much about the mundane dimensions of life (bread, milk, pasta) as the exotic (Jaguar cars, designer clothes). In addition the figures reveal the power and significance of tradition in our shopping patterns: the Christmas period is always the peak month for retail sales in New Zealand.

How we pay for our shopping and wider consumption items has changed with the advent and greater use of credit cards and EFTPOS (debit) cards. New Zealanders have resorted to greater use of credit over the 1990s. In March 1991, monthly credit card billings in New Zealand amounted to $303 million. By June 2000 this monthly figure had risen to $1,001 million. More significantly, outstanding credit advances rose from $918 million in March 1991 to $2.4 billion in June 2000.[7] People are using the credit system to consume today what would have been saved for in the past. Clearly, this move to credit-card consumption is proving profitable for banks. It is no wonder that financial institutions are using bonus schemes such as 'Fly-buys' to encourage people to make use of their plastic cards.

Not only are we spending more on shopping and increasingly resorting to credit, but where we are shopping is also changing. Shopping malls have become a major locus of consumption in the retail environment. The transition from the retail street to the mall entails a complex web of social significance and practice, which we will examine later, as well as valuable real estate. Significantly, the St Lukes Group, which owned 11 shopping malls in New Zealand in mid-2000, was also the largest property company listed in the country. Its total assets, consisting primarily of retail space, rose from $497.28 million in 1995 to $1,015.73 million in 1999.[8] The St Lukes Group operates some of the largest shopping malls in the country. St Lukes Shopping Centre in Auckland, which had a turnover of $238.6 million in 1999, is by far the busiest shopping mall, followed by Riccarton ($189.2 million) in Christchurch and Manukau Shopping Centre ($176.9 million). Table 10.1 sets out some of the business and physical dimensions of the St Lukes Group's retail interests. These details highlight the extent to which shopping malls act as business complexes. Interestingly, these 'factories of consumption'

Table 10.1: The St Lukes Group Shopping Interests 1999

Shopping Centre	Annual Turnover ($m)	No. of Retailers	Gross Lettable Area (sq.m)	Car Spaces
Chartwell Square	79.9	83	14,505	795
Downtown Shopping Centre	32.8	78	14,999	0
Glenfield Mall	83.4	51	17,872	860
Johnsonville Shopping Centre	35.2	56	6,165	515
Manukau Shopping Centre	176.9	127	36,088	1,821
Queensgate Shopping Centre	118	68	19,103	987
Riccarton Mall	189.2	93	29,103	1,411
St Lukes Shopping Centre	238.6	126	33,185	1,700
Shore City Galleria	84.2	74	13,085	853
The Plaza Pakuranga	109.3	75	20,428	918
Westcity Shopping Centre	113.9	92	16,088	1,010
Total	1261.4	923	220,621	10,870

(Source: St Lukes Group, Annual Report 1999)

are located in the Arcadian environs of residential suburbs, offering not only a venue for shopping but also a place to work.

In our discussions of shopping and consumption, it is possible to lose sight of the number of people earning their livelihood working in the retail sector. In 1996, 199,983 persons were employed in the retail trade and a further 69,408 persons were employed in the accommodation, cafe and restaurant sector.[9] The retail-trade sector alone employed more people than agriculture, forestry and fishing combined. Moreover, specific retail chains are significant employers in the New Zealand economy. For example, between 1991 and 1999, the Warehouse retail chain expanded its sales from $107 million to $932.8 million and its number of stores from 32 to 69. Whereas in 1991 the Warehouse was located in 20 cities and towns in New Zealand, by 1999 it had located in 46 towns and cities. This pervasive presence ensures that it has a significant local impact. In 1991 it employed 2,737 people; this had increased to 5,269 in 1999. Of the total employed in 1999 almost 50 per cent were part-time workers.[10] The importance of part-time workers in the retail sector is significant in several ways. Part-time employment is usually associated with a low-income and casualised labour force. Yet part-time work also affords income opportunities for groups that have difficulties accessing full-time employment, including women with childcare responsibilities and young adults (such as students).

Consuming Interests

The empirical dimensions of shopping (how much, when, where) offer insights into the magnitude of this set of activities. Yet shopping is embedded in a set of social and cultural practices that are not readily apparent in a cursory survey of facts and figures. In the remainder of this chapter, we seek to expand our discussion of shopping as an everyday economic practice by exploring links between place, identity and consumption.

Shopping implies the consumption of goods, services, and/or the spaces in which we browse and purchase. A great deal of social theory associated with (post)modernity, urbanism and social life has concerned itself with consumption over the last decade.[11] To consume implies sets of practices and perceptions that are predicated by, and embedded within, economic relations. This is because to consume implies the presence of something consumable. Likewise, buyers imply sellers. However, the simplicity of these relations, typified by negotiations at a village marketplace, are rendered complex and ambiguous within contemporary society.

Everyday economic practices are concerned with (re)constructing our personal identities, for such practices are a form of social participation. The experiences of having money and possessions (or even getting into debt), in other words, reflect degrees of 'fitting in' and participating in society. Micro-economic practices as routine as buying milk at the dairy or getting one's hair cut are, in small but significant ways, negotiated activities. This negotiation occurs in two contexts. The first context is a set of factors relating to what Lunt and Livingstone term 'positional goods': products and services through which people mark out their social class.[12] The second context involves psychological factors such as the moral connotations of 'appropriate' spending or being in debt. From this distinction, it follows that people's position in relation to their economic choices (i.e. how they engage with consumerism) may be ambivalent. This ambivalence occurs because routine economic practices may be inscribed with moral and social meanings. At the same time, everyday practices constitute social relations. Put another way, if one doesn't spend, one doesn't participate. Poverty, in other words, may well be more than lack of money and consequent hardship; within a consumption-driven culture, it can be an enforced withdrawal from a sense of participation and belonging in society. Thus, the key underlying ideas of a consumer society act in tension; the desire for security (the quest to save) and the desire for pleasure (the thrill of spending) can be seen as oppositional. As Lunt and Livingtone argue, 'being involved in a material culture is a way of locating oneself in a changing social and moral order'.[13]

In essence, shopping is a thoroughly spatial activity: we go shopping because the selling and buying of goods conventionally happens in particular places. Consumption and its implicit behaviour of 'shopping around' have been connected to three key processes within the postmodern era by influential writers such as Lash and Friedman:[14]

a)   The increasing commodification of social life, such that signs and images increasingly 'sell' consumption and intrude into the processes by which our identities are shaped. In other words, it matters to teenagers whether their clothes are known labels, or whether their running shoes are Nike (Seymour-East, 1993; Skelton and Valentine, 1998).[15,16] Thus the 'I shop therefore I am' slogan is ironic; it is both an appeal to enhance one's status through particular acts of shopping and a playful jest poking fun at the absurdity of this situation.

b)   Blurred social divisions in society. According to writers such as Bourdieu, a social implication of consumption is that the meanings of commodities become unstable, so that it is less easy to identify a person according to rank or class.[17] Thus advertising and fashion become tools in an attempt to stabilise meanings and create 'structures of taste'.

c) New forms of everyday life are generated via consumption, with an increased use and reliance upon created spaces of consumption such as malls, museums and theme parks.[18] For example, even in summer, families flock to the new 'Philips Aquatics Centre' in Auckland as an alternative to the beach, and shopping malls have become the preferred places to 'hang out' for teenagers. Such places allow the display of clothes, and even of bodies. Walter Benjamin calls these places 'dream worlds', noting the similarity with electronic media and the blurring of distinctions between representation and reality.[19]

The interaction of these three processes can be noted both in the story of consumption in New Zealand society and in the links between place, identity and consumption in everyday life.[20, 21] We now explore shopping as a routine and practical engagement with consumption in different geographical settings, and at various ages, and consider the ways in which it is being (re)shaped by technological developments.

Urban Change, Shopping Malls

We cannot separate developments in retailing from broader transformations in the city. In Auckland, for instance, the emergence of 'ethnoscapes' in which ethnic identity is 'mapped' onto the landscape is closely connected with the rapid diversification of immigration into the city.[22] An inner-city neighbourhood such as Sandringham, for instance, now features halal butchers that are both reflective of, and contributors to, a concentration of population from the Middle East and Asia. Examples of this type of diversification can now be found in most parts of New Zealand. Whereas two decades ago generic 'Chinese takeaways' outlets were the limits of cosmopolitanism in small towns, now it is not uncommon to encounter Indian or Thai restaurants in places with only modest populations.

Shopping has involved changes in the use of time as well as space. Until the Shops Trading Amendment Act (1980), Friday nights provided the only opportunity for people to shop outside of the 40-hour work week. Consequently, 'late-night Friday' became something of a social institution, especially in small-town New Zealand. In the words of a classic Topp Twins tune, people dressed for the occasion in their 'Friday night get-up'.

According to Bowler, the first mall to be opened in New Zealand was Lynn Mall in 1962. By 1993 there were over 90 malls.[23] The success of interiorised malls hinge on the opportunities for a range of people to be exposed to ideas of consuming. Thus, with the relaxation of trading hours, a new social context was born: the malling of New Zealand. One could rely on the mall being open on weekends, which in turn facilitated shopping as a family occasion. The Hillary Commission's 'Life in New Zealand Survey' found that shopping malls had become our most popular recreational places.[24]

What do we mean by a mall? A useful definition is 'a group of commercial establishments, planned, developed, owned and managed as a unit'.[25] Malls have their own internal geography. Because most are enclosed, they are easily controlled. Commonly, there are at least two 'anchor stores' – large department stores or supermarkets – with the space between these designed to resemble pedestrian-only streets containing a plethora of smaller businesses, mostly branches of larger chains. This commercial choreography, complete with public telephones, toilets and other non-consumption elements, is not the only way in which malls are designed for consuming. Writers such as Goss[26] and Hopkins[27] have pointed to the presence of 'placial icons' – installations that perceptually take us beyond the mall and into the realm of fantasy. These include water features, palm trees and ferns, Renaissance-like painted ceilings, temporary carnival features (e.g. carousels), fashion shows, pop concerts and trade displays, all of which are to be found to various degrees in malls around New Zealand.

The mall has been characterised as a predictable, safe and sanitised alternative to the city street, which remains prone to congestion, crime and bad weather. Malls may masquerade as public spaces, but are, in fact, privately owned and hence do not have to deal with the 'messier' aspects of public space such as persons regarded as 'undesirable'. Hence, it is not unusual to see a list of regulations discretely displayed in a mall. Indeed, the controlled nature of the setting is reflected in the presence of private security guards and CCTV cameras. Yet the boundaries between public and private are blurred, with a range of civic services frequently being found in malls (e.g. the library at Manukau Shopping Centre and the police station in Lynn Mall).

Increasingly we see the idea of the mall colonising other urban spaces. In Auckland, for instance, publicity hails the International Airport as 'A Whole New World of Shopping'. Elements of the mall can also be discerned in other 'public' spaces such as ferry terminals and hospitals. This appearance of shops within newly corporatised 'public institutions' has been seen as

'Americanisation'. Public outcry has been most shrill in the case of the volatile combination of children's health and an American fast-food giant. Indeed, an analysis of the arrival of a McDonald's at the Starship children's hospital reveals accusations of 'feeding junk food to sick children' and McHospitalisation.[28] While the fast food issue was bound to be controversial,[29] the fact that McDonald's is American feeds into a long-standing conflation of America with popular (low) culture in New Zealand, that developed in contrast to British culture as respectable (high).[30] The Starship, however, is an exceptional case. What of the 'ordinary' sites of shopping activity, and how have mall developments impacted on the conventional 'corner store'? Before answering these questions we need to look at how shopping malls work.

How are shoppers lured into these places?

- 'Anchor stores' serve to attract customers into the mall with the intent that they will spend at other stores during their visit.
- Malls are promoted as exciting places in themselves. St Lukes in Auckland, for instance, once described itself as 'The Centre of Auckland', more recently subtly changing the emphasis to 'The Centre for Auckland'.
- Shoppers are attracted by the provision of 'food courts'. Customers can be refreshed and sustained, and in so doing, spend more time at the mall.
- Malls invariably have large interior atrium spaces which might, through the course of a year, be host to a range of activities such as fashion shows or displays of vehicles. Some attractions, like Santa's castle at Christmas, are explicitly pitched at children who, since they must be accompanied, lure their parents into the mall environment. These events and installations are more than mere distraction. They both celebrate and promote consumption – in the foregoing examples, encouraging the purchase of clothes, cars and Christmas gifts respectively. Malls encourage shoppers through accessibility, with the hassles faced by drivers eased by extensive car parks. Within the mall, patrons are encouraged to circulate past the maximum number of stores, often assisted by escalators and moving walkways. The novelty of the mall is created through cyclical refurbishment. For instance, in 1998 Henderson Square was 'reinvented' as West City, replete with symbols such as nikau palms and mamaku tree ferns that reflect the 'Eco-City' image of Waitakere City. Here, natural light complements natural vegetation to encourage the shopper to feel in touch with the nearby Waitakere Ranges. When pedestrian counts begin to drop, refurbishment is contemplated so as to (re)fuel public interest and hence keep customer desire alive. In the words of the St Lukes website:

Shopping today is not just a necessity, it is one of the entertainment choices that people have. People have a conscious choice to stop at a particular centre. They are attracted by the ambience, the excitement, the variety, the convenience, to eat, to meet friends and for a day out.[31]

In sum, the advent of malls has intensified the fact that shopping is both a performance and a spectator sport. Desire is the key.[32] As Auckland songwriter Don McGlashan put it in a 1989 'Front Lawn' song, 'The beautiful things, the beautiful things ... we want them, we need them, to have and to hold'.

As indicated earlier, malls can be 'read' in diverse ways. This recognition leads Glennie and Thrift to be cautious about overattributing power to the mall itself. They contend that rather than 'drawing consumers to them in a trancelike state of desire, like moths to a candle ... such places meet the need to provide many different social groups (differentiated by class, ethnicity, gender and so on) with different information in the same place'.[33] Teenagers may meet at the mall to 'hang out', elderly people may see it as a safe place to linger and browse, and for parents it may be a place where the children can 'do their own thing' in play areas while they are grocery shopping.

These highly successful 'palaces of consumption' have affected the neighbourhood shopping areas around them. One impact of aggressive marketing by supermarkets and new shopping centres has been the relative demise of local shops such as dairies, butchers and chemists. Research in Christchurch has shown that restructuring in the retail sector heavily impacted on local services, affecting the role and viability of 'corner shopping centres' which Banks defines as 'those with between 10 and 15 shops serving everyday community needs' (see Table 10.2).[34] In his sample of 15 such centres, the services most likely to have disappeared were also the ones most likely to be represented in malls. Banks explains this trend by signalling that annual sales in dairies declined from $600 million to $350 million between 1982 and 1991, whereas over the same period supermarket sales increased from $600 million to $1,100 million.

The decline of the neighbourhood shop has implications for those whose lifeworlds are closely tied to their immediate locality, including the elderly, people with childcare responsibilities and those who lack access to private transport.[35] The routines of daily life can be disrupted as familiar shops and banks disappear from a neighbourhood. For those who own and operate small stores, the competition from shopping centres can represent considerable strain. In her examination of Indian dairy owners in Auckland,

Nandan records the experiences of shopkeepers who feel compelled to be open 15 hours a day in order to sustain business.[36]

Table 10.2: Changes in 15 Christchurch Local Shopping centres, 1978–91

Shop Type	No. in 1978	No. in 1991	Change
Dairy	23	17	-7
Butcher	13	6	-7
Drapery	11	4	-7
Chemist	8	7	-1
Fish Shop	6	5	-1
Post Office	5	0	-5
Takeaways	2	12	+10
Hairdressers	11	14	+3
Video	0	2	+2
All Others	46	65	+19

(Source: Banks, 1992)

Beyond the 'Big Smoke'

In rural New Zealand, opportunities for shopping are constrained by distance and the availability of outlets. To generalise, farm families typically make less frequent trips to urban shopping centres and rely to a greater extent on local produce such as meat and vegetables. However, new technology has revolutionised the accessibility of luxury items. A Hokianga resident recently remarked that he can now access a full range of speciality food items such as cheeses, wines and coffee via the Internet, and receive next-day delivery by courier. This level of availability is dependent on access to the technology and on purchasing power. Nearby in the Mangakahia Valley of Northland, some are opting for a more subsistence approach, spurred on by a mix of choice and necessity. According to one local, 'gardens provide food for the household and we still rely upon that river as part of food resources in terms of freshwater fish, and eels and watercress'.[37] For some Maori and 'alternative lifestylers', cultivating and catching food can represent a 'getting back to one's roots' and an active resistance to the seduction of shopping.

The effects of broader social and economic restructuring on the relative availability of places to purchase goods and services is most starkly evident in rural areas. In areas such as Northland and the West Coast, bank, hospital and post-office closures have precipitated behavioural change; in driving to larger centres for such services, residents bypass local stores and take their business elsewhere. In such 'changing places', closed stores are a common sight.[38] In another sense, banking and post-office functions have frequently been accommodated into the act of shopping itself. In Rawene, for instance, where the post office closed a decade ago, residents are now accustomed to using EFTPOS facilities at local stores (for both purchases and cash advances); the need for cash has been reduced by a range of services accepting both EFTPOS and credit cards.

Shopping, Commodification and the Everyday

Mass consumption and spectacle have often been constructed as a means of pacifying the public in capitalist society. Within these readings of consumption, cultural industries (advertising and marketing) are believed to have emerged with the purpose of manipulating people's desires and wants. In contrast to this notion of a mass market subject to manipulation, the notion of popular culture suggests that people resist and subvert dominant cultural ideas to create their own practices. Popular culture is often expressed in forms of music (rap, punk rock, country) and clothing. Ley and Olds note that, more often than not, the advertising agencies are followers of fashions rather than generators of trends.[39] In this section, we explore various elements of mass and popular consumption

Television has a pervasive place in New Zealand society and children are major consumers of its messages. De Boni reports that half of all New Zealand households have two or more television sets and that the average child watches for 20 to 24 hours per week.[40] This is a recipe, she says, for TV being 'the best channel to reach Kiwi kids'. Unlike other countries such as Canada and France, De Boni reports that 'New Zealand has happily rode almost every global marketing campaign from Teenage Mutant Ninja Turtles to Pokemon'.[41] It is thus no wonder that the issue of children's exposure to TV advertising entered the realm of political debate in 2000. As Gregory discovered in her research with Auckland children, their consumption of images and demand to consume goods are intimately related.[42] This link between image, desire and demand endures through youthful years, with clothes and music being key categories of consumption for adolescents in Auckland.[43]

The division of labour in the business of selling is such that it is not readily apparent who generates the message we are subjected to. As Jamieson writes, with respect to the notorious 'Bugger' ad, 'It's distressing to realise that Toyota has made a swear word, a term of sexual deviancy, commonly acceptable. I'd have written and protested when the advertisement came out – if only I'd known who to protest to.'[44]

Trolley Traffic

While advertising and television programmes promote new lifestyles, the experience of shopping may not always be fun and spectacle. Perhaps the least glamorous form of shopping is for groceries. One commentator recently described supermarkets as 'wearisome temples of today's avid consumerism';[45] the routine of shopping-trolley gridlock in the checkout aisles has resulted in one popular chain being colloquially known as 'Push 'n Shove'. What's more, Meagan Morris challenges accounts of shopping based on the notion of the *flaneur*-like shopper who slowly glides though the shopping centre observing life with a critical air.[46] She talks of the hard work that shopping sometimes entails and of those who do not enjoy shopping: the 'women who hate the car park, grab the goods and head on out as fast as possible'.[47]

One development changing the way that we shop is the Internet and, specifically, the first online supermarket (www.woolworths.co.nz). Web pages allow for virtual shopping behaviour, without the clatter of trolleys. The Woolworths' home page, for instance, invites progressive selections of 'Department', 'Aisle' and 'Shelf', then visual icons of a range of products. Preliminary research by Murphy signals lower-than-expected use of this service, with most common use by high-income customers.[48] These findings may be explained by the costs of access (i.e. Internet use, delivery fee), but may also be connected to a more fundamental facet of shopping: the corporeality of the act. George, for instance, writes of shopping for meat and vegetables by this means and having been concerned at 'not being able to see, feel and choose the best'.[49]

While New Zealand still has a low rate of participation in this form of shopping, retail executives in Europe and the US estimate that within three years 15 per cent of retail dollars will be spent on Internet shopping. George picks up on the hyperbole surrounding e-shopping when he states:

> Gone are the days of traispsing (sic) round the aisles, searching for one product stacked among hundreds ... having to backtrack for products

missed, tripping over crotchety children and bumping into their harried mothers, all the time bombarded by every impulse-buying trick in the book.[50]

Clearly e-shopping has a long way to go to out-compete shopping malls, but its advent has had an impact on the strategies of mall owners. Shopping-centre developments are beginning to anticipate this shift to cyber-shopping, offering more entertainment and spectacle in response.

Accessing Consumption

A prerequisite to consuming and, by extension, access to consumption spaces, is money. Increasingly, expenditure is by means of credit and direct debit (EFTPOS) cards. Acquiring these, in turn, is dependent on notions of 'creditworthiness', another aspect of contemporary identity. Without indications of likely spending, people are prone to be moved on from shopping centres and even entire parts of cities. In Los Angeles, for instance, Davis points to convex and hence thoroughly uncomfortable 'bum-proof seats' as symbolic of attempts to 'move on' those unlikely to consume and who by their very presence might detract from the appearance of the place.[51] From one perspective, being homeless or a street kid is an act of resistance to consumer society in itself.[52] Accordingly, criminal acts such as shoplifting represent a fundamental transgression against, and perhaps resistance to, the socio-legal order of commerce. There are other forms of less radical resistance to 'formal' contexts of shopping. Weekend flea markets, for instance, are now a part of life for many Aucklanders. Since their beginnings in the 1970s, markets such as those at Otara or Avondale have grown to the point that they are events drawing thousands of people who meet friends, haggle with dealers and enjoy a shopping environment quite different from enclosed and sanitised shopping malls.[53] If flea markets are the tax-free malls of the informal sector, then garage sales are the ephemeral corner dairies. Often advertised only by handwritten signs attached to suburban power poles, there are those who regularly cruise the early morning streets on weekends browsing for a bargain. Further, newspapers like *Trade and Exchange* represent a 'market outside the market' through offering opportunities to buy, sell or exchange second-hand goods in an informal manner beyond the reach of the Inland Revenue Department.

Conclusion

In this chapter, we have addressed a number of concerns relating to the material and social practices surrounding shopping. We have shown that shopping occupies a somewhat ambiguous position in academic texts. At one level, shopping is an ordinary everyday occurrence. It is about convenience as well as parking hassles, standing in long checkout queues, bargain-hunting and purchasing 'our daily bread'. Yet it often takes place in contrived spaces designed to encourage shopping: places that attempt to radiate images of spectacle, elsewhereness and pleasure.

Shopping is an activity fraught with contradictions. It can be viewed as a democratic activity, since the 'market' does not discriminate on the grounds of identity, nationality or culture. Yet it is a source of social exclusion that brings into relief emerging polarities of incomes in New Zealand. Amid the growth of shopping malls in New Zealand it is worth noting that one of the most successful retail chains to develop in the 1990s was the Warehouse, a discount shopping store 'where everyone gets a bargain'. The success of this chain represents the intersection of a number of processes involving business strategy, advertising and marketing. But this success also points to other issues. Clearly, there was a need for this type of development. In addition, the success of the Warehouse highlights the fact that shoppers are active agents in the consumption process. We make choices based on preferences, income and location. We participate, willingly or reluctantly, in shopping practices. We variously are persuaded by, enjoy, ignore or resist the onslaught of advertising from letterbox drops, local and national newspapers, radio, television and magazines.

In this chapter we have been concerned to expose the various levels of social interactions that surround a rather innocuous daily event termed 'shopping'. Our intention was to highlight the many interconnections that bind shopping, shoppers, workers and places together.

Acknowledgement

This chapter was written with the support of a Marsden Grant titled (Extra)ordinary Auckland: Exploring local meanings and evidence of globalisation. We are grateful to Matthew Henry and Burnetta van Stipriaan for research assistance in the preparation of the chapter.

Endnotes

1   Miller, D., Jackson, P., Thrift, N., Holbrook, B. and Rowlands, M. (1998) *Shopping, place and identity*, London: Routledge.
2   Spearritt, P. (1994) 'I shop, therefore I am', in Johnson, L. (ed.) *Suburban Dreaming: An interdisciplinary approach to Australian cities*, Geelong: Deakin University Press, pp. 129–140.
3   Frow, J. and Morris, M. (1993) 'Introduction', in Frow, J. and Morris, M. (eds) *Australian cultural studies: A reader*, St Leonards, N.S.W: Allen & Unwin, pp. vii–xxxii.
4   Eyles, J.D. (1985) *Senses of place*. Warrington: Silverbrook Press.
5   Kelsey, J. (1997) *The New Zealand experiment: A world model for structural adjustment?* Auckland: Auckland University Press & Bridget Williams Books.
6   Statistics New Zealand (2000) *PC Infos* (on line data base).
7   Reserve Bank of New Zealand (2000) website: www.rbnz.govt.nz.
8   St Lukes Group (1999) *Annual Report, 1999*, Auckland.
9   Statistics New Zealand (1997) *1996 Census of Population and Dwellings: Regional Summary*, Wellington: Statistics N.Z.
10 The Warehouse (1999) *Annual Report, 1999*, Auckland.
11 Shields, R. (1992) *Lifestyle Shopping: The Subject of Consumption*, London: Routledge.
12 Lunt, P.K. and Livingstone, S.M. (1992) *Mass Consumptrion and Personal Identity*, Buckingham: Open University Press.
13 Ibid., p. 166.
14 Lash, S. and Friedman, J. (eds) (1992) *Modernity and Identity*, Oxford: Basil Blackwell.
15 Seymour-East, B. (1995) *The teenage girl in Auckland city: Gender, place and identity in the city*, unpublished M.A. (Hons) thesis, Department of Geography, University of Auckland.
16 Skelton, T. and Valentine, G. (1998) *Cool places: Geographies of youth cultures*, London & New York: Routledge.
17 Bourdieu, P. (1984) *Distinction: A Social Critique of the Judgement of Taste*, London: Routledge and Kegan Paul.
18 Shields, R. (1992) *Lifestyle Shopping: The Subject of Consumption*, London: Routledge.
19 Benjamin, W. (1999) *The Arcades Project* (translated from German by H. Eiland & K.McLaughlin), Cambridge, Mass.: Belknap Press.
20 Glennie, P.D. and Thrift, N. J. (1992) 'Modernity, urbanism and modern consumption', *Environment and Planning D: Society and Space*, no. 10, pp. 423–443.
21 Mansvelt, J. (1999) 'Consuming spaces', in Le Heron, R., Murphy, L., Forer, P. and Goldstone, M. (eds) *Encountering Place: Explorations in Human Geography*, Auckland: Oxford University Press.

22 Murphy, L., Friesen, W. and Kearns, R.A. (1999) 'Transforming the City: People, Property and Identity in Millennial Auckland', *New Zealand Geographer*, vol. 55 no. 2, pp. 60–65.

23 Bowler, S. (1996) 'Planned Shopping Centres', in Le Heron, R. and Pawson, E. (eds) *Changing Places: New Zealand in the Nineties*, Auckland: Longman Paul, pp. 328–329.

24 Hillary Commission (1990) *Life in New Zealand Survey*, Dunedin: University of Otago Press.

25 Le Heron, R. and Pawson, E. (1996) *Changing Places: New Zealand in the Nineties*, Auckland: Longman Paul, p. 329.

26 Goss, J.D. (1993) 'The "magic of the mall": An analysis of form, function and meaning in the contemporary retail built environment', *Annals of the Association of American Geographers*, vol 83, no 1, pp. 18–47.

27 Hopkins, J.S.P. (1991) 'West Edmonton Mall: Landscape of myth and elsewhereness', *The Canadian Geographer*, no. 34, pp. 2–17.

28 Kearns, R.A. and Barnett, J.R. (2000) '"Happy meals' in the Starship Enterprise: Towards a moral geography of health care consumption', *Health and Place* no. 6, pp. 81–93.

29 Ritzer, G. (1988) *The McDonaldization of Society*, Thousand Oaks, Calif.: Pine Forge Press

30 Lealand, G. A. (1988) *Foreign Egg in our Nest. American Popular Culture in New Zealand*, Wellington: Victoria University Press.

31 St Luke's Group (2000) website: www.stlukesgrp.co.nz.

32 Shurmer-Smith, P. and Hannam, K. (1994) *Worlds of desire, realms of power: A cultural geography*, London: Edward Arnold.

33 Glennie, P.D. and Thrift, N. J. (1992) 'Modernity, urbanism and modern consumption', *Environment and Planning D: Society and Space*, no. 10, pp. 437–8.

34 Banks, G.A. (1992) 'Local shopping centres in Christchurch', in Britton, S., Le Heron, R. and Pawson, E. (eds) *Changing Places in New Zealand: A Geography of Restructuring*, Christchurch: New Zealand Geographical Society, p. 282.

35 Austin, P. A. and Whitehead, C. (1998) 'Auckland: Cappuccino city?', *Urban Policy and Research*, vol 16, pp. 233–240.

36 Nandan, R. A. (1994) *Open all hours: Indian dairy entrepreneurship in central urban Auckland*, unpublished M.A. (Hons) thesis, Department of Geography, University of Auckland.

37 Cited in Scott, K. and Kearns, R.A. (2000) 'Coming home: Return migration of Maori to the Mangakahia valley, Northland', *New Zealand Population Review* (in press).

38 Le Heron, R., Murphy, L., Forer, P. and Goldstone, M. (eds) (1999) *Explorations in Human Geography: Encountering Place*, Auckland: Oxford University Press.

[39] Ley, D. and Olds, K. (1999) 'World's fairs and the culture of consumption in the contemporary city', in Anderson, K. and Gale, F. (eds) *Cultural Geographies* (2nd ed.) Sydney: Longman, pp. 221–240.

[40] de Boni, D. (2000) 'Pester power costs parents dearly', *New Zealand Herald*, 30 May, p. C4.

[41] Ibid., C2.

[42] Gregory, S. (1997) *Consuming the 'cool': Children's popular consumption culture*, Unpublished M.A. (Hons) thesis, Department of Geography, University of Auckland.

[43] Seymour-East, B. (1995) *The teenage girl in Auckland city: gender, place and identity in the city*, unpublished M.A. (Hons) thesis, Department of Geography, University of Auckland.

[44] Jamieson, J. (2000) 'All credit to … whom?', *New Zealand Herald*, 1 June, p. A17.

[45] George, G. (2000) 'At home in the e-supermarket', *New Zealand Herald*, 1 June, p. A17.

[46] Morris, M. (1988) 'Things to do with shopping centres', in Sheridan, S. (ed.) *Grafts: Feminist Cultural Criticism*, London: Verso, pp. 193–225.

[47] Ibid., 203.

[48] Murphy, A. (2000) 'Internet Commerce: The New Zealand Context', Talk given at Department of Geography Departmental Seminar Series, June 2000.

[49] George, G. (2000) 'At home in the e-supermarket', *New Zealand Herald*, 1 June, p. A17.

[50] Ibid.

[51] Davis, M.(1992) *City of Quartz*, New York: Vintage Books.

[52] Lindsey, D. (1992) *Towards an understanding of situated practices: The spatiality of social life among Auckland's street kids*, unpublished M.A. (Hons) thesis, Department of Geography, University of Auckland.

[53] Milne, S. (1987) 'Formalising the informal sector', *New Zealand Geographer* no. 43, pp. 2–9.

Bibliography

Austin, P. A. and Whitehead, C. (1998) 'Auckland: Cappuccino city?' *Urban Policy and Research*, vol 16, pp. 233–240.

Banks, G.A (1992) 'Local shopping centres in Christchurch', in Britton, S., Le Heron, R. and Pawson, E. (eds), *Changing Places in New Zealand: A Geography of Restructuring*, Christchurch: New Zealand Geographical Society.

Benjamin, W. (1999) *The Arcades Project* (translated from German by H. Eiland & K.McLaughlin), Cambridge, Mass.: Belknap Press.

Bourdieu, P. (1984) *Distinction: A Social Critique of the Judgement of Taste*, London: Routledge and Kegan Paul.

Bowler, S. (1996) 'Planned Shopping Centres', in Le Heron, R. and Pawson, E. (eds), *Changing Places: New Zealand in the Nineties*, Auckland: Longman Paul.

Davis, M.(1992) *City of Quartz*, New York: Vintage Books.

De Boni, D. (2000) 'Pester power costs parents dearly', *New Zealand Herald*, 30 May, p. C4.

Eyles, J.D. (1985) *Senses of place*, Warrington: Silverbrook Press.

Frow, J. and Morris, M. (1993) 'Introduction', in Frow, J. and Morris, M. (eds) *Australian cultural studies: A reader*, St Leonards, N.S.W: Allen & Unwin.

George, G. (2000) 'At home in the e-supermarket', *New Zealand Herald*, 1 June, p. A17.

Glennie, P.D. and Thrift, N. J. (1992) 'Modernity, urbanism and modern consumption', *Environment and Planning D: Society and Space*, no. 10, pp. 423–443.

Goss, J.D. (1993) 'The 'magic of the mall': An analysis of form, function and meaning in the contemporary retail built environment', *Annals of the Association of American Geographers*, vol 83 no 1, pp. 18–47.

Gregory, S. (1997) *Consuming the 'cool': Children's popular consumption culture*, unpublished M.A. (Hons) thesis, Department of Geography, University of Auckland.

Hillary Commission (1990) *Life in New Zealand Survey*, Dunedin: University of Otago Press.

Hopkins, J.S.P. (1991) 'West Edmonton Mall: Landscape of myth and elsewhereness', *The Canadian Geographer*, no. 34, pp. 2–17.

Jamieson, J. (2000) 'All credit to … whom?', *New Zealand Herald*, 1 June, p. A17.

Kearns, R.A. and Barnett, J.R. (2000) "Happy meals' in the Starship Enterprise: Towards a moral geography of health care consumption', *Health and Place* no. 6, pp. 81–93.

Kelsey, J. (1997) *The New Zealand experiment: A world model for structural adjustment?* Auckland: Auckland University Press & Bridget Williams Books.

Lash, S. and Friedman, J. (eds) (1992) *Modernity and Identity*, Oxford: Basil Blackwell.

Lealand, G. A. (1988) *Foreign Egg in our Nest. American Popular Culture in New Zealand*, Wellington: Victoria University Press.

Le Heron, R., Murphy, L., Forer, P. and Goldstone, M. (eds) (1999)

Explorations in Human Geography: Encountering Place, Auckland: Oxford University Press.

Le Heron, R. and Pawson, E. (1996) *Changing Places: New Zealand in the Nineties*, Auckland: Longman Paul.

Ley, D. and Olds, K. (1999) 'World's fairs and the culture of consumption in the contemporary city', in Anderson, K. and Gale, F. (eds), *Cultural Geographies* (2nd ed) Sydney: Longman, pp. 221–240.

Lindsey, D. (1992) *Towards an understanding of situated practices: The spatiality of social life among Auckland's street kids*, Unpublished M.A. (Hons) thesis, Department of Geography, University of Auckland.

Lunt, P.K. and Livingstone, S.M. (1992) *Mass Consumptrion and Personal Identity*, Buckingham: Open University Press.

Mansvelt, J. (1999) 'Consuming spaces', in Le Heron, R., Murphy, L., Forer, P. and Goldstone, M. (eds), *Encountering Place: Explorations in Human Geography*, Auckland: Oxford University Press.

Miller, D., Jackson, P., Thrift, N., Holbrook, B. and Rowlands, M. (1998) *Shopping, place and identity*, London: Routledge.

Milne, S. (1987) 'Formalising the informal sector', *New Zealand Geographer* no. 43, pp. 2–9.

Morris, M. (1988) 'Things to do with shopping centres', in Sheridan, S. (ed.), *Grafts: Feminist Cultural Criticism*, London: Verso, pp. 193–225.

Murphy, A. (2000) 'Internet Commerce: The New Zealand Context', Talk given at Department of Geography Departmental Seminar Series, June 2000.

Murphy, L., Friesen, W. and Kearns, R.A. (1999) 'Transforming the City: People, Property and Identity in Millennial Auckland', *New Zealand Geographer*, vol. 55 no. 2, pp. 60–65.

Nandan, R. A. (1994) *Open all hours: Indian dairy entrepreneurship in central urban Auckland*, unpublished M.A. (Hons) thesis, Department of Geography, University of Auckland.

Reserve Bank of New Zealand (2000) website: www.rbnz.govt.nz.

Ritzer, G. (1988) *The McDonaldization of Society*, Thousand Oaks, Calif.: Pine Forge Press.

Scott, K.and Kearns, R.A. (2000) 'Coming home: Return migration of Maori to the Mangakahia valley, Northland', *New Zealand Population Review* (in press).

Seymour-East, B. (1995) *The teenage girl in Auckland city: Gender, place and identity in the city*, unpublished M.A. (Hons) thesis, Department of Geography, University of Auckland.

Shields, R. (1992) *Lifestyle Shopping: The Subject of Consumption*, London: Routledge.

Shurmer-Smith, P. and Hannam, K. (1994) *Worlds of desire, realms of power: A cultural geography*, London: Edward Arnold.

Skelton, T. and Valentine, G. (1998) *Cool places: Geographies of youth cultures*, London & New York: Routledge. ✗

Spearritt, P. (1994) 'I shop, therefore I am', in Johnson, L. (ed.) *Suburban Dreaming: An interdisciplinary approach to Australian Cities*, Geelong: Deakin University Press, pp. 129–140.

Statistics New Zealand (1997) *1996 Census of Population and Dwellings: Regional Summary*, Wellington: Statistics N.Z.

Statistics New Zealand (2000) *PC Infos* (on line data base).

St Lukes Group (1999) *Annual Report, 1999*, Auckland.

St Luke's Group (2000) website: www.stlukesgrp.co.nz.

The Warehouse (1999) *Annual Report, 1999*, Auckland.

11

Everyday Gambling in New Zealand

Bruce Curtis and Cate Wilson

Everyday Gambling

There is a sizeable body of statistics on gambling in New Zealand which points albeit unintentionally – to the everyday status of this activity. Max Abbott and Rachel Volberg,[1] two leading figures in the rapidly growing discipline of gambling studies, note that in 15 short years there have been no less than seven surveys on gambling in New Zealand (not including a large number of university theses). These include three assessments of people's participation in gambling by the Department of Internal Affairs,[2] plus two surveys funded by the department focusing on problem gambling.[3] To these can be added one conducted by a regional health authority, North Health, under contract to the Committee on Problem Gambling Management and one conducted on behalf of the Casino Control Authority.[4] This much research on gambling should suggest to the reader that there is something about gambling that piques the interest of government bureaucrats and agencies. Here the frequency of the phrase 'problem gambling' is the giveaway. In this section we will review some of the findings of this research and cover its more pathological rationale later.

The surveys commissioned by the Department of Internal Affairs indicate that gambling is an everyday or common activity for New Zealanders. Thus in the departmental survey of 1985, 85 per cent of respondents indicated that they had participated in at least one form of gambling that year.[5] In the 1990 and 1995 surveys this rose to 90 per cent.[6] A 1997 survey, commissioned by the Casino Control Authority, placed the participation rate in the previous twelve months at between 90 per cent and 95 per cent.[7]

Abbott and Volberg suggest 86 per cent for six months in 1999.[8] In other words participation in gambling seems to be increasing. Furthermore, in 1985 15 per cent of respondents reported participating in four or more activities. This rose to 40 per cent in 1990 and 41 per cent in 1995. Monthly or more frequent participation levels in the 1995 sample were: Lotto (55 per cent), Instant Kiwi (31 per cent), raffles/lotteries (19 per cent), gaming machines (9 per cent), track betting (7 per cent), Daily Keno (4 per cent) and housie (3 per cent).[9]

This recounting of rates of participation in gambling may (and should!) be of concern to readers, especially those with any familiarity of the longstanding criticisms of survey research. Undoubtedly these surveys suffer from a number of conceptual and methodological flaws.[10] At best they can be considered snapshots of the situation. The more we try to use them for detailed analysis, the more problematic they become. Nevertheless the sketch they offer of gambling's everyday status is confirmed by other sources, most notably the figures on consumer spending. The Department of Internal Affairs surveys of 1990 and 1995 estimated a 'mean expenditure' of $446 and $413 per gambler per annum, while the Casino Control Authority estimated it at $1,794. Abbott and Volberg suggest the amount was $492 in 1999.[11] More significantly the latest figures drawn from the returns of gambling operators suggest that New Zealanders spend around six billion dollars per annum on gambling. These figures tend to corroborate the high estimated mean expenditure of the Casino Control Authority vis-à-vis the low Department of Internal Affairs estimate. About five-sixths of the amount spent on gambling (this spend is usually called the turnover) is returned to individuals as prizes. What remains (that is, what is lost by gamblers) is called gross profits. The operators who sell gambling products retain these gross profits.

The principal gambling operators in New Zealand are a mixed lot. They include two state-owned enterprises, the Lotteries Commission and the Totalisator Agency Board (TAB); a handful of commercially owned casinos; several hundred clubs and pubs running gaming machines; and an even greater number of housie (or bingo) organisers. A breakdown of the expenditure on gambling and the shares of these operators is provided in Table 11.1.

The mix of gambling venues and products supplied by these operators provides further confirmation of the everyday status of gambling. Certainly the days are long gone when legal gambling options consisted of Golden Kiwi raffle tickets sold by stationers and tobacconists, and a few concrete-block TAB agencies hidden up side streets and alleys. Today gambling venues

Table 11.1   Licensed Gaming Activity: Estimated Turnover and
Expenditure $(million)

	1998	1999	2000
TAB-Racing			
Turnover	999	992	1009
Expenditure	190	188	192
TAB-Sports			
Turnover	53	64	69
Expenditure	7	8	9
Lotteries Commission			
Turnover	639	644	624
Expenditure	288	288	280
Clubs and Pubs/Trusts			
Turnover	2100	2600	2888
Expenditure	292	360	400
Casinos			
Turnover	3060	3675	4125
Expenditure	245	294	330
Housie			
Turnover	45	45	45
Expenditure	15	15	15
Other Forms (Raffles, etc.)			
Turnover	20	20	20
Expenditure	10	10	10

and products are on the main street, in the mainstream and advertised on prime-time television. They include racecourses, TAB agencies, lottery outlets, pubs, clubs, casinos, phone and Internet accessed betting, plus extensive television, radio, Internet and print coverage. Together these consumption opportunities ensure that gambling is a readily available activity for all New Zealanders.

But not everyone gambles equally. Returning to the survey results for a moment, and remembering their weaknesses, there are obvious disparities in the degree to which different types of people gamble, and on what. Much of this material confirms some stereotypes about gamblers: men spend more than women; seniors (55 plus) and the young (24 and under) spend less than average; Maori expenditure is roughly double that of non-Maori; Catholics spend more than non-Catholics; those with high educational qualifications spend less than those with low-level qualifications.[12] More interesting results can emerge when these sorts of socio-demographic divisions are used to delineate expenditure in terms of specific gambling products. Unfortunately because of limits in the existing research we can only get hints at what is unfolding in gambling. The most important trend could well be the 'proletarianisation' of gambling.

Proletarianisation is a term that refers to the middle classes assuming working-class values and habits. In this case we mean the growth of gambling – as a legitimate form of entertainment – beyond its stereotypical, masculine and labouring strongholds. Much of this transformation can be encapsulated in the shift from gambling to gaming. In the case of this terminology the proponents of gambling use the latter and its opponents the former. An important part of this sanitisation of gambling is that it is becoming more attractive to women, the educated and the middle class.[13] This is good news for gambling operators as these groups in New Zealand are notoriously antithetical to gambling. There is a separate article to be written on how respectable, essentially middle-class tastes became defined as 'public good' and codified through public policy. Here it is sufficient to note that historically a concern with respectability and the morality of others has meant policy-makers have done their utmost to limit and quarantine gambling (Austrin, 1998; Grant, 1994).[14] Vestiges of this moral imperative remain – indeed those currently running the Labour-Alliance Government are exemplars of the tradition – but the tide has for some years run with those in favour of the expansion of gambling in New Zealand.[15]

Defining Gambling

A definition of gambling is by no means as simple as it first appears. Recently an extensive literature review commissioned by the New Zealand Government could find no single definition. Instead Max Abbott and Rachel Volberg decided to cite a range of options.[16] The clearest of these is drawn from the work of Michael Walker, a psychologist. Here gambling is: 'Risking money in order to win money on an outcome that is wholly or partly determined by chance'.[17] This seems straightforward enough. All the elements that we might associate with gambling are there – risk, money, wins and losses, chance. But there are at least two deficiencies in this definition. First, it is exclusively money-focused. There is no acknowledgement of 'fun' as motivator for gambling. In part this reflects a blind spot of psychology in which fun – the social construction of fun – is more or less inexplicable. Among gamblers, having fun appears as the most common explanation for the activity.

Second, the psychological definition lacks specificity. It can be applied equally well to many forms of what we might call 'risk-taking'. For example, it applies in choosing a course of study at university. Selecting between majoring in sociology or accountancy is a form of risk-taking. Putting aside the thrill of the former and the drudgery of the latter for the moment, we can see that the choice of courses involves money (course fees), chance (the quality of teaching, developments in the economy), wins and losses (getting good grades or poor), and risk (potential career paths). But this sort of choice can't sensibly be described as gambling. Nor can the range of risk-taking activities that make up our everyday lives: starting a business, planning a marriage, buying a house, etc.

Fortunately sociologists have refined a definition. Gerda Reith provides a version that interestingly reworks notions of the everyday: 'Gambling can be defined as a ritual which is strictly demarcated from the everyday world around it and within which chance is deliberately courted as a mechanism which governs the redistribution of wealth among players as well as a commercial interest or "house"'.[18] This is a neat definition for a number of reasons. First, it captures the ritual aspects of gambling. By 'ritual' is meant the rules and practices particular to (forms of) gambling. These rituals must be learnt and to some extent understood in order to gamble. For example, none of us were born with an instinctual knowledge of how to buy Lotto tickets, nor of how to play multiple lines on a gaming machine, nor how to place a nullified field bet on the sixth race at Trentham. And despite the best advertising efforts of the Lotteries Commission and New Zealand On Air, this information is not readily available through our televisions or in schools. Rather, gambling remains demarcated from the humdrum experiences of the everyday. Consequently, in order to gamble we must seek out gambling possibilities.

The second important notion Reith uses is that of 'the house'. The house is central to gambling. 'The house' is the term used for the individual or business that accepts bets and pays out winnings (simultaneously keeping gamblers' losses). Sometimes the house is called 'the bank' and the range of gambling opportunities it offers 'banked games'. This terminology is largely associated with casinos, but every house/gambling operator acts as a bank. The most important aspect of the house/gambling operator is that inevitably it wins. In this sense the house does not operate simply as a clearing-house for bets. Gambling is not a nil-sum-game in which the winnings of some gamblers are offset by the losses of all the rest. Gambling operators are in the business to make profits, the only source of which are the net losses of their 'customers', the gamblers. Positioning the house and gamblers leads us to a discussion of the main elements of gambling.

Elements of Play

Odds and Handicapping

Gambling operators ensure they make a profit (in effect, that losing bets outweigh winning bets) in a multitude of ways. Most significantly, odds are used to determine the payouts made by the house for winning bets. These calculations are made in favour of the house and are used to minimise its risk. At the same time, odds and the schedule of payouts for bets on games and events are used to make gambling more attractive to players and hence viable in commercial terms.

Odds can be subdivided in terms of games for which probabilities can be determined and events for which they cannot. Odds are structured into the rules of games. Some odds are relatively easy to grasp, while others are exceedingly difficult. The simplest example of odds and the schedule of payouts is a lottery. If 1,000 tickets are sold in a lottery then the odds of holding the winning ticket in a single draw are 1 in 1,000 (1/1,000). There are obvious implications from this. Let us assume that the tickets are sold for $1 each. This creates the possibility of a prize pool of $1,000. Any more than this paid out in prizes and the organiser of the lottery (the operator) will lose money. Clearly for the lottery to generate gross profits (that is, what is lost by gamblers) the winning ticket(s) must have a total prize of less than $1,000 and all the tickets must be sold. But few individuals would buy the tickets if the winning prize was only $1 or $10. Thus to make the lottery more attractive the operator must offer a prize (a schedule of payouts) that is enticing, while leaving enough over to be retained as gross profits. Frequently the operator will offer a series of first, second or third prizes to make the lottery a more attractive proposition. This decision-making is of course a balancing act: the greater the share of prizes, the less the share of gross profits.

Most gambling today is far more sophisticated than the discrete lottery described above. Most commercial forms provide the possibility for continuous forms of gambling in which the process of selling tickets, establishing a prize pool, drawing the winner and making payouts becomes blurred. In these continuous or banked games the use of odds to determine payouts is also central. Here the game of roulette provides a good example. Roulette involves a wheel with 37 slots numbered from 0 to 36, and what is called a layout. The layout is also numbered from 0 to 36 and is used by players to bet which number will be selected by the roulette wheel. Half of the numbers from 1 to 36 are red and half are black (the zero is normally green). Players can bet on any single number (called a straight-up bet), a combination of numbers, red or black, odd or even. Each roulette game begins when the dealer spins the wheel in one direction, and then rolls a small ball along the inner edge of the wheel in the opposite direction. The ball eventually falls into one of the numbered slots. That number is the declared winner for the game and payouts are made. There are about 60 spins of the roulette wheel per hour.

In roulette the odds are structured to favour the house through the use of the number zero. Thus the chances of any straight-up bet being successful are 1 in 37; however, the scheduled payout for winning a straight-up bet is at '36 to 1' (thirty-six times the amount bet). Similarly the so-called 'even-money' bets, where a player picks 18 numbers (all blacks or all reds, all evens or all odds) and the scheduled payout is to '1 to 1' are misnamed, because if the ball stops on zero then all bets are lost. Two processes are in operation. The first involves aspects of a nil-sum-game wherein for the numbers 1 through 36 the house can rely on gamblers cancelling out each others' bets. The second involves the number zero, from which only the house can win. In total the use of the number zero gives the house an advantage or edge over roulette players of about 2.7 per cent.

Clearly the house/operator has an interest in obscuring the extent to which the odds and scheduled payouts favour them. For example, despite all the advertising encouraging us to buy Lotto each week there is no mention that the chance of winning the major prize is less than 1 in 3.8 million. However, what the sellers of Lotto and many other gambling products do is conflate the possible combinations of placing bets (buying the product) and the schedule of payouts with the actual odds on winning.[19] Thus a gambler may know that buying a ten-line combination rather than a 4-line combination means he or she has 2.5 times the chance of winning Lotto, without necessarily appreciating that the odds of any one of those lines winning is: 1/40 x 1/39 x 1/38 x 1/37 x 1/36 x 1/35 x 100 = 0.00000003587766048 per cent. Of course what makes Lotto viable is its massive ticket sales, which make it very likely that *someone* will win each week.

While the odds on Lotto are easy to calculate, the odds on other games are very obscure indeed. In this regard the odds for the gaming machines found in casinos, clubs and pubs are the exemplar. The chances of winning from any single spin of the reels on a gaming machine are rarely, if ever, given. While the schedule of payouts for the different combinations of symbols thrown up by the spinning reels are typically plastered across the front of the machine, the odds for these combinations are not. With the old-fashioned electro-mechanical reel machines it was just possible to work out how many symbols were on each reel and so calculate the odds of winning. But with the electronic video machines this is no longer a possibility. Consequently, one way or another, the players of gaming machines have to have faith.

Specifically, the players must believe that there is a genuine chance of winning. Whether or not they know it, this requires a faith in the software and hardware which run gaming machines. The core of this technology is the EEPROM (electrically erasable programmable read-only memory) which establishes a random number generator and links it to the rules of the game within the machine. Winning or losing results are produced by the EEPROM continuously, only some of which are selected by players dropping coins into the machine, pushing buttons or pulling a handle. The electronic impulses generated by the EEPROM are more rapid than any human reactions. Among other things this undermines the strategy of playing a machine continuously on the basis that it is due to pay out. Even if this was the case, the EEPROM generates far more winning and losing combinations than the player can access. At the same time faith in gaming machines can be diminished, as was the case some years ago when Sky City casino refused to pay out two cars won by a player in twenty minutes. Sky City argued that there was a fault in the EEPROM. This of course begs the question of what happens if the EEPROM is faulty but the malfunction is in favour of the house?

The odds which are structured into the rules of games can be obscure. In the case of wagering (betting on events) these odds are no more than a representational fiction. Thus the high-profile advertising campaign by the TAB – 'You know the odds, now beat them' – is doubly false. First, it is impossible to 'know' the odds of an event like a horse race or a rugby test in advance. Horse races and rugby matches are not analogous to the spin of a roulette wheel, or to the draw of a lottery, or even to the software in gaming machines which simulate these random selections. Horse races, rugby matches and all other sports events which people bet on are one-off events, which probability theory and statistics have little to say about. Second, it is impossible to beat the odds offered by the TAB.

The term for odds associated with wagering is 'handicapping'. Handicapping makes wagering on events involving dead certainties and long shots viable. In particular, it is used to minimise the house's exposure. For example, if the All Blacks were playing Italy at Eden Park then the TAB might offer payouts of $1.01 and $8.00 for the win, respectively. If the All Blacks win then successful bets make one cent on every dollar bet. If the Italians win then successful bets make $7.00 on every dollar bet. In terms of representing the underlying chances of winning, these payouts as odds clearly don't add up. If winning and losing are an either/or option (we'll forget the possibility of a draw) then the chances of someone winning must add to 100 per cent. The payout cited above for the All Black win suggests that they have a 99 per cent chance of winning. If this were so then the Italians should have a one per cent chance of winning. In this case the TAB should offer a payout of $100 on an Italian win. Conversely, the payout cited above for the Italian win suggests that they have a one in eight chance of winning. If this were so then the All Blacks should have a seven in eight chance of winning. In this case the TAB should offer a payout of $1.14 on an All Black win.

In practice the 'odds' posted by the TAB represent not so much its assessment of the chances of one team or horse winning an event, but its assessment of the punters' assessment. The TAB is centrally interested in making its product (betting on events) as attractive to the gambling public as possible, while at the same time minimising exposure and risk. This means that the TAB is involved in second-guessing the gambling public in the form of marketing a sports event as much as in predicting the outcome of that event.

Skill and Chance

The differences between odds and handicapping provide one important dimension of gambling. Ultimately this relates to the payouts made on winning bets and how they are represented. Skill and chance is an even more fundamental division and relates to the capacity of gamblers to influence their likelihood of winning. In skill-based games it makes a difference whether one is a good or poor player. In games of chance, player ability is of limited consequence.

For some games – like housie – the dimensions of skill and chance are somewhat blurred. Strictly speaking, housie games are a lottery. Players receive numbered cards, a 'caller' picks numbers from a barrel and players then cross out the selected numbers on their cards. Players can claim a prize only when they cross out a line or some other combination of numbers on their card. Here are the elements of chance: winning combinations are selected at random; good and poor players face the same odds; prizes are awarded to the winning combinations. But there are also elements of skill which centre on the capacity of players to use multiple cards in a single game or draw. Good players can keep track of the numbers called across four, six or more cards and thereby enhance their chances of winning. Thus the difference with a lottery is that in housie it takes skill to identify and claim a winning combination of numbers. Indeed it is this skill, displayed as it is in the noise, smoke and conviviality of a housie game, which arguably is as much prized as winning.

Skill is more clear-cut in wagering. In the case of betting on races or sports events, skill is expressed in terms of reading the form. Form relates to the past performances of the protagonists. Form guides for racing and sporting events take many forms, including specialist publications (e.g. *Turf Digest*, *Rugby News*), sections in newspapers, websites (e.g. http://www.tab.co.nz/yahoo.html), radio and television programmes (e.g. *Reunion*) and even dedicated sports stations (e.g. Trackside TV, Radio Pacific). It was argued in the preceding section that the gambling operator, the house, has no incentive to publicise the odds; however, the positioning of form is more problematic. Indeed, by and large the publication of form guides merges seamlessly with the advertising of related gambling products. As noted, the TAB advertising campaign challenges: 'You know the odds, now beat them'. This campaign emphasises form, form guides and all the related – some would say interminable – discussions of form. In so far as knowing the form gives confidence to gamblers (to gamble), then operators are supportive of guides. In truth this reflects the house's ultimate control, through odds and handicapping, over the payouts made on winning bets.

Nevertheless, gambling operators are particularly sensitive to form guides which they regard as cheating. Recently cricket and US college basketball have been wracked by match-fixing scandals. Putting aside these conspiracies for the moment it is also apparent that gambling operators are generally averse to form guides which operate in the realm of insider knowledge. Just as insider knowledge – insider trading – is supposedly disbarred in stock exchanges around the world, so it is illegitimate in gambling. In the case of gambling this insider knowledge is likely to relate to which players are carrying injuries, team strategies, personality conflicts, behind the scenes ructions, etc. Insider knowledge poses a problem for gambling operators at two levels. First, there is the outside chance that such knowledge might result in losses to the house. This could be the case if gamblers knew something that gambling operators did not. The exemplars of this are 'card-counters' who are able to memorise the order of cards in the five decks commonly used to play blackjack. Such a feat of memory, coupled with a similar memorisation of the odds on winning hands, gives the accomplished card-counter a slight edge over the house. Perhaps unsurprisingly, this form of expertise is constituted as cheating and is illegal in all gambling jurisdictions. The narrative of all form guides is precisely of such insider knowledge, but this is actually a representational device which hides their construction as advertising or marketing.

Second, and more significant, is the problem of form guides as esoteric knowledge. This speaks to the credibility of gambling and in particular the notion that all gamblers face the same odds. Insider knowledge gives rise to the possibility that those who aren't 'in the know' may become disgruntled. In this sense the possibility that a few insiders win against the house is less important than the need to keep the majority in the game. There are parallels here with the faith needed to play gaming machines. Gamblers also need to have faith that the events they wager on are not fixed, and that all gamblers are treated equally. This conflation of faith and equity are two elements in the displacement of a discourse of gambling by one of gaming.

In so far as there is a discernable trajectory, it is found in the reconstitution of gambling as gaming. The difference between gambling and gaming is more than semantic. It speaks to the need for expertise in gambling – what sociologists call cultural capital. The traditional forms of gambling required this. The imagery here is of James Bond playing baccarat, of card sharks, of skilled people doing tricky and risky things. The antithesis of forms of gambling as forms of cultural capital is found in Las Vegas.[20] Las Vegas casinos provide gambling as entertainment available to everyone. No expertise is required to play these games, in fact anyone with the wherewithal can play. Similarly, televised lotteries like Lotto draw on images of games rather than gambling.[21] This extends even into the skill-based games, one example of which is found in the TAB's 'Pick6' option for placing bets. The Pick6 selection introduces a random, lottery-like element into the selection process which deskills the process and supposedly broadens its appeal. Similarly, rule changes in the card games that can be played in casinos increase the chance component and decrease the scope for skill. Hence 'Caribbean Stud Poker' deskills traditional poker, while the use of multiple decks and continuous shuffling deskills blackjack.

Play and Pathology

So far we have discussed the prevalence of gambling, its main components and some of its contexts. What is left is to address the question: of why people gamble? In doing so, we immediately confront contesting, even oppositional, framings of gambling. These can be distilled in terms of the perspectives of play and pathology. Gerda Reith notes that:

> In order to pick through the many approaches that constitute the contemporary literature, it is useful to look first at their historical predecessors, and so outline their intellectual heritage. Out of this morass, two separate traditions gradually emerge, from which our modern perspectives can be traced. One condones all forms of play as manifestations of the sublime element of human nature, while the other regards play in general and gambling in particular as inimical to a healthy society. Within a changing terminology of criticism, the latter has persistently regarded gambling as fundamentally problematic and condemned it as variously sinful, wasteful, criminal and pathological.[22]

Reith further argues that pathological framings have dominated framings of play. In the contemporary literature the ascendance of pathology over play has a disciplinary locus: psychology dominates sociology.

We will return to the contesting frames of psychology and sociology in the following section. For now it is worth noting the claim by Wildman: 'The literature on gambling is the most disconnected, confused mass of materials that I have ever come across.'[23] This is not an encouraging starting point but it bears directly on the question of why people gamble. In short, there is no simple answer to this question or even agreement on how to go about answering it. Reith is correct to demarcate the approaches to gambling in terms of pathology and play, but at the level of explaining behaviour the discussion is indeed a morass. One symptom of this confusion is the plethora of literature reviews which never quite succeed in developing a synthesis from the mass of material they appraise. For example, the governments of New Zealand and the United States recently commissioned reviews of the literature.[24] These are characterised by their large size and lack of functional conclusion. Partly as a result, the typology of behaviour offered here is partial. Further, this abridgement is not intended as a set of exclusionary categories. The categories should not be read in terms of 'either or' statements but as potentially overlapping explanations.

Addiction

Logically the best explanation for gambling as pathology is that it constitutes a form of individual addiction. Gambling (meaning pathological gambling) can then be understood as analogous to alcohol and drug dependence.[25] Of course there is an obvious difference between gambling and substance abuse in that the latter involves the ingestion of something (such as alcohol, heroin, cocaine, marijuana, or even fatty foods) which generates a physiological response that is addictive. The lack of an obvious trigger to pathological gambling means that proponents of gambling addiction have to cast about for other causes of physiological responses. In this sense pathological gamblers might be similar to individuals with sex addictions or exercise addictions or even 'shopaholics'. In other words, gambling (like sex or exercise or shopping) stimulates changes in the brain and body that are addictive.

Anyone who has spent time watching a gambler feed coins into a gaming machine for hours on end should find the notion of addiction compelling. From the outside at least, little seems to be going on.[26] Indeed watching people gamble (especially with machines rather than with other people) is boring in the extreme. At the same time, there are plenty of potential triggers for addiction: the repetition of gambling, its periodic rewards, its exciting packaging, even its unquestioning inclusiveness. Perhaps some of these elements are responsible for raising (or lowering) dopamine levels, or serotonin levels, or heartbeat, or alpha-wave production. Maybe these physiological responses are addictive. At the same time an increasing body of research has stressed the comorbidity of pathological gambling – 'comorbidity is the medical term used to describe the cooccurrence of two or more disorders in a single individual.'[27] Again anyone who has spent much time around gamblers will be able to testify to the presence of at least one addictive substance – tobacco. Casinos, racecourses, TABs, housie nights, clubs and pubs are typically very smoky places indeed.

Perhaps what is going on at these sites of gambling is best explained in terms of multiple addictions. Certainly the recent court cases in the United States against the manufacturers of cigarettes show the mileage that can be gained from claims to addiction. However, there are a number of problems with addiction in the case of gambling. The first is the methodological one of measuring physiological responses. That is, it seems unlikely that gamblers at the Sky City casino or Riccarton racecourse, or anywhere else, will ever consent to giving blood and tissue samples while they are playing. Taking these sorts of samples in a laboratory situation is a distant second-best. Consequently, collecting the evidence to substantiate a physiological chain of addiction is a highly problematic endeavour.

An even more significant problem is the conceptual one. If we accept that addiction (pathological gambling) is caused by engaging in gambling activities (as opposed to ingesting certain substances), then the problem remains of how to define gambling. Here the problem is one of identifying the unique characteristics of gambling that can act as physiological triggers. Unfortunately no such definition exists, largely because of the boundary gambling shares with other forms of risk-taking. In this sense what makes gambling distinct are laws, norms, contexts and culture, and not its physiological imperatives. If we are to talk of gambling addicts, we can also talk of people as addicted to all the other and myriad forms of risk-taking and thrill-seeking. While this might have a certain journalistic purchase, it is a poor foundation for analysis.

Irrationality

Walker speculates on three core beliefs of regular gamblers:

> 1. That through persistence, knowledge and skill it is possible for a person to make money through gambling. 2. While many will fail in the attempt, the gambler believes that her or she, unlike those others, has the resources needed to win. 3. That persistence in applying oneself to the task will ultimately be rewarded.[28]

Walker regards these beliefs as irrational. And in so far as the intent of gamblers is to win money there can be little doubt that regular or sustained gambling is futile. Frederick Nietzsche long ago argued that when faced with limited resources and unfavourable odds, the most rational strategy for the gambler (in truth, all individuals) is the all-or-nothing wager. At least there is some, 'slim', chance of winning with such a wager, whereas a series of small bets only guarantees defeat. After all, the main operating principle of casinos is that if the gambler can be convinced to keep on gambling, he or she will eventually lose.

Psychologists explain this 'irrational thinking' in terms of cognitive dissonance. Gamblers, in order to justify their (losing) behaviour, deny the real odds and continue gambling under the misapprehension that they have a real chance of winning. The notion of addiction leads to abstinence as an appropriate response to gambling (or at least to problem gambling), while the notion of cognitive dissonance leads to harm-reduction strategies. Harm-reduction strategies centre on educating gamblers on the odds.[29] In effect they are about making gamblers better players so as to better limit their losses. Providing information is seen as the panacea for irrational thinking.

Sociologists are less certain about the divisions between rational and irrational thinking than are psychologists. For example, psychologists label one form of thinking as the 'illusion of control' (which refers to the 'locus of control'). Put simply, this refers to determining the internal or external control of situations individuals find themselves in. In this case, according to psychologists, the gambler irrationally believes that he or she has control of the situation. The gambler posits internal control, the psychologists external. The above discussion of the elements of play might suggest that external control (e.g. odds, chance and probability) is indeed the case, but Reith problematises even this.

Reith argues that probability theory can only describe the spread of events in the long run – the very long run – and certainly not what is going to happen next. This long-term aspect of probability is of little or no interest to gamblers. Gamblers are acutely interested in what will happen next, in the determination of a bet or wager. Consequently, framing gambling in terms of rationality is pointless as a scientific endeavour and, worse still, one which invalidates the lived experiences of most people. In following this line of argument we have arrived at what might be called the postmodern critique of science and its disciplines (including psychology *and* sociology). In this respect Reith posits the 'magical-religious worldview' as an alternative framing of gambling. Within this worldview luck and superstition are as valid as the measures of rationality. Indeed this type of approach aims to obliterate the distinctions between rational and irrational portrayals of human action.

There can be little doubt that gamblers rely on luck and superstition to guide them. Banal examples can be found in the wearing of a 'lucky rabbit's foot', or using birth dates to pick Lotto, or insisting that a particular gaming machine is due for a win.[30] More broadly still, most of us seem to hold to some aspects of the magical-religious worldview. In part this is because of the impossibility of calculating the odds in modern life. For example, who can say if our superannuation schemes will pay out in thirty years, or if our partners are truly faithful, or if choosing sociology rather than accounting was the right choice? Like players of gaming machines we are all forced to rely on faith. In essence we have to accept others' representations of the world.

The division between rational and irrational thinking is then not so obvious as psychologists are wont to claim. Furthermore, luck and superstition have the advantage of being able to explain the runs of good and bad luck which seemingly mark all of our lives. Not only are these aspects of luck and superstition inherently meaningful, they are ultimately irrefutable as analytical practice precisely because they are constituted outside the realm of evidence and rationality. However, while the postmodern critique has enjoyed considerable success in academic circles it is largely ridiculed outside of academe. This is deserved in so far as the critique ignores some fairly obvious aspects of everyday life. Most significant is the imbalance or asymmetry between framings of luck and probability.

The question should be asked: 'Which approach – luck or probability – is the better at explaining people's humdrum lives?' In this case luck opens up arguments about magic on the one hand and religion on the other. Magic offers the possibility for heightened forms of agency within which individuals can transcend the material constraints of their lives. Casting spells is one example of this transcendence, and positive visualisation is another. In contrast, religion engages with predestination and the omnipotence of an extra-human agency. The forms of agency made available through religion are that of the plaintiff and supplicant. But the issue remains of whether these framings of everyday life are credible. The short answer is no. The long answer is very long indeed. Suffice to say that the magical-religious worldview stumbles precisely at the point of inequality, at the distribution of results and life chances. That is, the inequalities of social life are so clearly patterned in terms of ethnicity, class, gender and wealth as to render the explanatory power of luck and superstition trivial in the extreme. In these terms the influence of probability swamps any of luck. Returning to gambling, the cliché is that places like Las Vegas are built on losers. This highlights that in the contest between the house and gamblers, probability inevitably beats out luck.

Action

Addiction is the classical psychological framing of gambling. Its counterpart in sociology is that of action. Action is a concept developed by Erving Goffman to describe the 'willful undertaking of serious chances'.[31] The manipulation of chance is understood here in very different terms to that of the psychologists. The psychological approach is to emphasise gambling as a means of exchanging (winning or losing) money. Given that the odds are stacked against gamblers, this is an unavoidably irrational undertaking. However the classical sociological approach is to view gambling as an arena for the exchange of an immaterial commodity, what we might call social honour. Clifford Geertz, an anthropologist now claimed by sociology, observed that wagering on cockfighting in Bali was as much about status as it was about the exchange of money.[32] Thus it was as important to be perceived as a good winner or loser as it was to win or lose wagers. From this perspective gambling, even where it sustains heavy losses, can be understood as rational. In short rationality is not universal but is bounded by the social context in which gambling takes place.

Goffman suggested that gambling represents one form of action, the purpose of which is to test and prove an individual's character. Winning money *per se* does not figure in this analysis, indeed it is the losing bets which best provide a test:

> Plainly, it is during moments of action that the individual has the risk and opportunity of displaying to himself and sometimes to others his style of conduct when the chips are down. Character is gambled; a single good showing can be taken as representative, and a bad showing cannot be easily excused or re-attempted.[33]

Goffman even categorised the major forms of character that are so tested and displayed: courage, gameness, integrity, gallantry, composure and confidence. While the concept of action does not rule out the possibility of pathological or problem gamblers, it certainly problematises them. In this sense Goffman, like most sociologists, is interested in the gambler as normal rather than in the psychologically constructed deviant.[34] We'll return to this issue in the closing section.

At this point it is useful to identify some limitations in Goffman's version of action. Firstly, it is imbued with a Hemingwayesque machismo. There are obvious parallels here between the gambler and the bullfighter, etc., but is it reasonable to draw these comparisons? Putting aside the sexism of the language used, is it valid to approach the everyday as a series of definitional struggles? Goffman seems to approach the hyperbole of Nietzsche in this regard. Possibly Goffman's dramaturgy overstates and glamorises the humdrum everyday. Secondly, and more clearly, is his focus on human interaction? The examples Goffman uses are card and coin games which provide face-to-face interactions, but in the case of gambling these interactions are increasingly mediated by technology. The extent to which technology (e.g. gaming machines, the Internet) runs with or counter to the notion of action is left hanging. For example, the concluding section in Goffman's article seems to problematise his own argument, in so far as face-to-face interaction is marginalised:

Commercialization, of course, brings the final mingling of fantasy and action. And it has an ecology. On the arcade strips of urban settlements and summer resorts, scenes are available for hire where the customers can be the star performer in gambles enlivened by being very slightly consequential. Here a person currently without social connections can insert coins in skill machines to demonstrate to the other machines that he has socially approved qualities of character. These naked little spasms of the self occur at the end of the world, but there at the end is action and character.[35]

Of course another take is to emphasise the experience of having fun, of entertainment. This approach seems particularly useful, given the ways in which traditional forms of gambling are ceding to gaming. In this sense the tensions found in Goffman's account relate to the restricted possibilities for 'action' in forms of gaming. In other words, how inconsequential can something be before it ceases to be open to action? Rather the linking of 'gambling as gaming as entertainment as fun' provides a useful starting point for analysis. Zygmunt Bauman suggests that capitalist society is founded on a work ethic which marginalises the possibilities for undisciplined behaviour, including fun.[36] In this regard, fun emerges as an aspect of entertainment which – as Goffman rightly identified – is thoroughly commercialised. Thus fun isn't a free-floating spontaneous experience, but is channelled through commercial outlets and sensibilities. George Ritzer has coined the term 'McDonaldization' to account for the commercialisation and disciplining of modern life. Bryman has extended this idea in terms of 'Disneyization', in which entertainment is simultaneously packaged and disciplined as forms of risk-taking, albeit in very anaemic forms.[37]

Framing Gambling

There can be little argument that psychologists rather than sociologists conduct the bulk of research on gambling. This is doubly true of research that is funded by agencies of government. In New Zealand, funded research on gambling has been monopolised by teams led by psychologists. Elsewhere in the world the dominance of psychologists in gambling research also holds. In part this reflects the focus of psychologists on pathological or problem gambling. Government funding is after all directed at solving social problems, and in this regard psychology is probably a safer bet than sociology. But this dominance is also the product of what Paul Starr calls 'the politics of numbers'.[38] The epistemology and methods deployed by psychologists result in an appeal to science, hypothesis testing, screeds of numbers and, most importantly of all, the promise of certainty. We might call this a positivist approach. From the perspective of most government agencies a sociological approach is much less appealing, precisely because it may seek to problematise what are commonsense assumptions and is more often than not anti- or post-positivist. Putting it simply, government agencies are more comfortable with the results of psychological research in so far as it is characterised by claims to objectivity and to the validity of individualised treatment.

Arguably the developments in sociology which emphasise the social construction of social problems and attack the rationality/irrationality dualism make the discipline even less attractive to the bureaucratic mindset.[39] Indeed for sociologists, the category of pathological gambling is of more interest than the characteristics of putative pathological gamblers. The main thrust of this study has examined the social construction of 'pathological gambling' as a vehicle for professional and popular claims-making.[40] This speaks to the possibility that by categorising tens of thousands of New Zealanders as pathological or problem gamblers we deny the lived experience of people, while creating an 'out' for the gambling industry. After all, if individuals have problems with gambling because they are sick, social problems cannot be said to lie with gambling itself. This is an attractive proposition for both gambling operators and the government, which collects significant revenues from gambling.[41]

Endnotes

1   Abbott, M.W. and Volberg, R.A. (1999) *Gambling and Problem Gambling in the Community: An International Overview and Critique*, Department of Internal Affairs: Wellington, 57–72.

2   Christoffel, P. (1992) *Peoples' Participation In and Attitudes Towards Gambling*, Department of Internal Affairs: Wellington; Reid, K. and Searle, W. (1996) *Peoples' Participation In and Attitudes Towards Gambling: Final Results of the 1995 Survey*, Department of Internal Affairs: Wellington; Wither, P. (1987) *Taking a Gamble: A Survey of Public Attitudes Towards Gambling in New Zealand*, Department of Internal Affairs: Wellington.

3   Abbott, M.W. and Volberg, R.A. (1991) *Gambling and Problem Gambling in New Zealand*, Department of Internal Affairs: Wellington; Abbott, M.W. and Volberg, R.A. (1992) *Frequent Gamblers and Problem Gamblers in New Zealand*, Department of Internal Affairs: Wellington; Abbott, M.W. and Volberg, R.A. (1996) The New Zealand National Survey of Problem and Pathological Gambling, *Journal of Gambling Studies*, 12,2: 143–160; Abbott, M.W. and

Volberg, R.A. (2000) *Taking the Pulse on Gambling and Problem Gambling in New Zealand: A Report on Phase One of the 1999 National Prevalence Survey*, Department of Internal Affairs: Wellington; Abbott, M.W., Williams, M.M. and Volberg, R.A. (1999) *Seven Years On: A Follow-Up Study of Frequent and Problem Gamblers Living in the Community*, Department of Internal Affairs: Wellington.

4　North Health (1996) *Interim Report on Problem Gambling Management*, North Health: Auckland; McMillen, J., Austrin, T., Curtis, B., Lynch, R. and Pearce, D. (1998) *Study of the Social and Economic Impacts of New Zealand Casinos*, Australian Institute for Gambling Research: Campbelltown.

5　Wither, op. cit.

6　Christoffel, op. cit.; Reid and Searle, op. cit.

7　McMillen *et al.*, op. cit.

8　Abbott and Volberg (2000) op. cit.: 4.

9　Abbott and Volberg (1999) op. cit.: 59.

10　Manly, B. F., Gonzalez, L. and Sullivan, C.(1992) Statistical errors in Abbott/ Volberg report (1992) on problem gambling in New Zealand, New Zealand Lotteries Commission: Wellington.

11　Abbott and Volberg (2000) op. cit.: 7.

12　Abbott and Volberg (1999) op. cit.: 58–61.

13　Howland, P. (1996) Benign Gambling to the New Zealand Good Life: *Lotto* Television Adverts from 1987 to 1992, *New Zealand Journal of Media Studies*, 1, 2: 46–58.

14　Austrin, T. (1998) Retailing Leisure: Local and Global Developments in Gambling, in Perkins, H.C and G. Cushman (eds) *Time Out? Leisure, Recreation and Tourism in New Zealand and Australia*, Longman: Auckland, 167–181; Grant, D. (1994) *On a Roll: A History of Gambling and Lotteries in New Zealand*, Victoria University Press: Wellington.

15　Curtis, B.M. (forthcoming), State Licensing, Taxation and the Marginalization of Community Forms of Gambling, *New Zealand Sociology*; Markland, J. (1996) Gaming in New Zealand, *Social Policy Journal of New Zealand*, 7: 79–92.

16　Abbott and Volberg (1999) op. cit., 17–18.

17　Walker, M. (1992) *The Psychology of Gambling*, Pergamon Press: Oxford, cited in Abbot and Volberg (2000) op. cit.: 17.

18　Reith, G. (1999) *The Age of Chance: Gambling in Western Culture*, Routledge: London: 1.

19　Howland, op. cit.

20　Austrin, T. and Curtis, B. (1999) Simulation and Surveillance: Developments in the Production and Consumption of Real and Virtual Gaming, in Collis, M. Munro, L. and Russell, S. (eds) *Sociology for a New Millennium: TASA Conference Proceedings*, CeLTS, Monash University, Melbourne: 483–490; Wolfe, T. (1965) 'Las Vegas (What?) Las Vegas (Can't hear you! Too noisy)

Las Vegas!!!', in *The Kandy-Kolored Tangerine-Flake Streamline Baby*, Farrar: New York: 15–32.
21 Howland, op. cit.; Munting, R. (1998) The Revival of Lotteries in Britain: Some International Comparisons of Public Policy, *History: The Journal of the Historical Association*, 83, 272: 628–646.
22 Reith, op. cit.: 3.
23 Wildman, R.W. (1998) *Gambling: An Attempt at Integration*, Wynne Resources, Edmonton: ii.
24 Abbott and Volberg (1999), op. cit.; Committee on the Social and Economic Impact of Pathological Gambling, Committee on Law and Justice, Commission on Behavioral and Social Sciences and Education, National Research Council, (1999), *Pathological Gambling: A Critical Review*, National Academy Press: Washington, D.C.
25 Walker, op. cit.: 171–189.
26 Austrin and Curtis, op. cit.
27 Committee on the Social and Economic Impact of Pathological Gambling, op. cit.: 127.
28 Walker, op. cit.: 1.
29 Cotton, P. (1994) Harm Reduction Approach May Be Middle Ground, *Journal of the American Medical Association*, 271, 21: 161–165.
30 Howland, op. cit.
31 Goffman, E. (1972) Where the Action Is, in Goffman, E. (ed.) *Interaction Ritual: Essays on Face to Face Behavior*, Allen Lane: New York: 149–270.
32 Geertz, C. (1983) Deep Play: Notes on the Balinese Cockfight, in Geertz, C. (ed.) *The Interpretation of Cultures*, Basic Books: New York: 412–453.
33 Goffman, op. cit.: 237.
34 Castellani, B. (2000) *Pathological Gambling: The Making of a Medical Problem*, State University of New York Press: New York; Kutchins, H. and S.A. Kirk (1997) *Making Us Crazy. DSM: The Psychiatric Bible and Creation of Mental Disorders*, Free Press: New York; Wedgeworth, R.L. (1998) The Reification of the 'Pathologic' Gambler: An Analysis of Gambling Treatment and the Application of the Medical Model to Problem Gambling, *Perspectives in Psychiatric Care*, 34, 2: 5–14.
35 Goffman, op. cit.: 269–270.
36 Bauman, Z. (1998) *Work, Consumerism and the New Poor*, Open University Press: Buckingham.
37 Bryman, A. (1999) The Disneyization of Society, *Sociological Review*, 47, 1: 25–38.
38 Starr, P. (1987) The Sociology of Official Statistics, in Alonso, W. and Starr, P. (eds) *The Politics of Numbers: Population of the United States in the 1980s*, Russell Sage Foundation: New York.
39 Best, J. (ed.) (1995) *Images of Issues: Typifying Contemporary Social Problems*, De Gruyter: New York.

[40] Castellani, op. cit.; Kutchins and Kirk, op. cit.
[41] Ereckson, O.H., Platt. G., Whistler, C. and Ziegert, A.L. (1999) Factors Influencing the Adoption of State Lotteries, *Applied Economics*, 31, 7: 875–891.

Bibliography

Abbott, M.W. and Volberg, R.A. (1991) *Gambling and Problem Gambling in New Zealand*, Wellington: Department of Internal Affairs.
Abbott, M.W. and Volberg, R.A. (1992) *Frequent Gamblers and Problem Gamblers in New Zealand*, Wellington: Department of Internal Affairs.
Abbott, M.W. and Volberg, R.A. (1996) 'The New Zealand National Survey of Problem and Pathological Gambling', *Journal of Gambling Studies*, 12, 2: 143–160.
Abbott, M.W. and Volberg, R.A. (1999) *Gambling and Problem Gambling in the Community: An International Overview and Critique*, Wellington: Department of Internal Affairs.
Abbott, M.W. and Volberg, R.A. (2000) *Taking the Pulse on Gambling and Problem Gambling in New Zealand: A Report on Phase One of the 1999 National Prevalence Survey*, Wellington: Department of Internal Affairs.
Abbott, M.W., Williams, M.M. and Volberg, R.A. (1999) *Seven Years On: A Follow-Up Study of Frequent and Problem Gamblers Living in the Community*, Wellington: Department of Internal Affairs.
Austrin, T. (1998) 'Retailing Leisure: Local and Global Developments in Gambling', in Perkins, H.C and Cushman, G.' (eds) *Time Out? Leisure, Recreation and Tourism in New Zealand and Australia*, Auckland: Longman, 167–181.
Austrin, T. and Curtis, B. (1999) 'Simulation and Surveillance: Developments in the Production and Consumption of Real and Virtual Gaming', in Collis, M., Munro, L. and Russell, S. (eds), *Sociology for a New Millennium: TASA Conference Proceedings*, CeLTS, Melbourne: Monash University, 483–490.
Bauman, Z. (1998) *Work, Consumerism and the New Poor*, Buckingham: Open University Press.
Best, J. (ed.) (1995) *Images of Issues: Typifying Contemporary Social Problems*, New York: De Gruyter.
Bryman, A. (1999) 'The Disneyization of Society', *Sociological Review*, 47, 1: xx–xx.
Castellani, B. (2000) *Pathological Gambling: The Making of a Medical Problem*, State University of New York: New York Press.

Christoffel, P. (1992) *Peoples' Participation In and Attitudes Towards Gambling*, Wellington: Department of Internal Affairs.

Committee on the Social and Economic Impact of Pathological Gambling, Committee on Law and Justice, Commission on Behavioral and Social Sciences and Education, National Research Council (1999) *Pathological Gambling: A Critical Review*, Washington, D.C: Academy Press.

Cotton, P. (1994) 'Harm Reduction Approach May Be Middle Ground', *Journal of the American Medical Association*, 271, 21: 161–165.

Curtis, B.M. (forthcoming) 'State Licensing, Taxation and the Marginalization of Community Forms of Gambling', *New Zealand Sociology*.

Ereckson, O.H., Platt. G., Whistler, C. and Ziegert, A.L. (1999) 'Factors Influencing the Adoption of State Lotteries', *Applied Economics*, 31, 7: 875–891.

Geertz, C. (1983) 'Deep Play: Notes on the Balinese Cockfight', in Geertz, C. (ed.) *The Interpretation of Cultures*, New York: Basic Books, pp. 412–453

Goffman, E. (1967) 'Where the Action Is', in Goffman, E. (ed.) *Interaction Ritual: Essays on Face to Face Behavior*, 14e–270.

Grant, D. (1994) *On a Roll: A History of Gambling and Lotteries in New Zealand*, Wellington: Victoria University Press.

Howland, P. (1996) Benign Gambling to the New Zealand Good Life: Lotto Television Adverts from 1987 to 1992, *New Zealand Journal of Media Studies*, 1, 2: 46–58.

Kutchins, H. and Kirk, S.A. (1997) *Making Us Crazy. DSM: The Psychiatric Bible and Creation of Mental Disorders*, New York: Free Press.

Markland, J. (1996) 'Gaming in New Zealand', *Social Policy Journal of New Zealand*, 7: 79–92.

McMillen, J., Austrin, T., Curtis, B., Lynch, R. and Pearce, D. (1998) *Study of the Social and Economic Impacts of New Zealand Casinos*, Campbelltown: Australian Institute for Gambling Research.

Munting, R. (1998) 'The Revival of Lotteries in Britain: Some International Comparisons of Public Policy', *History: The Journal of the Historical Association*, 83, 272: 628–646.

North Health (1996) *Interim Report on Problem Gambling Management*, Auckland: North Health.

Reid, K. and Searle, W. (1996) *Peoples' Participation In and Attitudes Towards Gambling: Final Results of the 1995 Survey*, Wellington: Department of Internal Affairs.

NB→ Reith, G. (1999) *The Age of Chance: Gambling in Western Culture*, London: Routledge.

Starr, P. (1987) 'The Sociology of Official Statistics', in Alonso, W. and Starr, P. (eds) *The Politics of Numbers: Population of the United States in the 1980s*, New York: Sage Foundation.

Walker, M. (1992) *The Psychology of Gambling*, Oxford: Pergamon Press.

Wedgeworth, R.L. (1998) 'The Reification of the 'Pathologic' Gambler: An Analysis of Gambling Treatment and the Application of the Medical Model to Problem Gambling', *Perspectives in Psychiatric Care*, 34, 2: 5–14.

Wildman, R.W. (1998) *Gambling: An Attempt at Integration*, Edmonton: Wynne Resources.

Wither, P. (1987) *Taking a Gamble: A Survey of Public Attitudes Towards Gambling in New Zealand*, Wellington: Department of Internal Affairs.

12

Death, Every Day

Tracey McIntosh

The Familiarity of Death

We encounter death every day of our lives. Most of these encounters are so much a part of our daily routine that we do not even recognise them for what they are. In the weeks preceding the writing of this chapter the New Zealand public had experienced, through newspapers and television screens; an 'outbreak' of suspicious deaths;[1] a debate around the use by Associate Maori Affairs Minister Tariana Turia of the term 'holocaust' to describe what Maori tribes suffered during the colonisation period; strike action by junior doctors; ongoing calls to seek strategies to redress our alarming child abuse figures and a deposition hearing to determine whether a former airline pilot should go to trial on four charges of manslaughter and three of injuring, resulting from an airline accident in the Tararua Ranges in June 1995. From a front-page shot of a bloodied telephone used by a brutally attacked man to contact the police, to the last-page 'births', 'deaths' and 'in memoriam' columns, our lives are awash with death.[2]

Giddens argues that when seen in a purely biological sense, death is relatively unproblematic: it is simply the cessation of the physiological functions of the organism.[3] In contrast to biological death, 'subjective death' is an absolute uncertainty, something which we truly have no way of knowing.[4] Giddens sees death as an excellent example of what he calls 'fateful moments', that is, moments where individuals have to confront problems which societies have kept away from public consciousness.[5] These fateful moments are paralleled by Berger's 'marginal situations'. Berger sees the confrontation with death (either the death of others or the thought of one's own death) as the most significant marginal situation:

Death radically challenges all socially objectivated definitions of reality – of the world, of others, and of self. Death radically puts in question the taken-for-granted, 'business as usual' attitude in which one exists in everyday life. There, everything in the daytime world of existence in society is massively threatened with 'irreality' – that is, everything in that world becomes delusions, eventually unreal, other than one had used to think.[6]

Kearl similarly notes that a basic accomplishment of any cultural orientation is its capacity to give symbolic order and meaning to human mortality. For the most part the majority of us rarely experience the precariousness of social life. We expect an ordered, predictable world, where our actions and the actions of others can be anticipated and understood. However, Kearl asserts that there are times when a 'reality rip' occurs within the fabric of this cultural canopy of security.[7] This reality rip may take the form of a natural disaster, such as the recent floods in Mozambique; a national tragedy, such as the explosion and sinking of the Russian submarine *Kursk* that led to the loss of 118 lives in the Barents Sea; the horror of a mass shooting, such as in Aramoana in November 1990; or a personal calamity such as losing a child to disease. For the survivors of such events the predictable world becomes malevolent.

The struggle merely to survive has for many of us become a thing of the past, yet modernity, while freeing us from the relentless quotidianal aspect of death, has presented us with the opportunity to witness death on the grand scale. Note, I say *witness:* death for the most part has become a spectator sport. This is not to argue that pleasure is extracted from watching this endless spectacle, but the evening news complete with its daily dose of death is absorbing while appalling, the action film (action here synonymous with creative violence and often innumerable deaths) or the medical drama which follows is seen at the very least as distracting. We are saturated with images of death. The mass media supplies us with a steady stream of encounters with a mortality that is always strangely 'other'. Apart from when we personally lose significant others to death 'the death lessons of modern individuals are primarily received from television, cinema, newspapers and the arts'.[8] We may practise death but it is of a particular type: careers, lifestyles, business affairs, relationships have a 'natural death'; bonds once considered permanent are now often seen as coming with an embedded use-by date. Bauman asserts that though death, that is personal death, is largely ignored in modern society it can be argued that '[d]eath is rehearsed repetitively, before we are widowed we are more likely than not to have faced the dissolution of a partnership. The new is celebrated, the "not so young" is revamped and revitalised'. [9] Death for the most part is second-hand and this distancing has, far from making us more secure, increased our anxiety and dread of it striking close. We live in a time in which we have created a vast array of sophisticated technological procedures for 'saving' life yet we have been unable to remove the shadow of the valley of death; if anything the shadow has darkened.

Death Systems

Momento mori – remember your death. In fifteenth-century Christian Europe this piece of advice underscored a death system that maintained that awareness and acknowledgment of one's mortality needed to be seen as a daily endeavour. In a time when religious beliefs were crucial to the way that the social world was perceived, it was seen as essential to be well prepared for the inevitability of one's demise. The emphasis was on the brevity of human life and the possibility of a sudden death. The reality of living conditions at the time meant that this lesson was reinforced with some frequency. For the most part, lives were likely to be relatively short and people died of acute rather than chronic illnesses. The Christian tradition meant that death was related to a number of images; it could be seen as both a punishment and a blessing. This specific knowledge of death and one's encounters with it determined the way that death was perceived and understood. Today, a preoccupation with mortality, a sense that there is a need to constantly envision those final moments, is unlikely to be seen as legitimate – indeed, it is likely to be viewed as at best a morbid curiosity, and at worst as a manifestation of a serious psychiatric disorder. The nature of death changes as the social fabric that it is embedded in changes.

When and under what circumstances did you first encounter death? The answer to this question is in part an exercise in identifying your social location. It is not uncommon for New Zealanders to attend their first funeral relatively late in life. Many people's first experience of the death of a significant other, usually a close family member, does not occur until they are in their thirties. For others, attending tangi from a very young age is an accepted part of the socialisation process. Our encounters with death are important to the way we understand death. Robert Kastenbaum describes a death system as being 'the interpersonal, sociophysical and symbolic network through which an individual's relationship to mortality is mediated by his or her society.'[10] A death system teaches us what to think about death, how to feel about it and what to do in regard to it. A death system is the total range of thought, feeling and behaviour that is directly or indirectly related to death. People, places and things that represent death or bereavement to us are part of our death system. In any society there may exist many death systems, offerring competing explanations on the way death is mediated within that society. In Aotearoa New Zealand, Maori death rituals highlight a distinct death system.

Tangihanga (Maori mourning and funeral rituals) remain an important element of Maori identity. It could be argued that tangi have come to have an even greater importance in Maori lives than previously. Tangihanga are often viewed by Maori as one of the few elements of their pre-contact lives that remain. Though there is a tendency to view tangi as immutable and unchanging – something that is clearly not the case – this does highlight an emphasis and need to stress a continuity with the past. More importantly, it reflects the very political element that tangi have come to play in Maori lives. Tangi are one of the ways that Maori reaffirm their collective identity and participate as a social group. Karen Sinclair, in looking at the part that tangi play in constructing a Maori identity, notes that these 'rituals punctuate the round of daily life by marking extraordinary events in a distinctively Maori manner'.[11] She argues that the modern tangi removes Maori from a world grounded by Pakeha rules and places them in a context perceived as a total Maori experience. The tangi and its values see Maori as social actors in an arena that is subject to Maori, not Pakeha, definitions. The tangi provides a refuge from a society that frequently marginalises Maori culture and an opportunity to redefine the position of Maori in New Zealand society.[12]

Harry Dansey underscores the importance of letting death have a place in life. He feels that whereas the Pakeha attitude towards death seems to be based on the belief (usually left unstated) that the dead must be hurriedly dealt with – with as little fuss as possible, for Maori death, ritual is about placing the dead and reaffirming the living:

> The death of a relation, even one whom I know so little, if at all, affects me deeply, just because of relationship. To many Maori, and certainly to me, it is enough that we were related, enough to give me reason to mourn. The comment 'why, I hardly knew him' does not have the same import as it has to Pakeha. My relation and I are a part of the same tree, we share the same ancestry and the claims of that ancestry are very real.[13]

Dansey states that the difference between the two cultures is not about how people feel about the dead, but how they express their feelings. Maori culture demands that the expression is a public one. 'The New Zealand European culture so firmly sets its face against public, visible, emotional expression of grief. I respect that difference and do not say that one way is better than another. But my way is my way and I will keep it.'[14]

It is interesting to note that we are now seeing Maori elements in non-Maori funerals.[15] Much of this is generated by a desire of many people to become more involved in the death process. Though many cultures had previously attended to the dead body at home, as little as thirty years ago in New Zealand this was an uncommon practice in non-Maori homes. It is now becoming more common, particularly in regards to the deaths of young people. Likewise, it is a mistake to believe that tangihanga have remained unchanged over time. Culture is dynamic not static, and the tangi has adapted to the impact of colonisation, introduced systems of belief, urbanisation and modernisation. As a child growing up with a Maori mother and a Pakeha father, I realised early that death was understood and expressed differently by different peoples. As I grew older I came to understand that the significance of the tangi went far beyond the farewelling of a loved family member, but was also inclusive of a political expression of solidarity and identity. Given the social reality of Maori, it needs to be noted that Maori are likely to have a far greater exposure to death than non-Maori. Our exposure to death and bereavement is an important factor that influences the way we perceive death.

Death Inequalities

Death, like life, is not equal. Social location, to a great extent, determines the type of death you are likely to experience. Class, gender and ethnicity play an important role in locating your probable cause of death. In the past hundred years the average life expectancy of New Zealanders has risen significantly. A temperate climate, low population density, lack of heavy industry and good nutrition meant that from the middle of the nineteenth century until the 1930s, New Zealand had the lowest mortality rate in the world.[16] The improvement in lifespan mostly occurred prior to the 1930s and was due to saving lives at younger ages. The infant mortality rate fell in association with a major reduction in infectious and respiratory diseases, which were previously the main cause of death. Recent data indicate that heart disease, cancer and cerebrovascular diseases are the three leading causes of death in New Zealand, and together account for three-fifths of all death among the adult population in any year. Respiratory diseases claim another ten per cent. Motor-vehicle accidents cause another three per cent of all deaths in a year, with people in the age group of 15–24 accounting for over four-fifths of these fatalities.[17] Since 1972 there has been a gain of a little over five years in the life expectancy at birth for men and four and a half years for women. Although the nation has benefited from better living standards, advances in medical technology and improvements in health services, these benefits have been unevenly distributed. In 1990–1992 the average life expectancy of Maori males was 68 years, compared with 73 years for Maori females, while for non-Maori, life expectancies were 73.4 years for males and 79.2 years for females.[18] Statistics are useful in giving an overview of a social phenomenon but there is a need to be mindful that numbers alone can obscure the lived reality for many people. What are the social consequences of Maori men living five years less than their non-Maori counterparts? People's health and life expectancy have always differed according to their position in society. The types of death may change, but overall 'wealthy people continue to have better health and live longer to enjoy it than poorer people'.[19]

There is strong evidence linking vulnerability to ill health with low income. Income inequalities in New Zealand diminished post-World War II until the 1970s, but increased markedly between 1987 and 1991. This growth in inequalities is particularly marked in relation to Maori and Pacific Island communities. Maori health status in the 1990s could be characterised by:

- higher risk of low birthweight and death during the first year of life than non-Maori;
- higher risk of injury, both accidental and non-accidental, during childhood and adolescence than non-Maori;
- higher risk of infectious diseases, including pneumonia, tuberculosis and rheumatic fever than non-Maori;
- higher risk of hospitalisation for and deaths from asthma than non-Maori;
- increasing rates of suicide and hospital admission for mental illness;
- higher risks of cancers, especially those of the lung, cervix, stomach, liver and uterus than non-Maori;
- higher risk of heart disease, especially coronary, hypertensive and rheumatic heart disease than non-Maori;
- higher risk of diabetes and its complications than non-Maori;
- higher risk of hospitalisation for and death from for road crashes than non-Maori;
- higher risk of injury and death from violence than non-Maori;

- a level of access to primary health services less than estimated need;
- institutional barriers to secondary or tertiary care;
- lower life expectancy, and life expectancy lived free of disability, than non-Maori;
- lower levels of health prerequisites such as education, adequate housing, income and employment than non-Maori;
- higher likelihood of belonging to a low socio-economic group than non-Maori;
- a greater likelihood of living in areas with higher rates of poverty and lower levels of servicing than non-Maori;[20]

Philippa Howden-Chapman notes that the behavioural and health effects of unequal resource distribution indicate a breakdown in social and community relations.[21] She further notes that health and wellness is more than just the absence of personal illness or injury: 'well-being involves consideration of collective well-being, sense of community and the community's pool of organised "social capital" from which individuals can draw'.[22] She feels that to arrive at more equal health outcomes in society there is a strong case for better distribution of economic and social resources.

Death Changes

An appreciation of death in an everyday context needs to acknowledge that death alters over time and place. Death changes. The death that we experience presently may have little in common with the death experienced previously. Philippe Ariès' *The Hour of Our Death* spans more than a millennium of European attitudes towards death.[23] Though his work has generated criticism. in regards to both method and interpretation,[24] it is still important in mapping the considerable changes in attitudes and perceptions of death. Though Ariès' work is geographically and historically specific to Christian Europe, it is useful in examining the provenance of ideas that have held or still hold currency in New Zealand. Ariès notes these changing responses towards death in what he sees as five distinct though often overlapping attitudes. Whaley argues that Ariès' entire work is based on the general proposition that an individual's relationship with death has become increasingly distorted as a result of human progress.[25]

The first attitude is what Ariès sees as being 'the tame death'. It is characterised by the total harmony of the living and the dead. Far from being something to fear, the condition is expected and accepted as inevitable. Indeed those who try and avoid it or stay too long in the world of the living are scorned. This is illustrated by La Fontaine's comment on the aged who appear to wish to cheat death: 'he who most resembles the dead is the most reluctant to die'.[26] Death is not over-dramatised, but is presented simply and appears, in a fashion, where:

> ... the death-bed ritual is the central and most symbolic aspect of death in a society which trusts in the ability of the Church to take care of the souls of the departed. Individuals accept death as a kind of extended sleep, confident in the ultimate resurrection of the body in the Last Judgement.'[27]

Ariès sees this acceptance of both death and dying as typical of most pre-modern societies. The next attitude Ariès sees as developing is the 'death of the self' – that is, the individualised death. Within Europe he locates this in the context of a small intellectual élite generating a specific version of the Last Judgement: '(t)he individual and his destiny takes precedence over the community – a change reflected in the institution of requiem masses for individuals rather than the occasional collective commemorations and in the new emphasis on the funeral rather than the deathbed'.[28]

This second attitude is also characterised by the increasing ostentatiousness of funerals, the tendency for these events to become celebrations that highlight the social status and material wealth of the deceased. There is a general ambiance of a vigour for life and its pleasures, and this is highlighted against the backdrop of the *danse macabre*. Ariès sees the *danse macabre* as a symbol of the love for life against the chance of death. 'In danse macabre the encounter between Man and Death is not violent. The gesture of Death is almost gentle: 'My hand must fall on you. Death warns more often than it strikes.'[29]

The third attitude is labelled 'remote and imminent death'. This is a complex phase and must be understood in the context that all the attitudes overlap and coexist. While there continues to be an élite obsessed with the death of the self, changes take place that are a reaction against the élitist attitude. Ariès notes a condemnation from certain quarters in the Lutheran and Catholic communities of excessive expenditure on elaborate funerals, and a plea for more modest internments. He argues that this attitude is transformed by the eighteenth century into what amounts to a denial of death by the Enlightenment. Enlightened medicine becomes fascinated with the biological realities of death, while early health reforms begin to demand the removal of the cemeteries from the churches, and their relocation of the city centres – the first symbolic expulsion or rejection of the dead from the community of the living.

Another feature of this phase is the emergence of a symbolic link between sex and death as a result of the scientific preoccupation with the corpse.

> Death becomes 'untamed' and 'savage' since optimistic enlightened doctors gradually become afraid of the one biological state they sense they will never be able to reverse.[30]

This third attitude is important in that Ariès claims that it pre-shadows the modern suppression of death. This third attitude is linked to the development of rationality and reason.

The fourth attitude is labelled 'the death of other'. The emergence of the modern family unit means that the attention is focused on the surviving family rather than the dying individual. This is also the era of romanticism and the cult of the tomb, regular visits to the graveyard and emotional expression and display of grief.[31]

The fifth attitude is that of the 'invisible death' or 'forbidden death'. It is characterised by the suppression of the idea of death and dying. It is in turn linked to a decline in the belief of an afterlife and to an increase in the medicalisation of death and dying.[32] According to Ariès the modern individual has attempted to 'suppress the frightening and scandalising knowledge' of his/her own mortality. Death is hidden in the sense that it is generally sequestered from the public space.[33] That is, my death is hidden. The death in focus is the sensational death, the atypical death, the death of the unlucky stranger or the celebrity. These are the deaths that are emphasised and awarded prominence. It is this attitude towards death that Ariès believes is the most dominant in modern Westernised societies. It is this attitude of death, or variations of it, that dominates in New Zealand society.

Finding Death

We die – everything dies – but we alone of earth's creatures are aware that we die. Heidegger remarked that life juts out into death, yet it is equally true that death juts out into life. Death shapes life: its drives, its desires, the whole of its emotional–intellectual existence.[34] What are the implications if we live in a time where, as some argue, death has become the modern taboo? A quick perusal of the anthropological and sociological literature on death alerts us to the thesis that death in modern society is often characterised as being taboo, or out of bounds. Philippe Ariès' work clearly indicates that death, while being a social and public fact has a tendency in the more industrialised, urbanised and technological areas of the Western world to be suppressed.[35] Death becomes expelled from daily life and the topic becomes one of disapproval and shame.

Geoffrey Gorer believes that the suppression of death has fuelled an appetite for violent and perverse portrayals of death – an effect which he pronounces as being an ethos of the 'pornographic' because it involves a twentieth-century prudery and denial similar to previous attitudes towards sex. As sex becomes pornographic when divorced from its natural human emotion (affection), so death becomes pornographic when it is severed from its natural human emotion, which is grief.[36]

Stephenson echoes Gorer's theme of death as pornography. He believes we:

> ...react to the reality of death with dread. The subject is obscene; it is pornographic. It is not polite to speak easily of death. We are too uncomfortable with it. Institutions are created to contain death, and emphasis is placed upon youth, for to grow old is to exemplify the decay of the body.[37]

Stephenson offers a response to those who ask how it can be alleged that modern culture shuns death when it is a constant theme of novels, television and news reports. He argues that much of our public treatment of death actually confirms the link to pornography. Drawing on Gorer he notes the parallel between the Victorian treatment of sexuality and contemporary death attitudes:

> The repression of sexuality brought with it a flourishing of pornography. The attempt to deny the existence of death by repressing the subject has brought about a popular fascination with violence. The similarities go further. As with sexual pornography, the pornography of violent death de-emphasises feelings – in sexual pornography there is little or no caring, tenderness or love. In necrography (violent pornography) people are 'wasted' or 'blown away'. The emphasis in both cases is upon the sensational.[38]

Within death literature, this taboo is not solely in the celluloid image or the representations of the popular press. It is thought to apply within the academic setting as well. Tony Walter believes that it is a strange taboo, that is 'proclaimed by every pundit in the land, and when virtually no Sunday is without at least one newspaper discussing death, bereavement, hospices or funerals'.[39] Walter accedes that Gorer's argument explicates a great deal. It explains how a society that refuses to talk of death in personal terms becomes obsessed with the horror of death. It explains how the mass media can be seen as obsessed with death, while individuals have difficulty articulating how they feel about their own deaths.[40] Like Gorer, Ariès argues that death, like sex, is one of the major ways in which 'nature' threatens 'culture'. Death must be tamed by cultural rituals, yet Ariès believes that individualism and secularism have undermined these rituals so that the modern individual is 'left naked before death's obscenity'.[41]

Walter argues that Gorer and Ariès are both guilty of romanticising the way that death and dying were ritualised in pre-modern societies. He perceives the modern death as being not so much forbidden, as hidden. Due to a lower death rate and an increased longevity, correlating to an increased medicalisation of death, death is relocated out of the public and into the private sphere. Moreover, in a discussion on frame analysis he notes that death competes for meaning through a range of disparate frames (public health frame, theological frame, psychological frame). This means that conceptions of death have become both fluid and fragmented. 'The traditional religious frames that tamed death have dissolved, laying bare the basic human anxiety at the unknown, an anxiety confused rather than confronted by the postmodern babel of languages.'[42]

Gorer does overstate the case when he argues that the modern depiction of death is devoid of emotion. Though it is true that our saturation with death images does little to assist us in examining our own mortality, popular culture would be less than successful if it relieved us of our ability to emote. We do react to images of death; and with mixed emotions. Gorer believes that the natural emotion in response to death is grief. Yet grief is just one of the many emotions that death elicits. Throughout all time it is highly probable that death has called forth a multitude of feelings. Grief may be to the forefront but guilt, fascination, relief, satisfaction and sometimes even joy are likely to be there as well. However, Gorer does create ways of understanding how it is that death images can overshadow us at a time when speaking of one's own death is seen as perverse.

Medicalisation and Modern Death

The medicalisation of our understanding of death, dying and bereavement is linked to this process of denial. The main characteristic of this process is the removal of death and dying from the community and its relocation in the hospital or similar institution. In New Zealand, as in many other countries, one is more likely to die within an institutionalised setting than in the home. Within the framework of modernity, medicine has replaced religion as the major institutional moulder of cultural conceptions of death.[43] Medicine can be viewed, like religion and law, as a moral enterprise that seeks to uncover and controls things it considers undesirable.[44] Ariès suggests that because the general attitude of Western societies towards death is characterised by fear and shame, it is now deemed appropriate that dying individuals should be removed from the community to die in pseudo isolation within a medical institution. Again, his analysis appears harsh in consideration of the fact that most of us hospitalise those close to us in the belief that we are doing the best for them, rather than in an attempt to remove them from our midst. However, it is true that we make this decision based on dominant medical models of the dying process. Our ability to care for the dying has become compromised by both the advances in medicine and a cultural acceptance of medical authority.

Elias notes a particular embarrassment felt by the living in the presence of the dying. Not knowing what to say, they feel relieved to be able to deposit the dying with specialists.[45] Elias attributes this muteness in the face of death to part of the civilising process that 'has lifted the threshold of shame'.[46] By privatising the personal, we are no longer adept at conversing with death when we encounter it. Bauman suggests that it is not just delicacy of manners that deprives us of speech, but also the fact that language, any language, is the language of survival. We have little to say to someone that we deem has no use of it. We may feel that using the language of survival will mean that whatever we say will sound false and meaningless.[47] He argues that we keep the dying at a distance so that communication is no longer possible: 'the dying die not so much in loneliness as in silence. There is nothing we can communicate about in the only language we both command and share – the language of survival.'[48]

For many, the 'appropriate' place of death is the hospital. Within the hospital system, death and dying are redrawn to meet new criteria. Sudnow's work explicates the social organisation of dying and emphasises the ways in which dying has been routinised and remodelled so that it becomes a piece with the day-to-day functioning of the hospital.[49] Moreover, who you are influences the dying process you will be presented with. The greater the social status, the more probable that extraordinary techniques and technology will be used to prolong the life. Lindsay Prior's work documents contemporary practices and notes the way they represent a particular version of death:

One dies from one's diseases rather than, say, old age, malfeasance or misfortune. Death and dying are hospitalised precisely because they are understood, first and foremost, as physical events. And the fact that it is the doctor rather than the priest who is summoned on the occasion says much about the ways in which human mortality is comprehended. Death is primarily regarded as an illness and an aberration rather than something that is natural and the physician is supposed to certify death and state its cause. These certificates also illustrate the belief that although human beings die from many causes at once, it is always possible to isolate a single and precipitate cause of death. Death is conceptualised as an ailment that is amenable to intervention.[50]

Unnatural Death

Doctors do not fight mortality, but they do fight mortal diseases. Death located in the modern project is far removed from Ariès' conception of the 'tame death'. Death has come to be seen as unnatural.

Our association with mortality is pushed to the margins. Certainty of death is seen as incapacitating, whereas the uncertainty of outcome is seen as fuelling energy and enticing one to action. Taking 'control' of one's body, by exercising, adhering to rules of nutrition, and avoiding smoking and smokers are all feasible tasks. They redefine the chaos of death (which one can do nothing about) into a series of manageable problems that one can do something about. This deconstruction of death is not an abolition of death but an attempt to strip it of significance. The rise of modern science, medicine and technology means that death becomes a project, something that can be understood, controlled and ultimately managed. The dilemma of human mortality is resolved by reducing it to smaller, potentially solvable problems. At last we are able to speak of the cause of death.

Nobody dies of mortality, instead, we die of individual causes. After our death these causes can be revealed; one dies of a disease or an accident, of suicide or murder. As individuals, we can constantly survey our lifestyles and abstain from unhealthy practices that might kill us and adopt practices that are good for us and which importantly, push the thought of death from our minds. Death is elsewhere, it is not here. Death happens to other people.

The pain of death is not lessened, yet mortality has lost its sting. Our battle is with diseases and the search for a 'cure'. Cancer research and AIDS research can be likened to crusades; the flocks may be ravaged but the good fight continues. As a community we can support Daffodil Day for cancer research or Red Nose Day for cot death research. We can at least pretend to rob death of its dominion. As Bauman asserts: death has been turned from a hangman into a prison guard. Mortality has been 'sliced from head to tail into thin rashers of fearful, yet curable (or potentially curable) affliction'.[51]

Managing Death

For many then, death has come to be seen as a failure. A failure 'of science and a failure of the individual, who is supposed to be a master of his or her own fate'.[52] Death may be viewed as an 'emphatic denial of everything that the brave new world of modernity stood for'.[53] One way we may cope with or manage death is to see life as a series of risk preventions. As a child, my idea of a child safety restraint in a car was my mother putting her arm across me as she braked. Now we are compelled to wear seatbelts and our children must be in approved car seats. To do otherwise would not only be illegal but also irrational and unreasonable. We are expected, in the appropriate situations, to wear bicycle helmets or motor bike helmets, to use condoms and to read and take tobacco warnings seriously. In many ways these are an attempt to write death small. The monolithic becomes manageable.

However, this skirting of death has meant that death is written over every facet of our lives. For those of us fortunate enough not to have to worry about basic survival needs, our lives become a series of checks and prescriptions against possible causes of death. As individuals we may find ourselves in a cultural ethos where we become responsible for our own fate. Smoking, eating fatty foods, having a sedentary lifestyle, and promiscuity are all choices we can make, but only at our own risk. Moreover, when individuals or groups of individuals choose to ignore these social prescriptions then there may be punitive action.[54] While not disputing the value of medical advances in our society and the need to live sensible, collectively caring lives, there is a need to understand that death is among us. A societal approach that focuses on equal life and death outcomes may move towards ensuring a greater level of social health. Paradoxically, the pushing of death to the outer boundaries of our existence has made death itself more present in our daily lives.

Endnotes

1   For the week August 26–September 2 the New Zealand Police were investigating 6 suspicious deaths / homicides.
2   *NZ Herald*, August 30, 2000.

3   Recent studies would suggest that the definition of biological death is also problematic. Kastenbaum (2000: 34–41) notes that the biomedical definitions of death are subject to change. When is somebody dead? Medicalised certification of death means that we now speak of being brain dead, or suffering cerebral or neo-cortical death (seen as different conditions). Death may be ascertained as having occurred when the heart has stopped beating, when there is no pulse or when blood circulation has ceased. Technological advances continually change and challenge the way we determine that death has occurred. Kastenbaum notes that there are now echelons among the dead – some appear deader than others.

4   Giddens, A. (1991) *Modernity and Self Identity,* Cambridge: Polity Press, p. 49.

5   Mellor, P. (1993) 'Death in High Modernity: The Contemporary Presence and Absence of Death', in *The Sociology of Death,* Oxford: Blackwell, p. 13.

6   Berger, P. (1967) *The Social Reality of Religion,* Middlesex: Penguin Books, p. 52.

7   Kearl, M. (1989) *Endings: A Sociology of Death and Dying,* Oxford: Oxford University Press, p. 24.

8   Ibid., p. 379.

9   Bauman, Z. (1992) *Mortality, Immortality and Other Life Strategies,* Cambridge: Polity Press.

10   Kastenbaum, R. (2000) *Death, Society and Human Experience,* 7th Edition, Boston: Allyn and Bacon.

11   Sinclair, K. (1990) 'Tangi: Funeral Rituals and the Construction of Maori Identity', in Linnekin, J. and Poyer, L. (eds) *Cultural Identity and Ethnicity in the Pacific,* Honolulu: University of Hawaii Press, p. 221.

12   Ibid., pp. 227–232.

13   Dancey, H. (1981) 'A View of Death', in King, M. (ed.) *Te Ao Hurihuri: The World Moves On,* Auckland: Longman Paul, p. 133.

14   Ibid., p. 139.

15   The funeral of Sir Robert Muldoon at the Auckland Town Hall is a good case in point. The incorporation of Maori elements in public funerals obviously speaks to political considerations as well.

16   Statistics New Zealand: Te Tari Tatau (1998) *New Zealand Official Yearbook 1998,* Wellington: GP Publications.

17   Ibid.

18   Ibid.

19   Evans *et al.* (1994) in Davis, P. and Dew, K. (eds) (1999), *Health and Society in Aotearoa New Zealand,* Auckland: Oxford University Press.

20   Reid, P. (1999) 'Nga Mahi Whakahaehae a Te Tangata Tiriti', in Davis, P. and Dew, K. (eds) *Health and Society in Aotearoa New Zealand,* Auckland: Oxford University Press, pp. 89–90.

21   Howden-Chapman, P. (1999) 'Socioeconomic Inequalities and Health', in Davis, P. and Dew, K. (eds) *Health and Society in Aotearoa New Zealand,* Auckland: Oxford University Press, p. 73.

22 Op. cit., pp. 80–81.

23 Ariès, P. (1981) *The Hour of Our Death*, New York: Alfred Knopf.

24 See Elias, N. (1985) *The Loneliness of Dying*, Oxford: Basil Blackwell; Walter, T. (1991) ' Modern Death: Taboo or Not Taboo', *Sociology*, Vol. 25: 293–310, Mellor, P. & Shilling, C. (1993) 'Modernity, Self-identity and the Sequestration of Death', *Sociology*, Vol 27; and Derrida, J. (1993) *Aporias*, Stanford, Calif.: Stanford University Press.

25 Whaley, J. (1981) *Mirrors of Mortality: Studies in the Social History of Death*, London: Europa.

26 Ariès, op. cit., p. 9.

27 Whaley, op. cit., p. 5.

28 Ibid., p. 6.

29 Ariès, op. cit., p. 116.

30 Whaley, op. cit., p. 6.

31 Ibid., p. 7.

32 Ibid.

33 Mellor, P. (1993) 'Death in High Modernity: The Contemporary Presence and Absence of Death', *Sociology*, vol. 27:3

34 Metzger, A. (1973) *Freedom and Death*, London: Chaucer Publishing, p. 5.

35 Ariès, op. cit., p. 560.

36 Kearl, op. cit., p. 387.

37 Stephenson, J., in Killilea, A. (1988) *The Politics of Being Mortal*, Lexington: The University Press of Kentucky, p. 5.

38 Ibid.

39 Walter, T. (1991) 'Modern Death: Taboo or Not Taboo?', *Sociology*, Vol. 25, p. 293.

40 Ibid.

41 Ibid., p. 296.

42 Stannard in Walter, op. cit., p. 303.

43 See Segerberg, O. (1974) *The Immortality Factor*, New York: EP Dutton; Harrington, A. (1977) *The Immortalist*, Millbrae, Calif.: Celestial Arts.

44 Kearl, op. cit., p. 406.

45 Elias, N. (1982) *The Civilising Process*, Oxford: Basil Blackwell.

46 Elias (1985) op. cit.

47 Even though many studies show that the dying often crave to be talked to as they were talked to before they became ill – That discussion of the small and the inconsequential allows them to be still a part of life rather than outside it.

48 Bauman, op. cit., p. 131.

49 Sudnow, D. (1967) *Passing On: The Social Organisation of Dying*, New Jersey: Prentice-Hall.

50 In Bauman, op. cit., p. 139.

51 Ibid., p. 140.

52 Stephenson, J. (1985) *Death, Grief and Mourning: Individual and Social*

Realities, New York: Free Press.
53 Bauman, op. cit., p. 134.
54 From anti-smoking laws to compulsory bicycle helmets the state has intruded increasingly in a domain previously left to personal responsibility. When we are unable or unwilling to 'save' ourselves from death then the state may see fit to intervene. Much legislation is responding forcefully to economic criteria (the cost of hospitalisation for respiratory failure and trauma, for example), but the legislation is presented on preventative and safety grounds. Papaarangi Reid notes that the emphasis on the individual has led to 'victim-blame' members of Maori communities who practise 'health-risk behaviours' and to withdrawal from collective solutions to health problems (Reid, op. cit., p. 92).

Bibliography

Ariès, P. (1981) *The Hour of Our Death,* New York: Alfred Knopf.
Bauman, Z. (1992) *Mortality, Immortality and Other Life Strategies,* Cambridge: Polity Press.
Berger, P. (1967) *The Social Reality of Religion,* Middlesex: Penguin Books.
Dancey, H. (1981) 'A View of Death', in King, M. (ed.) *Te Ao Hurihuri: The World Moves On,* Auckland: Longman Paul.
Derrida, J. (1993) *Aporias,* Stanford, Calif.: Stanford University Press.
Elias, N. (1985) *The Loneliness of Dying,* Oxford: Basil Blackwell.
Elias, N. (1982) *The Civilising Process,* Oxford: Basil Blackwell.
Giddens, A. (1991) *Modernity and Self Identity,* Cambridge: Polity Press.
Harrington, A. (1977) *The Immortalist,* Millbrae, Calif.: Celestial Arts.
Howden-Chapman, P. (1999) 'Socioeconomic Inequalities and Health', in Davis, P. and Dew, K. (eds) *Health and Society in Aotearoa New Zealand,* Auckland: Oxford University Press.
Kastenbaum, R. (2000) *Death, Society and Human Experience,* 7th Edition, Boston: Allyn and Bacon.
Kearl, M. (1989) *Endings: A Sociology of Death and Dying,* Oxford: Oxford University Press.
Killilea, A. (1988) *The Politics of Being Mortal,* Lexington: The University Press of Kentucky.
Mellor, P. (1993) 'Death in High Modernity: The Contemporary Presence and Absence of Death', in *The Sociology of Death,* Oxford: Blackwell.
Mellor, P. & Shilling, C. (1993) 'Modernity, Self-identity and the Sequestration of Death', *Sociology,* Vol. 27.
Metzger, A. (1973) *Freedom and Death,* London: Chaucer Publishing.
Reid, P. (1999) 'Nga Mahi Whakahaehae a Te Tangata Tiriti', in Davis, P.

and Dew, K. (eds) *Health and Society in Aotearoa New Zealand*, Auckland: Oxford University Press.

Segerberg, O. (1974) *The Immortality Factor*, New York: EP Dutton.

Sinclair, K. (1990) 'Tangi: Funeral Rituals and the Construction of Maori Identity', in Linnekin, J. and Poyer, L. (eds) *Cultural Identity and Ethnicity in the Pacific*, Honolulu: University of Hawaii Press.

Statistics New Zealand: Te Tari Tatau, (1998) *New Zealand Official Yearbook 1998*, Wellington: GP Publications.

Stephenson, J. (1985) *Death, Grief and Mourning: Individual and Social Realities*, New York: Free Press.

Sudnow, D. (1967) *Passing On: The Social Organisation of Dying*, New Jersey: Prentice-Hall.

Walter, T. (1991) ' Modern Death: Taboo or Not Taboo', *Sociology*, Vol. 25:293–310.

Whaley, J. (1981) *Mirrors of Mortality: Studies in the Social History of Death*, London: Europa.

Index

Contributors

Claudia Bell is Senior Lecturer in Sociology at the University of Auckland. Previous books include *Inventing New Zealand, Putting Our Town on the Map* (with John Lyall), and *Community Issues in New Zealand*. Her main research interests are local and national identity, tourism and heritage, cultural studies, and sociology of the arts. Her next book, also with John Lyall, is on landscape, tourism and identity, to be published in the USA in 2001.

Ian Carter is Professor of Sociology at the University of Auckland. His latest book, *Modernity's Epitome: Railways and Culture* will be published by Manchester University Press in 2001. Current research interests include trying to make sense of debates swirling around food, diet and health, and the sociology of enthusiasm.

Bruce Curtis is Lecturer in Sociology at the University of Auckland. He has wide-ranging research interests, including gambling, health, work, and the state. He is currently editing a book called *Gambling in New Zealand*.

Ward Friesan lectures in Geography at the University of Auckland, specialising in economic, population and urban geography, with particular focus on demographic change, migration, and ethnicity in New Zealand and the Pacific. His recent research projects have included the Chinese community in Auckland, the changing nature of Tangata Pasifika in New Zealand, demographic and social change in the Solomon Islands, and New Zealand's position within APEC.

Ruth Habgood recently completed her PhD thesis at the University of Auckland: 'A study of the constraints to sharing domestic responsibilities and resources in double income families in New Zealand'. She is currently lecturing at the School of Education and Social Sciences, Auckland

University of Technology (AUT), Auckland, teaching methodology and social theory.

Wayne Hope is Senior Lecturer in Communications Studies at AUT. His principle research interests are critical theory, political economy, globalisation, public sphere analysis, and sport–media relationships. He co-edited and contributed to *Critical Theory, Post Structuralism and the Social Context* (with Michael Peters, James Marshall and Stephen Webster). Wayne is a regular contributor to the Political Economy stream of the International Association of Media Communication Research (IAMCR). He writes for *New Zealand Political Review,* and is a regular radio commentator on broadcasting issues.

Rosser Johnson teaches in the School of Communication Studies at AUT. His research centres on developing a critical appreciation of advertising in relation to both traditional mass media and new communication technologies. His MA (Communication Studies) thesis examined the infiltration of the infomercial into mainstream primetime television. He is currently designing a doctoral research proposal.

Robin Kearns is Senior Lecturer in Geography at the University of Auckland. He completed an MA (Hons) at Auckland and a PhD in social geography from McMaster University (Canada). His research and teaching interests centre on geographies of health and health care, the cultural politics of place, and research ethics. He has published over 50 refereed articles and co-edited *Putting Health into Place: Landscape, Identity and Well-Being* (Syracuse University Press).

Mike Lloyd is Senior lecturer in Sociology at Victoria University of Wellington. His publications have been wide-ranging in topic, including studies of male infertility, yoga, accidents, epidemiology, and island spatiality, but all have a common desire to analyse the fine detail of social organisation.

John Lyall is an artist and Head of Sculpture at UNITEC, Auckland. He exhibits in the genres of installation, photography, performance and sound. He co-wrote with Claudia Bell *Putting Our Town on the Map,* which was also a television documentary and a travelling photographic exhibition. John performed his cyber-opera *Requiem for Electronic Moa* at SoundCulture Auckland 1999, and in Lancaster, UK in 2000. He works in the areas of landscape, the sublime and hyper-nature, with particular reference to Feral Theory.

Steve Matthewman lectures in the Sociology Department at the University of Auckland. His research and teaching interests include cultural studies, social theory and the sociology of science. He is currently working on a book about scientific attempts to change the weather and the public responses that such actions precipitate.

Angela Maynard lectures in Sociology at Manukau Insititute of Technology and at Unitec, Auckland, while working on her doctorate on the sociology of the New Zealand food system, including an investigation of whether there is a distinctive New Zealand cuisine. She is also a community worker for the Auckland District Council of Social Services.

Tracey McIntosh (Tuhoe) is a Lecturer in the Sociology Department at the University of Auckland. Prior to joining the department she was lecturing at the University of the South Pacific in Suva, Fiji. She teaches and researches in the areas of death, crime, deviance, politics and religion.

Laurence Murphy is Senior Lecturer in Geography at the University of Auckland. He has published in a variety of journals on topics relating to housing issues and housing policy in New Zealand, urban social geography, geographies of finance, and urban property processes. His current research examines the socio-spatial impacts of contemporary processes of globalisation in metropolitan Auckland.

Camilla Obel is a Lecturer in the Sociology Department, Canterbury University, where she is currently completing her PhD thesis on the organisation of rugby union in the 1990s. Camilla teaches a sport and leisure course and has published on the sports of bodybuilding, rugby union and rugby league. Apart from sport, her academic interests include media and culture.

Harvey Perkins is Associate Professor in the Human Sciences Division, Lincoln University, New Zealand. His main research and teaching interests are in the social geography of human settlement. Current research projects focus on the meaning of house and home, urban change and environmental planning, place promotion and the social geographical aspects of leisure and tourism in New Zealand. Recent publications include *Time Out? Leisure, Recreation and Tourism in New Zealand and Australia* (with Grant Cushman) and *Environmental Policy and Management in New Zealand* (with Ali Memon).

David C. Thorns is Professor of Sociology at the University of Canterbury, New Zealand. He is the author or co-author of eight books, including *Fragmenting Societies* and *Understanding Aotearoa* (with Charles Sedgwick). He has published extensively in the fields of housing, urban and regional restructuring, tourism and the understanding of home and identity. His current research includes work on globalisation and urban change, the meaning of home and urban sustainability.

Farida Tilbury has recently completed her PhD at Victoria University of Wellington. Her research, following on from an Honours project looking into neighbouring interactions, investigated friendships between Maori and Pakeha. Using contact theory, she analysed how individuals' friendship networks relate to their sense of ethnic identity and attitudes to race relations issues. She has recently moved to Australia where she is teaching at the University of Western Australia and is engaged in health research.

Martin Tolich is Senior Lecturer in the School of Sociology and Women's Studies at Massey University, Palmerston North. His recent textbook publications have been *Starting Fieldwork, Social Science Research in New Zealand* (both with Carl Davidson) and *Research Ethics in Aotearoa New Zealand*. His interest in the workplace can be found in recent volumes of *Journal of Management Studies, Gender Work and Organization* and the *Australian and New Zealand Journal of Sociology*.

Cate Wilson is a PhD candidate in psychology at the University of Waikato. Her research interests include community psychology, youth issues and health. Her PhD examines deliberate self-injury amongst young women.

	Sol
weather	x
housing	EL
housework	EL
friendship	x
food	EL
work	EL
media	media
aesthetic leisure	PC ?
sport	PC
shopping	consumption or EL ?
gambling	PC
death	? body ec ?

refs.

Reith, gambling, p. 232

Rowe, sport, p. 187

Ley + Olds, cult. geog p 208

Miller, shopping, p 208

Skelton + Valentine, youth, p 209.
[order for Lib]

Bennett et al, taste, p. 164